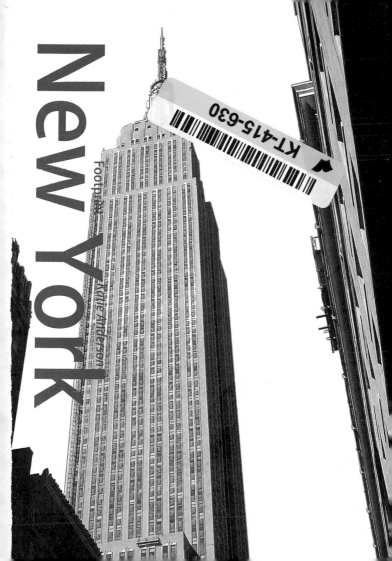

New York

Footprint

Katie Anderson

Contents

About the author

From an early age Katie Anderson had an urge to explore foreign lands, so she travelled the world in search of adventures and stories to tell. After living in Paris and London, working in various editorial roles and earning a Master's degree in International Journalism, she returned to New York. When she's not out and about, enjoying the city's cosmopolitan restaurants or planning her next trip, she works as a journalist.

Acknowledgements

Big thanks to the following friends who helped in various ways: Matt Godson, who wrote and researched various sections; Ally Longfield and Rosa Chang for having their fingers on the pulse; Terry Brennan for his architectural know-how; Sharon Klah, who helped with the shopping chapter; the Valentis for their experience of posh New York dining; Sophie Blacksell for editing; Nadim Barakat, Francesca de Chatel and Sara Candy; the Broken Cup Café and, especially, Mom and Dad.

"new york metro"
on line – v. gd
for latest on
restaurants

However many times you visit, New York is sure to move you. Its mesmerising appeal comes in different forms from other world-class cities: the lights that hold back the night, the zany characters on the streets, the neck-wrenching buildings and the exhilarating pace. A tranquil moment in New York is undoubtedly fleeting but it is this endless, inexhaustible energy that makes the city inimitable.

In no other city is more top-notch culture, architecture, food, entertainment, excitement and glamour caught within the confines of a net-like grid of streets. Perhaps the reason that New York is so frenetic is that visitors and locals simply feel there's not enough time to sample everything that this extraordinary city has to offer.

International village

Despite the protestations of other world cities, New York is the planet's urban epicentre and New Yorkers believe that anyone who chooses to live elsewhere must, in some sense, be kidding. Little Korea is just one block away from Little Brazil, Little Italy jostles for elbow room with Chinatown, which, in turn, merges into the Hispanic Lower East Side. This cosmopolitan diversity means that the city is open to visitors who pick out a little corner to claim as home, even if temporarily. Spend enough time in one neighbourhood and the local deli, grocer and dry-cleaner will greet you on a first-name basis, erasing the impersonal stigmas too often associated with the concrete façade of Manhattan. Following the events of September 11th 2001, New Yorkers feel even more fiercely tied to their city and its myriad communities.

Sensational

New York is cinematic, the backdrop for more than 200 movies a year. It is musical, getting name-checked in more songs than any other place on earth. It is endlessly mobile: see schoolgirls cutting loose on the subway to the beat of drummers. Sample foods from all around the world, watch fashionistas strut their stuff and media empires flash neon news to a soundtrack of roaring traffic and taxis horns. New York is a city of sights, sounds, smells and tastes and it won't take you long to feel the vibe. The air is thick with potential; literally anything could happen and every visit is an adventure.

Grid and bear it

The mass of high-rise buildings that constitute this endless urban jungle is really a network of finely tuned neighbourhoods divided up neatly into blocks. Although visitors might first experience the city as an imposing amount of concrete and an undying amount of chaos, New York's grid of avenues and streets is a carefully orchestrated system that somehow keeps the anarchy in check, while allowing the spirit of the city to soar free.

At a glance

New York City consists of five boroughs: Manhattan, Brooklyn, Queens, the Bronx and Staten Island. The heart of the city is undoubtedly Manhattan Island, which is divided, at least in the minds of its inhabitants into Uptown and Downtown, a distinction that defines social heirarchies and personality stereotypes. Downtowners, technically those living below 14th Street, regard themselves as the cutting-edge, liberal darlings of New York. Those living Uptown, anywhere alongside Central Park, claim to be genteel, while being labelled as a bit staid and unadventurous by their southern neighbours. During the week, Midtown is the centre point of it all, bringing together the arty Downtown folk and their well-groomed Uptown rivals. Broadway threads through the whole of Manhattan from north to south, distinguishing the more laid-back west side from the more upscale east side of the island and often intersecting drastically varied neighbourhoods.

Lower Manhattan

The starting point for many visitors to New York, including the original Dutch settlers of 1624, the tip of Manhattan is a place of stunning views towards the Statue of Liberty, Ellis Island and the surrounding boroughs. Following the tragedy of September 11th, it has also become a place of pilgrimage for genuine mourners and morbid tourists. The location of many of the country's federal and financial institutions, including the New York Stock Exchange, this area is lively during the week but clears out at the weekends. Locals stick around only to enjoy Battery Park and the recently done-up Hudson River Park.

Chinatown, Little Italy and Nolita

A perfect example of how tolerant New Yorkers can be, Chinatown and Little Italy snuggle up to each other closely enough to be sharing dim sum and ravioli recipes. Gregarious Chinatown, between Grand Street to the north and Worth Street to the south, features colourful food stalls and cheap-and-cheerful stores. The tinselled streets and espresso stops of Little Italy flow out of Chinatown's north end from Canal Street up to Grand Street, trying to hang on to their traditions despite the infringement of their more populous neighbours to the south. Super-cool Nolita (north of Little Italy), the artsy extension of Little Italy, has trendy Elizabeth and Mott Streets at its heart, where bars, French cafés and one-of-a-kind boutiques are found.

SoHo and Tribeca
Formerly the Downtown home of artists and bohemians, the funky, cobbled streets of SoHo and Tribeca are now the stomping ground of models, movie stars and well-to-do artists. SoHo (South of Houston, pronounced *How-stun*) is a perfect place to stroll. Its cast-iron buildings from the turn of the 19th century form a dramatic backdrop to narrow, touristy streets, lined with art galleries and shops. Tribeca (Triangle below Canal) lies immediately west of Broadway, between Canal Street and Chambers Street, and is a smaller area of pricey loft conversions, high-end galleries and chic New York restaurants. It also hosts an important annual film festival, created in part by local resident Robert De Niro.

Greenwich Village and Chelsea
Set apart from the grid system, Greenwich Village is best seen by foot, with a map or enough time to get lost. Wander west from Washington Square Park to the charming streets of the West Village or head south to where New York University students still hang out in the cafés where beatnik culture was born. The axis of Bleecker Street spans the whole of the Village, with narrow tree-lined streets trickling off in all directions. On its north border is the hottest real estate in town. The Meatpacking District combines

a working meat market with trendy bars, restaurants, clubs and all-night diners to create an edgy, glamorous vibe. Neighbouring Chelsea, north of 14th Street along Seventh and Eighth Avenues, is the centre of gay New York, known for its beautiful 'Chelsea boys' and chic art galleries.

Lower East Side and the East Village
Romanticized as a former haven for Irish, then Italian, then Jewish, and, most recently, Puerto Rican immigrants, the Lower East Side lies south of Houston Street from Bowery over to the East River. Although the boutiques and bars around Rivington, Ludlow, Clinton and Orchard Streets are signs that the tenement days have long gone, this area is still a bit grimy-chic. Just north, the rapidly gentrifying East Village, from Houston up to 14th Street, is home to a wayward set of punks, hippies, vintage shoppers and artists.

Flatiron District
Considered the entrance to Downtown, Union Square sits neatly between 14th Street and 17th Street, bordered by Broadway and Park Avenue South. Just north of the square, the Flatiron District houses creative and media types between 17th and 23rd Streets, connecting over to the smart shops of Fifth Avenue, while further east, stately streets surround Gramercy Park, the only private park on Manhattan.

Midtown
New York's grid system is never so clear-cut as in the wide, straight avenues of Midtown. Midtown is the businesss centre of the city and the place where those unmistakable New York symbols are found: skyscrapers, yellow taxis, corner diners, the flashy lights of Broadway and many celebrated buildings and department stores. Heading west, the once shabby area of Hell's Kitchen, around Eighth and Ninth Avenues, is now teeming with artists and yuppies, who enjoy its ethnic restaurants and its close proximity to Central Park.

▶ City on the move

Reinvention is New York's favourite hobby and even its most famous museums and landmarks are susceptible to makeovers and upgrades. Grand Central Terminal, Bryant Park, the Museum of Modern Art, the Morgan Library and the Museum of Modern Art have all undergone massive renovations, the American Museum of Natural History and the Guggenheim have gained numerous extensions and the unfortunate Guggenheim SoHo has closed down altogether.

Relocation is another big theme these days. The Museum of African Art is now in Queens, the Dahesh Museum has spacious new digs and the American Folk Art Museum has moved to Midtown. To avoid ending up in the wrong place, check museum addresses carefully before visiting.

Upper East Side

Stretching up from 59th Street to 96th Street, between Central Park and the East River, the Upper East Side is distinguished and uppity but many locals prefer its tidy appearance and safe streets to the buzz of Downtown. The grandiose mansions around Fifth and Park Avenues have been home to America's wealthiest families over the years – the Kennedys, Vanderbilts, Astors and the Whitneys – but although this area may reek of old money, its famed Museum Mile won't disappoint culture addicts. Highlights include the Metropolitan Museum of Art, the Frick Collection and the Cooper-Hewitt National Design Museum.

Upper West Side

Bordered to the east by the sprawling green sanctuary of Central Park, the Upper West Side is home to New York's cultural elite – artists, journalists, Ivy League students and well-off locals, whose

slice of Manhattan has a more bohemian edge than the Upper East Side. The affluence here is combined with a vibrant atmosphere that is particularly apparent around the Lincoln Center and around Columbia University at 116th Street. The Upper West Side is also the location of one of world's largest cathedrals – the unfinished Cathedral of St John the Divine.

Harlem
North of Central Park, Harlem is rich in culture, music, cuisine and art. Its fast gentrification and increasing popularity mean that this historic community is setting trends once again.

Outer boroughs
Separated from Manhattan only by narrow strips of river, the surrounding four boroughs couldn't really be more different. Brooklyn, easily accessible from Downtown, has its own New York jive, a thriving art and music scene and some of the best parks in the city. Queens is its less-glamorous northern neighbour, home to JFK and La Guardia airports. Staten Island to the south of Manhattan holds little appeal for the short-term visitor apart from the unbeatable view from the boat that ferries back and forth, while the Bronx, to the north, is well worth a visit for baseball or zoo fans.

Trip planner

Every season in New York is accompanied by new attractions. Although New York's temperatures range from frigidly cold to brutally humid, the sun tends to poke out more often than not and the weather shouldn't hold back your plans. With the freezing December temperatures arrive the holiday lights and spectacular window displays in the city's department stores, while the summer heat brings with it some of New York's best street entertainment and sidewalk dining. The ideal times to visit temperature-wise, though, are probably the spring, from March until May, and again in the autumn, with warm Indian summer nights often lasting until mid-November. Bear in mind, however, that the weather can vary drastically from year to year. New York, believe it or not, does get quieter at weekends during the summer, when many city dwellers clear out for beach homes or upstate retreats. Although this is the city that never sleeps, many shops and sights close earlier on a Sunday and most museums are closed for one day a week.

A long weekend

Manhattan's grid layout and accessible transportation make getting around quite manageable. Resist the urge to cram as many sights as possible into a short trip, since New York is as much about its atmosphere as it is about specific sights and museums. A weekend in New York will allow you to gain a striking impression of the city's myriad personalities; you'll have time to take in a view or two from one of the many skyscrapers and to enjoy a stroll through one of the Downtown neighbourhoods. Be sure to sample the city's restaurant scene and non-stop nightlife and to gain a glimpse of the surrounding boroughs from New York's harbour.

Kick off any New York visit with a strong coffee and a visit to Lower Manhattan. Get there early, before the crowds turn up, and take the free **Staten Island Ferry** over and back for astounding views of the city, the Statue of Liberty and Ellis Island. If you're feeling energetic, walk through **Chinatown** on the way to a leisurely brunch at **Café Lebowitz** or **Café Gitane**. Afterwards, stroll the streets of **Greenwich Village**, browse the galleries in **SoHo**, rummage through **Chelsea flea market** to find some interesting bric-a-brac or enjoy great views of the Hudson River from the roof of the **Dia Center for the Arts**.

Then, head northeast to be awed by the dizzying skyscrapers of Midtown. Check out the **Chrysler Building**, probably the most stunning example of art deco in the city, and **Grand Central Terminal**, where you may have time to sneak a drink in the **Campbell Apartment** bar. The shops of **Fifth Avenue** are temptingly close but save some cash for a sunset drink Downtown, in the rooftop **Rise** bar at the Ritz-Carlton. After dinner at **Pfiff**, pay a brief visit to **Times Square**, either to catch a Broadway show or just to ogle at all those neon lights and pandemonium. You can sip a fancy cocktail as you people watch at the **Blue Fin** bar or peer down on the crowds from the sophisticated surroundings of the **Ava Lounge**. Late night head to **Bungalow 8** for some classy clubbing.

Get up early on Sunday, if possible, when hardly a soul is awake, and stroll up to **Central Park**, for an exploration of New York's favourite garden. The museums along the east side make a welcome change from hectic Midtown, but choose just one if you're short on time. The **Metropolitan Museum of Art** is worthy of several hours, but the nearby **Frick Collection**, **Guggenheim Museum** and **Whitney Museum** are each possible on their own in an hour or two. Stop at **Serafina's** for a late Italian lunch or indulge in coffee and cakes at the lovely Viennese **Café Sabarsky** inside the Neue Galerie. Later on, take in a comedy show, such as the **Upright Citizens' Brigade**, or hear some jazz in Harlem or Greenwich Village.

One week or more

After a few days, New York's pace and character will start to become familiar. Take a walking tour of one of Manhattan's historic districts to deepen your understanding of the city but also find time to visit the outlying areas. From Uptown you can continue north to **The Cloisters** for tranquillity and culture. Alternatively, cross the unmissable **Brooklyn Bridge** and then go on to explore **Williamsburg**'s buzzing art scene or to enjoy the raucous seaside fun of **Coney Island**. Sports fans may want to take in a **Yankees** game at the famous stadium in the Bronx, while shoppers should visit the quirky boutiques of **Nolita** and the **East Village**. Spend an evening at an Off-Broadway play or catch a modern dance performance at the **Joyce Theater** in Chelsea.

★ **Ten of the best**

1   Statue of Liberty and Ellis Island Miss Liberty stands gracefully at the tip of Manhattan, a potent symbol for the millions of immigrants who arrived on Ellis Island, p35

2   Central Park This vast green space has something for every child, adult, athlete, outdoor lover, exhibitionist or people-watcher, p91

3   Metropolitan Museum of Art The Met houses a superb collection of paintings, sculpture and artefacts from all over the world. It's particularly enjoyable on a Friday or Saturday evening when it's open late, with wine and jazz, p83.

4   Brooklyn Bridge Architecturally magnificent, the 19th-century bridge offers breathtaking views of Downtown Manhattan, p107

5   Grand Central Terminal This beaux arts beauty reminds us of the days when travel was elegant. Soak up the atmosphere in one of the bars on the balcony, p71

6   New York Public Library and Bryant Park This landmark library is splendid, even for those who are not pursuing academic endeavours. Behind it is French-inspired Bryant Park, a lovely place to relax, p74

7   Rooftop bars Enjoy the best views of the city's skyline, preferably with a Martini in your hand, p69.

8   Brunch in Greenwich Village Munch your way through a New York institution before exploring the historic, narrow off-grid streets, p54 and p143.

9   Chinatown With plenty of gaudy gifts, bargain foodstuffs, Formica and fluorescent lights, this colourful neighbourhood is sensory overload, p46

10 The Cloisters An unmissable collection of medieval art is housed in a monastery at leafy Fort Tryon Park, with lovely views of the Hudson River, p105

Contemporary New York

New York finds itself in a unsettled situation at the moment. It's still recovering from the terrorist attacks, still wobbling out of its recession and the Republican mayor (an anomaly in this typically Democrat city) is still trying to figure out where he's heading. However, this self-styled world capital always seems to be able to pull itself out of any slump or hardship thanks to a single-minded belief that it really can do anything it sets its mind to. A city always on the go, New York doesn't have much time for mood swings.

The defining moment of 2001 was followed by a series of downturns: a decline in tourism (which has recently reversed itself), a plunge in the stock market, rampant corporate scandal, which unfolded like a soap opera, and layoffs in nearly every sector. The cost of everything in the city, from parking tickets and subway fares to cinema seats and a decent lunch all seemed to rise in response to the looming financial crisis.

Mayor Michael Bloomberg had a tough act to follow in the form of outgoing Mayor Rudolph Giuliani, whose hard-nosed, imperious management style was quickly forgiven in the aftermath of September 11th. Rudy, as New Yorkers fondly called him, handled the city's worst disaster with confidence, gaining respect even from diehard Democrats, who had held his 'zero tolerance' policies in the 1990s responsible for the perceived demise of New York's quirky character.

Bloomberg has spent most of his tenure cutting back on everything possible – including rubbish collection, recycling, library hours and even fire houses – in order to get New York's finances back on an even keel. And the city seems to be responding, albeit slowly. Wall Street has started to rally, jobless rates continue to fall and the weak dollar has lured overseas visitors back to the city. What's more, although party-going folks complain that the Republican duo have stripped the city of its naturally maverick ways, New Yorkers are living it up in style in all corners of the city. Even Bloomberg's 2003 ban on smoking inside all bars, clubs and restaurants has failed to stub out New York's rebellious party spirit.

Many social commentators are comparing today's city to the New York of the 1970s, citing the similar fiscal situation and the reawakening of New York's identity as a city of artists, dreamers, immigrants and bohemians. Although the free-wheeling 1970s disco days of Studio 54 are long gone, New York is certainly revelling in a rowdier manner as its inhabitants begin to buck against the gentrifying trends of the 1990s. Big nightclubs are reopening, the no-dancing cabaret laws, enforced in many bars since Prohibition days, are being fought aggressively and even a handful of smoking bars are clinging to existence.

New York remains one of the most progressive places on earth and its inhabitants seem to gain enormous reassurance from the city's ability constantly to reinvent itself. Despite the recession, there's enough construction in progress to keep New York's makeover obsession alive and well. The futuristic towers of the Time Warner Building are transforming Columbus Circle; the Museum of Modern Art is undergoing a massive facelift that will double its size; the New Museum of Contemporary Art is moving to a much larger home on the Bowery; the formerly seedy and rundown Garment District has numerous new luxury high-rises and even the Lower East Side, known for its former sweat shops and tenements, has gained a sparkling glass designer hotel. Something new is always rising up on the New York skyline that is sure to draw both praise and ridicule. As witnessed in the feuding between architects of the Freedom Tower at the World Trade Center, New Yorkers are passionate about their buildings.

All this construction work is nothing new, of course. Urban architects have always had a heyday in New York. The city is scarcely 300 years old, a blink of an eye compared to its European peers and it seems almost inconceivable that so much has been built here in such a short time. What's more, the night-time vision

The world at your feet
Manhattan's panoramic cityscape encompasses myriad neighbourhoods and communities.

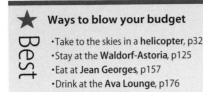

★ **Ways to blow your budget**

Best
- Take to the skies in a **helicopter**, p32
- Stay at the **Waldorf-Astoria**, p125
- Eat at **Jean Georges**, p157
- Drink at the **Ava Lounge**, p176
- Shop at **Barney's**, p205

of Manhattan's skyscrapers shimmering across the East River elicits a tingly feeling in even the most hard-bitten traveller, conjuring a dreamy starlit city where anything is possible. For many hard-working New Yorkers, however, the city's crammed living spaces, humid summers, clamorous noise, hordes of people and high cost of living are more stress-enducing than inspiring. And yet, New Yorkers have learned to adapt to their ever-evolving city with munificent patience and always with zeal. The blackout of 14 August 2003 was the biggest power outage in the country's history and a frightening reminder of what life would be like without modern conveniences. But just as in the aftermath of September 11th, New Yorkers pitched in to get the city back on its feet. Neighbours served food to people on the street, city dwellers offered sofas to commuters stuck in town. The communal feeling throughout the darkened city belied New York's fast-paced, self-absorbed, cold-hearted reputation.

Despite life's uncertainties, New York still charms with its outrageousness, baffles with its impulsiveness and teases with its romantic lights and flirtatious structures. No other city is so easy to navigate and yet so maddeningly complex, so sociable and yet so boorish at the same time. It's understandable why New Yorkers take pride in calling their city the capital of the world.

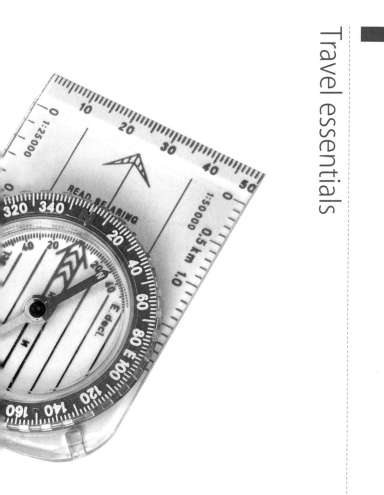

New York is accessible by plane from just about anywhere, with bargain flights available from London and other European cities. The last few years have seen a surge in cheap airfares and, as competition remains fierce, a trip to the world's fastest city is less likely to speed up your travel debt. Getting around the city need not be a concern either. Unlike other US cities, New York has an excellent public transportation system. The subway and bus services are inexpensive and efficient, many sights are within easy walking distance of one another and the city's 60,000 or so cabs are always swirling around, waiting for you to raise your arm or shout 'taxi!' in true New York style. These ubiquitous yellow cabs are affordable and available 24 hours, only becoming scarce at rush hour or when it's raining. Boat tours around Manhattan are popular, but guided tours by foot, bike or even helicopter are also possible. The layout of the island is easy to grasp thanks to its straight lines and numbered streets. Ask locals for directions and you may be surprised at the helpfulness of many New Yorkers.

Getting there

Being a 24-hour city, New York welcomes visitors at all hours. Taxis and public transportation are available around the clock, although few flights arrive after midnight. If you're arriving in the middle of the night, check with your hotel or accommodation ahead to see if they have night service. New York, especially Manhattan, is generally safe at night as long as you're streetwise and don't dawdle in unlit or unpopulated areas.

Air

From Europe There are direct flights to New York from most European cities including Amsterdam, Athens, Barcelona, Berlin, Brussels, Copenhagen, Frankfurt, Geneva, Lisbon, London, Madrid, Nice, Paris, Prague, Vienna and Zurich. *British Airways, Virgin Atlantic* and most major US airlines frequently offer fare deals, with return tickets from London sold for as little as £200 or less in the off-season. Higher fares from £300-£480 resurface in the summer months (June to August) and during the Thanksgiving, Christmas and New Year holidays. Fares usually cost slightly more from continental Europe, depending on the time of year, but special prices of £230 and up are not uncommon. The frequency of trans-Atlantic flights means last-minute discounts often get posted on airline or travel websites. Recently, some airlines have started to include a couple of nights' accommodation as part of the fare deals.

From North America Most US and Canadian airlines including *American Airlines, United Airlines, Delta Air Lines, Continental Airlines* and *Air Canada* fly direct to New York from all major cities, many arriving in **La Guardia Airport** (see p26). Prices vary depending on the season and on how far in advance tickets are purchased. There are special deals to New York from many US cities for under $99 each way, while return tickets from Montreal and Toronto often cost around C$250 or US$160.

→ Airlines and travel agents

Air Canada, 15 W 50th St, T 1-888 247 2262, www.aircanada.ca
Air France, 120 W 56th St, T-1800 237 2747, www.airfrance.com
American Airlines, 18 W 49th St, T-1800 433 7300, www.aa.com
British Airways, 530 Fifth Av, T 1-800 247 9297,
www.british-airways.com
Continental Airlines, 100 E 42nd St, T 1-800 525 0280,
www.continental.com
Delta Air Lines, 100 E 42nd St, T 1-800 221 1212, www.delta.com
Northwest Airlines, 100 E 42nd St, T 1-800 225 2525,
www.nwa.com
Qantas Airways, 712 Fifth Av, T 1-800 227 4500,
www.qantas.com.au
United Airlines, 100 E 42nd St, T 1-800 241 6522, www.ual.com
US Airways, 101 Park Av, T 1-800 428 4322, www.usairways.com
Virgin Atlantic, JFK International Airport, T 1-800 862 8621,
www.virgin.com

Travel websites
www.orbitz.com
www.travelocity.com
www.cheaptickets.com
www.expedia.com
www.priceline.co.uk
www.statravel.com

From Australia and New Zealand *Qantas* flies via Los Angeles
from Brisbane, Cairns, Melbourne and Sydney for around A$3000.
United also flies these routes, often at lower fares of A$2400. To
take advantage of the cheapest fares, tickets should be bought at
least 21 days in advance.

Airport information

Flights from abroad arrive at **John F Kennedy International Airport** in Queens, or at **Newark International Airport** in New Jersey. **La Guardia Airport** in Queens is only used for domestic flights. There are a variety of options for getting into the city: buses, shuttle vans, subway or taxis. Unless you're travelling alone, it often makes sense to take a cab. Otherwise, locals say the best value from JFK and Newark are the private buses, which go directly to Grand Central Terminal and Penn Station. Check the Port Authority of New York and New Jersey's **Air Ride Line** (**T** 1-800 247 7433, www.panynj.gov) for information on transportation to and from the airports.

JF Kennedy International Airport (**T** 1-718 244 4444, www.panynj.gov/aviation/jfkframe.HTM) is 15 miles from Manhattan. Each terminal has money-changing facilities, ATMs, tourist information desks and some have newsagents and souvenir shops. Transportation to the city is available from all terminals, just outside the baggage reclaim area. Taxis are the easiest way into the city but charge a flat rate of $35 plus toll and tip, bringing the total up to $44 or so. A cheaper option are the buses or shuttles, which circle around the terminals.

New York Airport Service Express (**T** 1-718 875 8200, www.nyairportservice.com) runs every 15 to 30 minutes from 0600 to 2300. The journey into the city takes 50 minutes and costs $13 one-way or $23 return. Buy a ticket from the agent standing outside baggage claim or you can book online for a slight discount. The buses drop passengers off at Penn Station, Grand Central Terminal and the Port Authority bus station.

To be dropped off right at your hotel's door, consider using one of the two shuttle services. **Gray Line** (**T** 1-800 451 0455, www.graylinenewyork.com) charges $14 for a journey into town, $19 out to the airport or $28 return. **SuperShuttle** (**T** 1-800 BLUE VAN) serves all of Manhattan 24 hours a day and charges $15 to hotels and $19 to residences. Look for the bright blue vans with yellow lettering that swing by each terminal every 15 to 20 minutes; tickets can be purchased inside by baggage claim. For those on a very strict budget, there is also a free shuttle bus that will drop you off at the Howard Beach A subway stop: from here it's about an hour's journey into Manhattan ($2).

Newark International Airport (**T** 1-973 961 6000, www.newarkairport.com) is 16 miles from Manhattan across the Hudson River. It has a new international arrivals terminal and often less traffic hiccups than JFK. The **Newark Airport Train** run by NJ Transit is the best way to get into Manhattan from the airport. A free monorail will take you to the airport station and, once on board, it's a 20-minute journey to Penn Station ($11.55). Otherwise, the best alternative is the **Olympia Airport Express** (**T** 1-212 964 6233), which runs buses every 15 to 20 minutes to Grand Central Terminal, Penn Station and Port Authority. Tickets ($12 one-way and $19 return) can be purchased just near baggage claim or outside by the bus.

La Guardia Airport (**T** 1-718 533 3400, www.new-york-lga.com) Mostly used for domestic flights, this airport is the closest to Manhattan. **New York Airport Service** buses go to Grand Central and Penn Station for $10, leaving from outside all terminals every 15 minutes. The **SuperShuttle** is just as frequent and charges $14 for direct services to hotels. Taxis cost $17-25 plus toll and tip. There's also a public bus that connects with the subway at 125th Street in Harlem. It only costs $2 but is not recommended for first-time visitors, late-night arrivals or those with heavy luggage.

Bus

Located in a rather grimy area of Downtown, the **Port Authority Bus Terminal** (41st St at 8th Av, **T** 1-212 564 8484) is the major hub for short- and long-distance buses, including national

Greyhound services (**T** 1-800 231 2222) and regional bus companies such as **Peter Pan Trailways** (**T** 1-800 343 9999). Those wanting to travel to/from Philadelphia, Washington DC or Boston, however, should consider the Chinatown bus services, which run from 139 Canal St at the Bowery every hour or so. The tickets are a bargain at $10 each way.

Train

If you travel into New York by train you'll arrive at either **Grand Central Terminal** (42nd St and Park Av), or **Pennsylvania Station** (32nd St between 7th Av and 8th Av). Both are in the centre of town, connected to the subway and are within easy walking distance of many attractions and hotels.

    Amtrak (**T** 1-800 USA RAIL, 1-212 582 6875, www.amtrak.com) runs services between Penn Station and New Jersey, Philadelphia, Boston and Washington DC; the NJ Transit and the Long Island Rail Road operate from here, too. From Grand Central, the Metro North line heads to the New York suburbs, Hudson Valley and Connecticut.

Getting around

The MTA

The **Metropolitan Transportation Authority** (**T** 1-718 330 1234, www.MTA.info) operates New York's thousands of buses and subway carriages. Maps and other information are available on the MTA website. A **MetroCard** allows unlimited use of the subway and MTA buses (with free transfers) for a day, a week or a month and can be purchased with cash, debit or credit cards from subway vending machines or ticket booths. Pay-per-use MetroCards are also available and are ideal if you're unsure how much you are going to use the MTA or if you're travelling in a group. A $10 MetroCard, for example, is valid for six journeys.

→ Travel extras

Safety

New York's reputation as a dangerous city is largely a thing of the past. However, as in any big city, pickpocketing takes place in touristy areas such as Times Square and other Midtown locations. You should keep an eye on your belongings at all times and stick to streets where others are walking late at night. Most of the avenues are always full of cabs, if you find yourself feeling lost or uncomfortable. For emergency numbers, see Directory p234.

Tipping

Almost everyone working in a service industry in New York will expect a tip, so keep some one-dollar bills handy at all times. In **restaurants** the rule of thumb is to double the tax, which works out as a 17% tip. If service is lousy you are under no obligation to tip, although 15% is usually regarded as the decent minimum. Some restaurants automatically add a service charge on to the bill, especially for groups of six or more, so make sure you check before handing over more money. **Bar staff** expect $1 per drink. You should tip **taxi drivers** about 15-20% or you can round up to the next dollar or two depending on the total fare. **Hotel attendants** and doorman will expect a tip of $1 per bag for delivering luggage to your room.

Visas

Due to the tightened security situation, visitors from many countries now require visas to enter the USA. However, citizens of Australia, Austria, Denmark, France, Germany, Ireland, Italy, Japan, the Netherlands, New Zealand, Portugal, Singapore, Spain, Sweden, Switzerland and the UK, who are in possession of a valid passport, do not require visas for visits of up to 90 days. Canadians must show proof of citizenship in the form of an ID card or passport.

Subway

Five million people use the subway each day, proof that this is the most reliable and handiest way to manoeuvre around the city, despite its rather grungy appearance at some stations. The system encompasses a massive area without zones or fare restrictions; for $2 you can travel to any of the five boroughs as far as the end of the line. The system can seem complicated at first but it's logical once you get the hang of it. Letters or numbers are used to distinguish the trains and colours are used to denote different lines, with stations named after their street location. 'Express' trains only call at major stops, while 'local' trains stop at each station.

Bus

The bus system is far-reaching and allows great views of New York street life at a more leisurely pace. Buses only accept exact change (no pennies or half-dollars), so it's best to buy a **MetroCard** (see p27), which will allow you to ride two buses within two hours for one fare. Otherwise, ask for a transfer when you board if you want to ride another bus within two hours. Buses generally travel in straight lines up and down the Manhattan grid but ask the driver if you need guidance. Pick up a bus map at the airport or subway.

Ferry

The **Staten Island Ferry**, (T 1-718 815 BOAT) runs from the terminal on South Street at the end of Whitehall Street in Lower Manhatten. This local commuter ferry is one of the best means of catching a free glimpse of the Statue of Liberty and the Manhattan skyline. Grab a seat near sundown for romantic views of the city. It runs 24 hours daily, every 15 to 20 minutes during the day and every hour at night, with less frequent services at weekends.

Cycling

Cycling around the streets of New York requires nerves of steel. As an alternative, use the cycle lane that circles Manhattan – the

→ Street talk

Manhattan's grid system is easy to negotiate once you've understood a few basic principals. The grid operates in earnest above Washington Square Park in Greenwich Village (Downtown is chopped up differently), with Fifth Avenue separating the east and west sides. Avenues run north to south throughout Manhattan from First Avenue on the east side to 12th Avenue on the west side. The avenues are intersected north of Houston Street by numbered cross streets that run east to west, with house numbers increasing as you move away from Fifth Avenue. Uptown, Central Park marks the division between the east and west sides. When calculating distances, it's important to note that avenues are much larger than cross streets.

West Side is the most developed. It offers a more relaxed ride around town and fine views. Hiring a bike at Central Park is also a safer option (see p31). Consult www.nycvisit.com for further information on New York bike paths or **Transportation Alternatives**, www.transalt.org, which offers practical advice on cycling around the city. It also organizes the annual **Bike Week**, a 42-mile, five-borough cycle ride.

Taxi

Wave your arm an inch on a New York street and most likely you'll have hailed a cab. Inexpensive compared to most other major cities, New York's yellow cabs are loved by most city dwellers. Fares start at $2 until 8pm or $2.50 thereafter. The meter then runs at quarter-mile increments. You'll need to hold on, though, since most city cab drivers feel it's their duty to drive you along at neck-whipping speeds.

Walking

Manhattan is best seen by foot. Although the city may seem intimidating and enormous, it's really great for walking as it can be broken down easily into manageable sections and the subway is always nearby if you need to cover a larger distance. For many New Yorkers a 40-block walk is nothing unusual. Put on your best walking shoes and see what it's all about. Always obey pedestrian signs and look both ways before crossing a road as cars, taxis and bikes can make the streets dangerous for pedestrians. Don't worry about jaywalking – all New Yorkers do it when it's safe.

Tours

Adventure on a Shoestring, **T** 1-212 265 2663. *Sat and Sun; call for times and meeting place. $5 per person.* Howard Goldberg has been running a variety of tours for over 40 years. Each one lasts 90 minutes and may cover Marilyn Monroe's Manhattan, Haunted Greenwich Village, A Salute to Jackie Kennedy Onassis or a *Little Odessa* tour of Brighton Beach.

Big Onion Walking Tours, **T** 1-212 439 1090, www.bigonion.com *$12 per person.* Well-run and lively tours that focus on a variety of themes, such as the Gangs of New York or the Gay and Lesbian Village. The guides are all well-versed and entertaining. Call or check online for further information and to confirm tour times.

Central Park Bicycle Tours, meet outside 2 Columbus Circle, **T** 1-212 541 8759, www.centralbiketour.com *1000, 1300 and 1600. $35, $20 children.* Choose between a Central Park Movie Scenes, a Celebrity Trivia Bike Tour or a three-hour Manhattan Island Bike Tour. The friendly guides allow you the chance to stop and rest every so often. Bike rental is also available: $20 for two hours or $35 for a whole day.

Circle Line Harbor Cruise, Pier 83 at W 42nd St and 12th Av, **T** 1-212 563 3200, www.circle-line.com *Check website for times. $13-26 depending on length of tour.* This narrated tour, with stops at the Statue of Liberty and Ellis Island (see p35 and p36), is popular with tourists and a good way to see the city from afar.

Gray Line Bus Tour, Port Authority at 8th Av and 42nd St, **T** 1-800 669 0051. Probably the best of the familiar hop-on/hop-off double-decker tour buses. They don't provide much insight into the city as they whizz by but can offer a quick overview, if you're really short of time.

Liberty Helicopter Tours, 30th St at the Hudson River, **T** 1-212 967 4550, www.libertyhelicopters.com *$49 for 7 mins to $155 for 15 mins*. An expensive but unforgettable view of Manhattan.

Talking Street, **T** 1-800 644 3545, www.talkingstreet.com Anyone with a mobile phone can take this free self-guided tour of the Lower East Side, which explores the Jewish history of the area. There are 13 stops on the one-hour tour, starting from the Visitors' Center at 261 Broome Street, where you'll find free maps.

Tourist information

New York City's Official Visitor Information Center, 810 Seventh Av between 52nd St and 53rd St, **T** 1-212 484 1222, www.nycvisit.com *Mon-Fri 0830-1800; Sat, Sun and holidays 0900-1700. Subway B, D, E to 7th Av. Map 4, E5, p266* This is the city's official source for information and free maps, brochures and discount coupons to sights and theatres. It also has a MetroCard vending machine. The **Times Square Visitors Center** (*1560 Broadway between 46th St and 47th St, **T** 1-212 869 1890, daily 0800-2000*), is also helpful for free city and theatre information.

Lower Manhattan

Lower Manhattan has, perhaps, a more palpable sense of history than any other part of the city. **Bowling Green Park**, *a little patch of green near the tip of the island, is where Dutch general Peter Minuit bought the whole island of New Amsterdam from the American Indians in 1626 for roughly $24 in trade goods. The district has been shaped by trade ever since. As the city's oldest quarter, Lower Manhattan today is a hodgepodge of skyscrapers, churches, statues and financial institutions, with the money-making machine of the New York Stock Exchange on* **Wall Street** *sitting right smack next to a church dating back to the 17th century.*

However, Lower Manhattan is symbolic of more than financial wheeler-dealing these days. Downtown is still dotted with memorials, flowers and peace signs, but the sombre atmosphere that permeated Manhattan's financial district after September 11th 2001 is giving way to a renewed sense of purpose, with plans approved in late 2003 for construction of the **Freedom Tower** *on the World Trade Center site. Quite apart from the morbid allure of Ground Zero, the area has plenty of appeal for visitors, with some of New York's most iconic symbols,* **Brooklyn Bridge** *and the* **Statue of Liberty**, *within easy reach.*

▸▸ *See Sleeping p118, Eating and drinking p137, Bars and clubs p165*

 Sights

★ Statue of Liberty

T 1-212 363 3200, www.nps.gov/stli *Circle line ferry from Battery Park daily 0900-1700 in winter, 0845-1845 in summer. Admission to Liberty Island free. Ferry tickets $10, $8 seniors, $3 children (sold at Castle Clinton). Map 1, H3, p261*

New York's most recognized symbol carries even more significance these days due to the gap in the Manhattan skyline. Modern-day

Ms Liberty and her torch now seem more emblematic of the struggle for harmony than the promise of opportunity. The statue was the brainchild of the French statesman Edouard de Laboulaye, who wanted to honour the friendship between France and the USA. Sculptor Frederic-August Bartholdi was responsible for building it and Gustav Eiffel helped design a metal framework to support the base of the structure. It took 20 years to get the project finished but finally, in 1886, the 151-foot statue was unveiled. The famous poem by Emma Lazarus at the base reads, *'Give me your tired, your poor, your huddled masses yearning to breathe free. The wretched refuse of your teeming shore. Send these, the tempest-tossed to me. I lift my lamp beside the golden door'*.

In the 1980s, the grimy statue underwent a massive $100-million renovation to clean her up and replace her torch. Since September 11, the statue, crown and museum have remained closed but visitors can still walk around the grounds. The Circle Line ferry runs to the Statue every 30 minutes from Battery Park but queues can be ridiculously long in the summertime unless you arrive early or go on a weekday.

Ellis Island

T 1-212 363 3200. *Circle line ferry from Battery Park daily 0900-1700 in winter, 0845-1845 in summer. Admission to Ellis Island free. Ferry tickets $10, $8 seniors, $3 children (sold at Castle Clinton). Map 1, H3, p261*

The second stop on the Circle Line ferry, Ellis Island was the point of arrival for more than 12 million immigrants who came to the United States between 1892 and 1954. As many as 12,000 people per day were processed through Ellis Island, after medical examinations and interviews with immigration officers. The **Museum of Immigration** offers a fascinating glimpse in to the lives of the immigrants who passed along the human production line through the cavernous Registry room, where criminals,

> ### CityPass
>
> **CityPass** (www.citypass.net) is an affordable way to see six attractions over a nine-day period . It can be purchased at any of the attractions and includes entry to the American Museum of Natural History, the Guggenheim Museum, the Museum of Modern Art (currently in Queens), the Intrepid Sea Air Space Museum, Circle Line Harbor Cruise and the Empire State Building Observatory & NY Skyride. It costs $45 for adults and $39 for children 17 and under.

disease-ridden immigrants and anarchists were turned back after failing inspection. Items of clothing, faded photographs and other artefacts are organized according to cultural origin to show the contrasting items that families from different parts of the world brought with them to start their new lives in America. The hereditary database allows visitors to search for family roots.

● *Between Brooklyn and Manhattan is Governor's Island, which was home to the US Coastguard for 200 years.*

Battery Park
South end of Broadway. *Subway 4, 5 to Bowling Green.*
Map 7, H2-3, p272

At the tip of Manhattan, congested Battery Park has splendid views of the Statue of Liberty, Ellis Island and Governor's Island. If you don't have time to take the Circle Line Harbor Cruise, you can enjoy the panorama from the Rise bar at the Ritz-Carlton Battery Park (see p165). Within the park is the façade of **Castle Clinton**, built as a fortress for the War of 1812, before being decommissioned and turned into a garden and renowned concert hall in 1824. The shell now serves as a ticket booth for the Circle Line ferry (see p32).

Smatterings of monuments throughout the park commemorate immigrants from around the world. More recently, the park has acquired *The Sphere*, a bronze and steel sculpture built in 1971 to honour world peace. It was the only salvageable piece of artwork from the World Trade Center.

● *Just across the road from Battery Park is 7 State Street, the only survivor of a series of waterfront homes built in the 1790s. The elegant Georgian-style house is a* **Shrine to Saint Elizabeth Ann Seton**, *who was born on Staten Island and canonized as the first saint in the USA in 1975.*

National Museum of the American Indian
One Bowling Green, **T** 1-212 514 3700, *Mon-Wed, Fri-Sun 1000-1700, Thu 1000-2000, free. Subway 4, 5 to Bowling Green. Map 7, H3, p272*

North of Battery Park is one of the city's most enduring beaux arts structures, the former **US Customs House**. Built as a monument to the Port of New York, it is now home to the Smithsonian's National Museum of the American Indian, a collection of artefacts from nearly every tribe in the USA, including crafts, rodeo items and contemporary art.

Outside the museum is New York's oldest park. **Bowling Green**, where the Dutch general Peter Minuit made his deal with the American Indians in 1626 (see p240). It became a Dutch cattle market but was transformed into a space for bowls by the British in the 1730s. Just up the street is the brazen **Wall Street bull**, an icon of the economic strength of the city in the 1990s.

● *A few blocks east of Bowling Green is refurbished Stone Street, a colourful, historic two-block area filled with restaurants and bars. Lively during the day and night with Downtown bankers, tourists and locals, it provides a welcome change of pace from the otherwise lacklustre eating spots around here.*

▶ The Great Hoax

In 1824, a year of economic depression and newspaper sensationalism, two men by the names of DeVoe and Lozier caused consternation in New York's Central Market by claiming that Manhattan was sinking. The weight of the inhabitants and buildings was, according to the pair, threatening to unbalance the southern part of the island and tip the city into the harbour. The duo announced they had been hired by Mayor Stephen Allen to solve the problem by sawing Manhattan in half, towing the lower portion in to the harbour, turning it around and then reattaching it. The most heavily populated section of Manhattan would thus be situated in the middle of a more balanced island and the danger of its tipping into New York harbour would be overcome. Rumour has it that DeVoe and Lozier signed up hundreds of eager workers for their project and on the appointed day an estimated one thousand volunteers turned up. After a long wait, a message was finally delivered to the expectant crowds, announcing that DeVoe and Lozier had left town on health grounds. This extraordinary hoax remains one of New York's most enduring legends.

Fraunces Tavern Museum

54 Pearl St, **T** 1-212 425 1778, *Tue, Wed, Fri 1000-1700, Thu 1000-1900, Sat 1100-1700, $3, students $2. Subway 4, 5 to Bowling Green, 1, 2 to Wall St Map 7, G4, p272*

This was where George Washington sent his troops out to recapture New York from the British in 1782 (see p240). The tavern of Samuel Frances was destroyed in the 1800s by fires that wiped out many Dutch structures in Lower Manhattan but was restored in the early 1900s. The museum feels a little cobbled together but it has two period rooms showing the history of the tavern and of Manhattan in the late 1700s, as well as a working bar where you can raise a toast to George.

Wall Street
Subway 1, 2, 4, 5 to Wall St, J, M, Z to Broad St.   Map 7, E3-F6, p272

Wall Street takes its name from the wooden barricade, or 'wal', that the Dutch constructed along the edge of their settlement in 1653, as protection from the English colonies to the north. These days it's a narrow mile-long strip synonymous with capitalist wagering. The most noticeable landmark is the **New York Stock Exchange**, whose neo-classical façade built in 1903 has witnessed more money changing hands than anywhere else in the world. Now covered in an enormous American flag and with armoured military personnel outside, it is currently closed to visitors. Brokers and traders who formerly shouted on the floor are more likely to be sitting behind computer screens elsewhere these days.

At the western end of Wall Street sits **Trinity Church**, an anomaly amongst the city's financial buildings. The church, originally constructed in 1697 but rebuilt in 1846 after a fire, hosts music concerts during the week. **Federal Hall**, at 26 Wall Street, is where George Washington took the oath of office in 1789 and briefly served as the first US Capitol. Across the street, **No23** (now the Morgan Guaranty Trust Company but formerly JP Morgan's office) was the site of a massive explosion in 1920 when an anarchist killed 33 with a wagonload of explosives. Scars of the blast are still evident. Other noteworthy buildings include **No14**, the former abode of financier JP Morgan's mistress, which now houses a chic bar and restaurant on the 31st floor, and the **Merchants Exchange**, an Ionic temple at No55, that is now a Cipriani's restaurant.

South Street Seaport

Pier 17, at the East River and eastern end of Fulton St, **T** 1-212 732 7678, www.southstseaport.org *Subway 1, 2, 4, 5, J, M, Z to Fulton St-Broadway Nassau Map 2, F7, p263*

Located on the site of the city's former fish market, this is one of the best surviving examples of what 18th-century New York was like. It underwent a major renovation in the late 1960s, following the construction of Franklin D Roosevelt Drive, which still roars overhead. Pier 17 now serves as a tourist destination with some breezy views and nautical appeal but little charm thanks to the herds of visitors. Within easy sniffing distance is the **Fulton Fish Market**, where New York's restaurants stock up on seafood. The **South Street Seaport Museum** (213 Water St at Beekman St) encompasses a series of restored warehouses and recounts the history of the once-thriving seaport with displays of sailing vessels and tugboats as well as some maritime goods for sale.

City Hall

Broadway at Park Row, **T** 1-212 788 3000, *Subway 4, 5, 6 to Brooklyn Bridge-City Hall or J, M, Z to Chambers St. Map 7, B3-4, p272*

The heart of the city's rather insipid civic centre, City Hall was intended to be the northernmost point of Manhattan when it was built in 1812. The building has a formal, federal air, with large columns and a spiral staircase inside. Abraham Lincoln lay in state here in 1865 before his funeral procession. Outside is the little green space of **City Hall Park**, recognizable to locals as the site of press conferences, political protests and countless marriages over the years. Most recently, it was the site of the shooting of a local councilman by a political rival in 2003. Across the street to the east is **Park Row**, formally known as Newspaper Row. This was New York's version of Fleet Street in the late 1800s, with 19 newspapers clustered together here. A bronze statue of Benjamin Franklin holding his *Pennsylvania Gazette* sits at the intersection of Park Row, Spruce and Nassau Streets.

Woolworth Building

233 Broadway between Park Pl and Barclay St. *Subway 2, 3 to Park Pl. Map 7, C2-3, p272*

This elegant skyscraper across from City Hall Park is a Gothic masterpiece and tribute to architect Cass Gilbert's designs (he also built the US Customs House, the US Courthouse and the New York Life Insurance Company building). When it was finished in 1913, it was the tallest building in New York at 60 stories, and remained so until 1931 when the Chrysler Building was completed. Its church-like design ensures that its elongated shape stands out in the otherwise modern landscape of Downtown. Nicknamed the Cathedral of Commerce, the Woolworth Building has a decadent lobby with mosaics, gargoyles and vaulted ceilings that is open to visitors during the day. Try to find the gargoyle of Woolworth himself counting nickels and dimes and the image of Gilbert holding a model of his building.

St Paul's Chapel

Broadway between Vesey St and Fulton St. *Subway 2, 3 to Park Pl. Map 7, C3, p272*

Two blocks south of the Woolworth Building on Broadway sits the oldest church in Manhattan, St Paul's Chapel. Dating back to British rule, it was designed in 1766 to look like St Martin-in-the-Fields in London. George Washington came here to pray; his pew is still on display. Despite its location just opposite the World Trade Center, St Paul's remarkably survived September 11th unscathed and played a big role as a refuge for the workers at the site.

▶ **9-11-2001**

Manhattan

The Twin Towers of the World Trade Center had a short life of only 29 years. They were reviled by some, admired by others but were undisputed as a symbol of New York's strong, often arrogant nature. As the centre of the world's financial markets, they were also perceived by some as emblems of the greed of a privileged, capitalist country. In reality, the towers were filled with workers from around the world.

In 1993, the World Trade Center was bombed by a terrorist group, leaving six people dead and thousands injured. However, this shocking event was eclipsed by the total destruction that took place on September 11th 2001, when two hijacked planes were deliberately flown straight into the Twin Towers by members of the Al-Qaida terrorist network.

Since that fateful day in 2001, New York has changed forever. The physical collapse of the towers and the motivation of those responsible shocked the city to its core. Despite its self-assertive and maverick personality, this mighty city was shown to be vulnerable. New York's loss of innocence was a sobering reminder of how quickly lives and skylines can change. Yet, despite the tragedy, many New Yorkers believe the events have created a sense of community and friendliness that has made the city an even better place to live.

World Trade Center site
Subway 1, 2 to Chambers St. Map 7, D1, p272

Visiting the World Trade Center site will give you a sense of the enormity of what is missing but there's little actually to see from the viewing platform, apart from a big open pit, a few signs of construction and street vendors, still capitalising on tourists' morbid fascination, by selling souvenirs nearby.

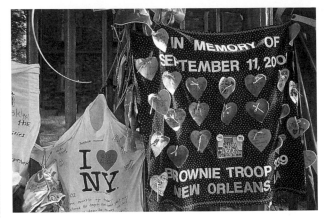

In memoriam
*Messages of sympathy still shroud the World Trade Center site,
Ground Zero for the terrorist attacks on September 11th 2001.*

The plan for the redevelopment of the World Trade Center site
was finally agreed in late 2003 after months of creative wrangling
between the original architect, Daniel Libeskind, and David Childs,
who was brought in to work on the project by the leaseholder,
Larry Silverstein. The highly sensitive redevelopment has had many
groups to please, not least the families of the victims of the
September 11th attacks. Architects, government officials, civic
groups and property developers have all had a say since
consultation started in 2002.

At the heart of the new design is the 1,776- foot **Freedom
Tower** (taller than the original towers), whose asymmetric form
and 276-foot spire echo the Statue of Liberty. The tower will be
accompanied by a memorial called 'Reflecting Absence' by Michael
Arad and Peter Walker, consisting of a grove of trees reflected in
two deep pools. However, some victims' families have voiced

concern that the memorial lacks a clear connection to the human cost of the attacks. A new transportation terminal designed by the Spanish architect Santiago Calatrava is also included in the plans, with construction due to start in summer 2004.

Battery Park City
from Pier 1 to Chambers St, **T** 1-212 267 9700, www.bpcparks.org
Subway 4, 5 to Bowling Green.   Map 2, p262

This peaceful 30-acre stretch of Downtown was created from the rock and other debris deposited here when the Twin Towers were built in the early 1970s. The landscaped Esplanade is used by roller-bladers, joggers and lunching office workers and is a pleasant place for a stroll. Walking tours are available.

At the southern end of the Esplanade, close to Battery Park, is the interesting and well-presented **Museum of Jewish Heritage** (*18 First Pl, T 1-212 509 6130, www.mjhnyc   Sun-Wed 1000-1745, Thu 1000-2000, Fri 1000-1500. $7, $5 seniors and students*), a memorial to Holocaust victims and to the survivors who found new lives in New York. Nearby, sculptures adorn **Robert F Wagner Park**, a fine place to take in the waterside views of New Jersey and the Statue of Liberty.

Chinatown, Little Italy and Nolita

The cluttered, untidy streets of Chinatown can be brash and overwhelming, but with the right attitude their fluorescent lights and kitschy spirit can also be a hoot. Home to roughly 125,000 of New York's 400,000 Chinese inhabitants and almost as many faux designer accessories, Chinatown has been steadily expanding in recent years, keeping its title as the largest Chinatown in the western hemisphere. With twice as many people per acre as the rest of Manhattan, this area is not for those who suffer from claustrophobia. It's a jumble of market-style shops, restaurants, fish and fruit stands. Pagoda-style storefronts pour out onto the sidewalks of Mott, Bayard and Canal Streets. Buddhist temples, the **Museum of Chinese in the Americas**, a Confucius statue and the oldest Roman Catholic church in town are packed in here, too. Bring your earplugs in January and February during the celebration of the **Chinese New Year**; although fireworks were officially banned under the Giuliani administration, you'll find no shortage of them amid these bustling streets.

At the north end of Chinatown and increasingly crowded out by its neighbour, **Little Italy** hosts a ten-day festival in September to honour the patron saint of Naples, **San Gennaro**. The restaurants on Mulberry Street tend to be touristy and tacky, with most true Italians having long since moved elsewhere, but if tinselled streets and strong espressos appeal, stop here for a break from the bargain shopping. Further up the road, trendy **Nolita** springs out of Little Italy, with happening cafés and some of the city's best boutiques.

▸▸ See Eating and drinking p138, Bars and clubs p166,

Sights

★ Chinatown
Canal and Grand Streets, between Broadway and The Bowery.
Subway J, M, N, R, Z, 6 to Canal St. Map 2, B5-C6, p262

The colourful pagoda-style storefronts aligning **Canal Street** are the most popular destination for shoppers hoping to take home some discounted goods. Bargain-hunters will enjoy the extensive collections of counterfeit designer handbags, fake Rolexes, bootleg CDs and DVDs, unique Asian imports and pop-culture kitsch, not to mention jewellery, T-shirts, pashminas, dishes, paper lanterns, slippers, toys and just about anything else you might want. Further north at the markets on **Grand Street**, Chinese-Americans and other savvy New Yorkers shop for fish, fruit and vegetables. Snow peas, spices, dried foods and seafood of every sort add to the general chaos of the narrow sidewalks. Countless restaurants serve up dim

Dressing up
Shop till you drop at the stalls and shops along Grand and Canal Streets in Chinatown.

sum and Cantonese and Szechwan delicacies at affordable prices, while nightlife options include clubs and karaoke bars.

Bordering Chinatown to the east is **The Bowery**, a broad and dusty street lined with a smattering of speciality shops. In its heyday, before Times Square made its mark, this street was the heart of the city's glamorous theatre district. At the junction with Worth Street is a monument for the Chinese-American soldiers of World War II, while at No18 is the oldest row house in Manhattan, built in 1785. Note the Romanesque facade of the former **Bowery**

! Between 1880 and 1926, the sharp turn on Doyers Street, just below Pell Street, was known as the Bloody Angle. It is where notorious gangs On Leong Tong and Hip Sing Tong fought for control of opium trafficking and gambling in the area .

Savings Bank at No130. Built in 1894 by Stanford White, the gold-leafed interior is deluxe with a capital D.

You can salute the statue of Confucius in the plaza just off The Bowery before browsing the many peculiar shops and restaurants that fill the small, sinuous area around Pell, Mosco and Doyers Streets. West of Mosco Street is **Columbus Park**, where locals practise tai-chi and place wagers on the game of mah-jongg. The **Eastern States Buddhist Temple** (64 Mott Street, **T** 1-212 966 6229) is an incense-infused shrine with some significant Buddhas.

Museum of Chinese in the Americas
70 Mulberry St, 2nd floor, *T* 1-212 619 4785, www.moca-nyc.org, *Tue-Sun noon-5pm. $3, students and seniors $1, children under 12 free. Subway J, M, Z, N, Q, R, W, 6 to Canal St. Map 2, C6, p262*

Recommended for those who want to see more of the area than fake Gucci handbags, this small museum consists of two rooms shaped in the style of a 15-sided Chinese lantern, containing interesting exhibits on Chinese immigrants around the world. Check out the permanent Family Portraits display, put together by photography students at the Fashion Institute of Technology, and the 'Where Is Home?' exhibit, which shows the evolution of New York's Chinatown and explores issues of migration, women, faith and home. The museum also offers an informative tour of Chinatown at 1300 on Saturday and Sunday for $10.

Church of the Transfiguration
29 Mott St, **T** 1-212 962 5157. *Subway 4, 5, 6, J, M, Z at Brooklyn Bridge. Map 2, C6, p262*

Incongruously sited amid dim sum restaurants and souvenir shops and offering a quiet reprieve from all the chatter outside is New York's oldest Roman Catholic church. A Georgian structure built in

1801, the church started as a place of worship for the many Italian and Irish immigrants in the area but now hosts the largest Chinese-American congregation in the country for masses in Cantonese and English. The Saint of All Immigrants, Mother Frances Cabrini, set up a school here in 1899.

Little Italy
between Houston St, Canal St, Lafayette St and The Bowery. *Subway J, M to the Bowery. Map 2, B6, p262*

The electric lights and al fresco dining of Little Italy are best enjoyed during the 10-day **Feast of San Gennaro** in September (see p199), at other times the area retains little of its original Italian charm. Southern Italians first made this part of New York their home in the 1850s but today the area seems to be struggling to keep its roots alive. Although you'll still find the best pizza in the city on Spring Street at **Lombardi's** (see p139), and **Mulberry Street** is fun for a coffee and a gelato, unfortunately most of the restaurants are tourist traps; better Italian food can be found elsewhere. Mulberry Street will be familiar to many from *The Godfather* movies; it features in the christening scene in part one and as the setting of the Genco Olive Oil company. Film director Martin Scorsese grew up on Elizabeth Street but, like many other Italians, he has long since left the neighbourhood. Many New York Italians now live in areas outside Manhattan, particularly parts of Brooklyn around leafy Cobble Hill.

Nolita
From Houston St to Grand St, between Lafayette St and the Bowery. *Subway J, M to the Bowery. Map 2, B6, p262*

The northern part of Little Italy between Spring and Houston Streets is known as Nolita (**no**rth of **Li**ttle **Ita**ly), where cutting-edge designers have boutiques and old-time locals mingle with trendy Downtown-types. Undoubtedly one of Manhattan's coolest spot these days, the area resembles SoHo in the 1970s, with a similar sought-after grungy appeal. Explore the shops and restaurants and soak up the fashionable atmosphere, particularly around Elizabeth and Mott Streets. This area is at its best around brunchtime or when SoHo becomes too crowded.

● *Old St Patrick's Cathedral at 263 Mulberry Street, built in 1815, has now been restored after a fire. This is where John F Kennedy Jr's memorial mass was given after his death in 1999.*

SoHo and Tribeca

If the hustle and bustle of Chinatown is too much, a short stroll away lies SoHo, Manhattan's eternally hip and stylish district. Architecturally as good-looking as its inhabitants, SoHo continues its run as the city's cast-iron delight. The area's beautiful ironwork was developed in the 1850s as an ornate but inexpensive way to assemble buildings. SoHo was the industrial heart of the city at the time, with numerous factories and sweatshops producing china, glass, silk, satin, lace, ribbons and furs. By 1960 the fabric trade had declined and SoHo was a run-down slum known as 'hell's hundred acres'; there was even talk of building an expressway through the area. Fortunately, the developers didn't get their way and SoHo became an enclave of artists seeking cheap rents and large work spaces. They converted vacant warehouses into studios, galleries and homes. Andy Warhol, Chuck Close and Cindy Sherman were a few of the famous names that inhabited the area. By 1971, the SoHo artists were strong enough to force the city to change its zoning laws and, soon after, a 26-block area of SoHo was designated a historic district. Now most of the 'art enthusiasts' in the neighbourhood are, in fact, multi-millionaires and models.

Despite its sometimes pretentious air, SoHo on a sunny morning is one of New York's most appealing backdrops. **Sullivan Street** *still retains its Italian heritage, with long-established restaurants, some great bakeries and mellow cafés. Bustling Prince and Spring Streets slice*

► **Cast-iron crew**

Check out the following buildings for the best of SoHo's cast-iron architecture:

Haughwout Building (490 Broadway and Broome St) The oldest and, many say, the finest cast-iron structure in SoHo was built in 1857 with majestic columns and arches adorned with little motifs.

Little Singer Building (561 Broadway at Prince St) This handsome red-brick building was constructed in 1903 by Ernest Flagg as the main office of the sewing machine company. It is now partly a co-op for artists. The Singer name, cast in iron, can still be seen on the Prince Street side.

Roosevelt Building (478 Broadway) A picturesque 1874 structure with eye-catching columned windows, especially on the decorative third floor.

Frederick Clark Withers Building (448 Broome St) Gothic revival meets cast iron in this 1871 building. Note the rosettes between the windows on each floor and the decadent design of the roof.

across Broadway where the **New Museum of Contemporary Art** sits among galleries and busy clothing stores. Design enthusiasts won't want to miss the landmark **Prada** store, designed by Dutch architect Rem Koolhaas. Local artists flank the pavement along **West Broadway**, the main shopping thoroughfare, to sell their art and crafts. Sit at one of the many cafés to watch New York's chicest residents saunter by or have a fancy Martini at one of the swanky hotel bars. Just west lies **Tribeca** where more funky buildings, trendy people and high-end stores share space with Robert De Niro's **Tribeca Film Center** and **Duane Park**.

►► See Sleeping p119, Eating and drinking p140, Bars and clubs p168

▶ Gallery gallop: SoHo

SoHo's many art galleries aren't always obvious from the street as many are located above the ground floor. Usually signs are posted on a building's entrance.

For an overview of the area's art scene start at Houston Street on Broadway, walking down to Spring Street and then weaving around Mercer, Greene and Wooster Streets before ending up at West Broadway. The area between Houston Street and Grand Street houses a great deal of art and photography, although the trend to move Uptown to Chelsea has left some of the former SoHo spaces empty.

Serious art buffs should be sure to pick up the *Gallery Guide*, a comprehensive listing of many of the 500 or so galleries in New York, from one of the featured venues. However, if you just want to dip in to the SoHo art scene, check out the following art spaces – most are on Wooster Street (the area's main gallery thoroughfare).

June Kelly Gallery, 591 Broadway, between Houston St and Prince St, Flr 3, **T** 1-212 226 1660, Tue-Sat 1100-1800. Contemporary painting, sculpture and photography.

Peter Blum Gallery, 99 Wooster St, **T** 1-212 343 0441, Tue-Fri 1000-1800, Sat 1100-1800. Contemporary paintings, photographs and art installations.

Spencer Brownstone Gallery, 39 Wooster St, **T** 1-212 334 3455, Tue-Sat 1100-1800. Conceptual contemporary art installations.

The Drawing Center, 35 Wooster St, **T** 1-212 219 2166, Tue-Fri 1000-1800, Sat 1100-1800. Contemporary and historic drawings.

Deitch Projects, 18 Wooster St, and 76 Grand St, **T** 1-212 343 7300, Tue-Sat 1100-1800. Contemporary sculptures, paintings, collages and more.

Sights

New Museum of Contemporary Art

583 Broadway between Houston St and Prince St, **T** 1-212 219 1222, www.newmuseum.org *Tue-Sun 1200-1800, Thu 1200-2000. $6, $3 students and seniors, free to all on Thu 1800-2000. Subway 6, C, E to Spring St, N, R, W to Prince St.   Map 2, A5, p262*

The prototype of all that's cutting-edge in contemporary art, this cast-iron SoHo space displays work by a selection of rising artists from the past decade. Known for its controversial exhibitions, the museum shows pieces in various media by local and international artists, whose work is too risqué to be taken on by other galleries. An excellent bookstore and reading room are nestled downstairs, where debate and discussion are encouraged through performances and new media. Like many museums in New York, the New Museum will be moving in 2006 to a bigger space, a few blocks over on The Bowery.

Tribeca

Broadway to Canal St between Greenwich St and Chambers St. *Subway 1, 2 to Chambers St or Franklin St. Map 2, D3-D5, p262*

Like SoHo, Tribeca's appeal for the visitor is more to do with ambling around, poking into galleries and absorbing the neighbourhood's architecture and ambience than the chance to visit any landmark sights. Located just a few blocks from the former World Trade Center, Tribeca has suffered greatly since September 11th, when many residents and visitors abandoned the badly damaged neighbourhood. In response, the city has been promoting the area, even running ad campaigns to get New Yorkers back to this part of Downtown.

Tribeca is the film production centre of New York. Robert De Niro's **Tribeca Fim Center** (375 Greenwich St), boosted the

Downtown effort by launching the successful **Tribeca Film Festival** in 2002 (see p196). The area is ideal for an afternoon's shopping followed by a night out in a chic warehouse bar.

Duane Park
Duane St between Hudson St and Greenwich St. *Subway 1,2 to Chambers St. Map 2, D4, p262*

This small slice of green is a good place to gain a feeling for Tribeca's lofty 19th-century industrial architecture. It is surrounded by some noteworthy red-brick and brownstone houses, with a view of the Woolworth Building to the southeast. Once the butter, egg and cheese market, this little patch of land was bought by the city as a public park in 1797 for five dollars.

Greenwich Village and Chelsea

The area of Manhattan now known as Greenwich Village was first developed as farmland by the Dutch in the 17th century, gradually becoming a desirable residential area of large land plots and notable mansions. By the 19th century the Village's crooked layout was already well established, so it escaped the grid that was imposed on the rest of the city in 1811. The twisting, leafy streets are now one of the defining characteristics of Greenwich Village, attracting wealthy New Yorkers who've moved into the area to enjoy its beautiful townhouses, European-style cafés and lack of high-rise buildings.

*New York University started building around **Washington Square Park** in 1836 and, soon after, the area became an enclave of art clubs, literary salons and learned societies. Today, students, chess players, artists, break dancers and families fill the streets around the Square, following in the footsteps of writers, painters, actors and musicians who made this area a focal point for the Beat movement in the 1950s. **Bleecker Street**, the busy thoroughfare that spans the Village, is the most commercial part of the area, while **Sheridan***

Square at Christopher Street is where the gay rights movement was born in 1969. The peaceful streets tucked off Seventh Avenue in the **West Village** feel a world apart from one of the world's fastest cities. The best way to see them is by spending a couple of hours exploring on foot or by joining an organized walking tour. Charm oozes from every square inch and former carriage houses make for some of the most expensive real estate in the city.

The genteel crowd of the West Village contrast with the hip inhabitants of the **Meatpacking District** to the north. This cobbled area is getting trendier by the minute as big-name designers, bars and clubs move in to share space with a working meat market. Further north again is **Chelsea**, where art galleries, a thriving gay scene, the best weekend flea market in the city, food lovers' **Chelsea Market** and a buzzing, cruisy nightlife make for a don't-miss destination.

Fashionable theatregoers and film studios located here in the early 1900s, but the area's proximity to the river and railroad lines saw industrial breweries and tenements take over and, like much of Downtown, Chelsea became dilapidated and run-down. In the 1980s money was invested to spruce up its tree-lined streets and these days Chelsea is one of the most vibrant areas, filled with handsome gay men called Chelsea boys, the **Joyce Dance Theater**, more galleries than anywhere in the city and a vast choice of bars and restaurants.

➤➤ *See Sleeping p120, Eating and drinking p144, Bars and clubs p169.*

◉ Sights

Washington Square Park
5th Av at Washington Sq North. *Subway A, C, E, F, S, V to West 4th St. Map 3, G6, p264*

Once a burial ground for the poor and the site of public executions, this mostly concrete square now serves as one of the best people-watching areas in town. Political activists and polemical ranters, artists, chess players, break dancers and street loafers are joined in the autumn by students from the **New York University** campus to create a hubbub of activity.

The 77-foot-high **Washington Square Arch** was built to honour George Washington in 1889 and redesigned in marble in 1891 by Stanford White (the man responsible for building much of New York at the turn of the 19th century). Herman Melville, Mark Twain, Henry James and Edgar Allen Poe are a few of the famed literary characters who lived in the houses around the square.

Although West Villagers point out that their neighbourhood technically starts west of Seventh Avenue, many New Yorkers consider Washington Square Park to be the dividing mark between the East and West Villages. It is certainly the logical starting point for a walk through Greenwich Village, as you can either go south to one of the many cafés along MacDougal or Bleecker Streets, or head west into the tranquil streets beyond Seventh Avenue.

● *On the southeast corner of the square, just below W Third Street is Minetta Lane, the home of Café Wha? Although its heyday has long passed, this is where Bob Dylan and Jimi Hendrix once played.*

Bleecker Street
between Hudson St and The Bowery. *Subway A, C, E, F, S, V to West 4th St. Map 3, G3-H7, p264*

To the south of Washington Square, cafés, bars and souvenir shops line Bleecker Street, some more appealing than others. **Caffe Reggio**, just off Bleecker Street at 119 MacDougal Street (see p148), claims to own the first-ever espresso machine to arrive in the USA. Writers and poets first made this area famous but now the scene is rather touristy. However, among the tacky shops are some outstanding bars and music venues, notably the **Blue Note** (see p189), where many jazz greats can still be heard.

Jefferson Market Library

425 Sixth Av, **T** 1-212 243 4332, www.nypl.org *Subway A, C, E, F, S, V to West 4th St. Map 3, F5, p264*

Gables, Gothic trimming and a clock tower make this one of the area's most recognized landmarks. The Venetian-style structure was built in 1875 as a courthouse, served as a jail for troublesome women and was then converted into a public library in the 1960s. Across the street, notice the small alley of **Patchin Place**, where EE Cummings, Djuana Barnes and Marlon Brando all lived at various times.

● *The lopsided townhouse at 18 West 11th Street was blown up in 1970 by the radical Weathermen Group, who accidentally ignited their basement bomb factory. Kathy Boudin, a member of the group, managed to escape (naked) and evade police for ten years after the blast. She was released in 2003 after two decades in jail.*

West Village

From 7th Av to the Hudson River between Houston St and 14 St. *Subway 1, 9 to Christopher St. Map 3, p264*

Considered the most liberal part of Manhattan, **Christopher Street** is the focal point for the city's gay community. The Stonewall Rebellion of 1969, when the gay rights movement was established, happened outside the Stonewall bar on Sheridan Square following riots with the police. Christopher Street remains at the cutting edge of New York's gay scene, as evidenced by the many condom and leather shops in the area.

Wander just off Christopher Street, however, and the country-like streets taper off into some seriously off-grid sections of town, creating a village atmosphere that was central to New York's literary and artistic development from the 1830s onwards. Stroll around the West Village to see the row houses on Barrow, Bedford and Grove Streets, between Seventh Avenue and Hudson Street. The 9.5-foot wide house at **75½ Bedford Street** is allegedly the narrowest in the Village and is situated on one of its loveliest corners. Some well-known people lived here including the poet Edna St Vincent Millay, Cary Grant and Margaret Mead.

At 86 Bedford Street is a former speakeasy from the Prohibition era, known to locals as **Chumley's**. Note the back door of the bar, where patrons would sneak out in the 1920s.

Hudson Street intersects many of the leafier thoroughfares and is a good stopping point for a drink or meal. Dylan Thomas frequented the **White Horse Tavern** at 11th and Hudson Street and died after leaving the bar one night in 1953 (see p169).

● *Those wanting to take in a sunset should head over to Hudson River Park, which borders the West Village and has many renovated piers with views across the water.*

Meatpacking District
14th St down to Little W 12th St, between 8th Av and the Hudson River. *Subway A, C, E to 14th St or L to 8th Av. Map 3, p264*

It would be difficult to imagine any area of Manhattan achieving greater social status than this industrial, cobbled northern border of the West Village called the Meatpacking District. The working market has been infiltrated by sought-after designers, including Stella McCartney, chic bars and cutting-edge nightclubs to create an unusual combination of meatpacking by day, socialising with the stars by night. Even London's exclusive **Soho House** has opened a branch here, while the restaurant **Pastis** literally packs 'em in every night; stop for a drink at its impossibly handsome French bar (see p144).

Chelsea Historic District
20th to 22nd St between 8th and 10th Av. *Subway C, E to 23rd St. Map 3, D2-3, p264*

Bargain hunt
Root around for the perfect souvenir among the bric-a-brac at Chelsea Flea Market.

The patchwork of beautiful brownstone houses, housing projects, warehouses, art galleries, restaurants and factories from 14th to 26th Streets between Broadway and the Hudson River make Chelsea one of the most vivid neighbourhoods in the city.

At its heart is the **Chelsea Historic District**, which escaped destruction when elevated train lines ripped up the rest of the neighbourhood in the 1870s. It contains some of Chelsea's best architecture from the 1800s, including dignified blocks of townhouses, elegant apartment buildings and the peaceful General Theological Seminary and its garden.

! Edith Wharton was born in 1862 at 14 West 23rd Street, once the most fashionable part of town.

Dia Center for the Arts
548 West 22nd St, **T** 1-212 989 5566, www.diachelsea.org
*Wed-Sun 1200-1800. $6, $3 students and seniors. Subway C, E to
23rd St. Map 3, D1, p264*

Nestled among the myriad galleries of Chelsea's warehouse district
is the pioneering Dia Center for the Art, the first gallery to open
in Chelsea in 1974. Internationally recognized artists, such as Andy
Warhol and minimalist Sol LeWitt got their early breaks here and it
now shows designers and contemporary artists from the 1960s and
1970s over three floors. The lobby, tiled in lime patterns, resembles
an empty retro swimming pool and has one of the best art
bookstores in New York, while the plexiglass water tower on the
rooftop enjoys views of the Hudson River.

Dia's stunning warehouse conversion, the **Dia: Beacon**
(*3 Beekman St, Beacon, NY, **T** 1-845 440 0100. Thu-Mon 1100-1800.
$10*) is located sixty miles north of the city in a former printing
plant. It has an enormous exhibition space for art installations.

Lower East Side and East Village

*The working-class **Lower East Side** may not be beautiful yet its
history-laden, grungy streets are among the most interesting
destinations on New York's social scene. Puerto Rican bodegas share
space with restaurants, boutiques, live music venues and galleries to
create an all-night buzz. Real estate in this area, once considered
the last bargain in town, is on the rise thanks to an influx of flash
hotels and restaurants.*

*In the mid-1800s, the area's crowded tenements were home to
immigrants from Ireland and Germany. They were followed between
1870 and 1930 by Italians, Jewish, Polish, Romanians, Chinese and
Ukranians who came here to work in the garment industry. After
World War II, Puerto Rican and African Americans also moved into
the area. The Eastern European influx to the area is still evident in the*

▶ Gallery gallop: Chelsea

One of the best ways to see art in New York is to stroll through Chelsea's gallery district, which stretches from 17th Street up to 26th Street between 10th and 11th Avenues. Most galleries are free, except for the Dia (see p60). Keep wandering until one sparks your interest, there are literally dozens filling the warehouse buildings, with the largest concentration centred around 20th to 22nd Streets. The following contemporary art galleries run south to north. For further information consult www.westchelseaarts.com See also p52.

Matthew Marks, 529 W 21st St, and 523 W 24th St, **T** 1-212 243 0200, Tue-Sat 1100-1800. New paintings, drawings, photographs and video installations by established artists are displayed in two contrasting spaces.

303 Gallery, 525 W 22nd St, **T** 1-212 255 1121, Tue-Sat 1000-1800. Mixed-media work by cutting-edge artists.

Barbara Gladstone, 515 W 24th St, **T** 1-212 206 9300, Tue-Sat 1000-1800. High-class sculptures, installations and more by well-known artists.

Gagosian Gallery, 555 W 24th St, **T** 1-212 741 1111, Tue-Sat 1000-1800. Top-notch painting and sculpture in a vast space.

Miller/Geisler Gallery, 511 W 25th St, Ste 305, **T** 1-212 255 2885, Tue-Sat 1000-1800. Displays a range of contemporary photographs, paintings and sculptures

*diners lining Second Avenue, selling matzoh ball soup, cured roast beef and the like; the Irish have left their mark, too, especially at New York's oldest drinking den, **McSorley's Old Ale House**. Join a walking tour run by the **Lower East Side Tenement Museum** for a fascinating insight into the area's poverty-stricken past.*

*Just across Houston Street is the non-conformist **East Village**, where the city's zanier students, punks, bums, artists and eccentrics keep a scruffy and lively neighbourhood awake all night. This edgy, politically-active area was home to many of the Beat artists in the 1950s, including WH Auden, Allen Ginsburg, Jack Kerouac and William Burroughs, who used to hold poetry readings together. Musically, it's been the launching pad for big names such as the Talking Heads, the Ramones, Blondie and Patti Smith, many of whom were first heard at legendary **CBGB's** on The Bowery. Boutiques and bars cluster around **Tompkins Square Park** at the heart of this area, nudging up to the Hispanic neighbourhood of **Alphabet City**.*
▶ *See Sleeping p122, Eating and drinking p148, Bars and clubs p172*

 ## Sights

Lower East Side Tenement Museum

90 Orchard St at Broome St, **T** 1-212 431 0233, www.tenement.org *Visitor center Tue-Fri 1300-1600, Sat-Sun 1100-1630. Museum Tue-Sun by guided tour only; phone ahead for times and reservations. $9, $7 students and seniors. Subway F to Delancey, J, M, Z to Delancey-Essex St.   Map 2, A8, p263*

Visit refurbished former tenements to witness the lifestyles of German Jewish or Sicilian Catholic immigrants in the 19th century. Three tenements have been recreated to show how immigrants lived without water or electricity, often cramming several families into one room. Far from being hokey, the tours are an excellent and interesting way to learn about the hardships and unbelievably crowded living conditions that accompanied the American dream.

! By the 1880s the Lower East Side was the most densely populated area in the world with 240,000 people per square mile. Between 1863 and 1935 one address, 97 Orchard Street, was home to 7,000 immigrants from 20 countries.

Rivington Street

between Allen St and Essex St. *Subway F, J, M, Z to Delancey St-Essex St. Map 2, A8, p263*

The many cafés, restaurants, boutiques and bars around Rivington Street make this an ideal starting point for exploring the area. Proof that the East Village has aspirations beyond its working class roots is proved by the opening of the flashy, glass-fronted **Surface Hotel** in 2004 (see p122). Luckily, the wine and matzo-making shops, kosher of course, can still be found here too. At the east end of Rivington Street, wander into **Essex Street Market** (*120 Essex St, Mon-Sat 0800-1800*), a large market hall with dozens of food vendors and bakeries. It attracts a mixed shopping crowd of working-class locals and incoming hipsters.

Tompkins Square Park

Av A to Av B between 7th and 10th St. *Subway 6 to Astor Pl. Map 3, F10, p263*

The punk and grunge atmosphere gives way to a more village-like vibe towards **Alphabet City** and **Tompkins Square Park**, where the streets have inviting cafés, second-hand shops and attractive townhouses. During the 1980s Tompkins Square Park was the hangout for drug dealers, squatters and the homeless, until former Mayor Giuliani added it to his zero-tolerance crackdown list in the 1990s. Now, this lively, anything-goes part of the East Village provides hippies, punks, chess players, musicians and dogs a place to mingle. The square hosts musical performances, festivals and rallies by individuals and groups, but usually people watching is entertainment enough.

● *Look out for pretty Grace Church at 48 E 10th Street and Broadway, particularly at night when white lights illuminate the Gothic structure. The marble for the church was quarried by prisoners at Sing Sing, the notorious state penitentiary on the Hudson River.*

St Mark's-in-the-Bowery

131 E 10th St at 2nd Av, **T** 1-212 674 6377. *Daily 1000-1800. Subway 6 to Astor Pl.   Map 3, F8, p263*

This striking, steepled Episcopal church with a cast-iron entranceway was built in 1799 on the former home of Peter Stuyvesant, a Dutch governor of New York. It is now famous as the place where many art groups meet and perform, with poetry readings, dance shows and other events taking place regularly.

New York Marble Cemetery

41½ Second Av between 2nd St and 3rd St, www.marblecemetery.org *4th Sun of the month 1100-1500. Subway F, V to Lower East Side-2nd Av.   Map 3, H9, p263*

Hidden away, like many of New York's treasures, this private 1830 cemetery is the oldest non-sectarian burial ground in the city. If you are lucky enough to be visiting on the fourth Sunday of each month, it is well worth a look, providing a half-acre oasis of calm amid the bustle of the East Village.

Six and B Community Garden

Av B and 6th St. *Subway F, V to Lower East Side-2nd Av. Map 3, G10, p263*

The hippies who flocked to the East Village in the 1960s have done a fine job of setting up communal parks around the neighbourhood. The Six and B park is open most days and is worth visiting to see the funky collection of objects and people, including a giant tree sculpture that resembles the imaginings of some hallucinogenic dream. There are a number of other community gardens between Avenues B and D, especially on Eighth Street.

● *Curry lovers take note, Sixth Street between First and Second Avenues is home to dozens of Indian restaurants.*

★ **Squares for people watching**

Best

- Washington Square, p55
- Union Square, p66
- Tompkins Square, p63
- Madison Square, p67

Manhattan

Flatiron District and around

Flowers, park benches and a farmer's market have made spruced-up **Union Square** *a popular spot for lunchers, strollers and dog lovers, students, breakdancers and peace protesters, who consider this the gateway to Downtown. From the square, Broadway leads north through the* **Flatiron District**, *home to interior designers and the advertising set. The area takes its name from the landmark* **Flatiron Building**, *whose distinctive, 20-storey, triangular form was once the tallest building in New York. This area was nicknamed Silicon Alley in the late 1990s but these days the dotcom businesses have given way to more traditional forms of media and print and left room for photo labs and designer shops to move in. Also here is* **Madison Square Park**, *a lovely revived square flanked to the east by banks and restaurants.* **Ladies' Mile**, *where beautiful old department stores lined Fifth and Sixth Avenues in the 1800s, is today characterized by retail chains of all sorts. Heading north from the east side of Union Square is* **Park Avenue South**, *which has been transformed from a shambles a few years ago to a hotbed of trendy sushi bars and happy-hour spots. World's away, tucked just off Park Avenue at the end of Lexington Avenue, is stately* **Gramercy Square**, *built in the 1830s as New York's answer to London's private parks. Only those living in the posh townhouses and apartments on the square may enter but visitors can walk by for a peek.*

▶▶ *See Sleeping p124, Eating and drinking p151, Bars and clubs p175*

Sights

Union Square

14th St to 17th St between Broadway and Park Av South. *Subway L, N, R, Q, W, 4, 5, 6 to 14th St-Union Sq. Map 3, E6, p264*

Union Square has attracted all sorts of opinionated folk, activists, workers' rallies, unions and political protests over the years. The area became home to the Communist and Socialist parties in the 1920s and continued to develop as a place of civil unrest in the following decades. By the 1960s and 1970s, it was grungy, dangerous and drug-infested. However, following a injection of funding in the 1980s, it has regained its status as a pivotal point in this part of Manhattan. Bars, restaurants, shops, cinemas and a bowling alley are all within easy reach of the Square, which hosts the **Greenmarket Farmers' Market** four days a week. Inspired, perhaps, by the statue of Mahatma Gandhi on the southwest corner, peace vigils took place in Union Square after September 11th, followed by protests against the invasion of Iraq in 2003.

● *Until the 1960s, the stretch of Broadway south of the square down to Astor Place was called Booksellers Row, due to the number of bookshops along its length. One of the few survivors is The Strand, an independent store, whose slogan promises 'Eight Miles of Books'.*

Flatiron Building

23rd St between 5th Av and Broadway. *Subway N, R to 23rd St. Map 3, C5, p264*

When this famous, much-photographed, 20-storey building was first constructed in 1902, it was the tallest in the city. Now, as well as striking a distinctively narrow, triangular pose, the limestone building marks the entrance to the Flatiron District. Designed by the architect Daniel Burnham to fit into the awkward space where Broadway and Fifth Avenue diverge, it has angled corners that give it dramatic flair. The best place to view it is a block or two north, from where it's said to resemble a ship sailing up the avenue.

Gramercy Park

20th St to 21st St between Park Av and 3rd Av. *Subway 6 to 23rd St. Map 3, D7, p265*

Only a few are lucky enough to hold a key to the city's only private park. Built in the 1830s to mimic the leafy squares in London, it is worth a glance for its dignified setting and for the well-to-do dogs cruising the perimeter. Some famous members' clubs line the square, too. **The Players**, at No16, was a theatre club owned by the actor Edwin Booth and frequented by the likes of Mark Twain, Frank Sinatra and Winston Churchill. Booth is commemorated with a statue in the middle of the square, which can be seen through the gate. Next door at number 15 is the stately **National Arts Club** (*www.nationalartsclub.org*), where members still sip drinks under an original Tiffany stained-glass ceiling. **Irving Place** just south of the square has a smattering of restaurants, cafés and **Irving Plaza**, a popular venue for rock bands (see p188).

Madison Square Park

23rd St to 26th St, 5th to Madison Av. *Subway N, R, 6 to 23rd St. Map 3, C6, p264*

This dusty square had a facelift a few years ago but still remains one of the most overlooked parks in the city. Located at the border of Downtown and Midtown, with views of the Flatiron and the Empire State buildings, it's a pleasant place to rest in the sunshine,

! At the famous hot dog stand in Madison Square Park you can win a dog on the house if you can answer a trivia question correctly.

with free concerts in the summer. The **Metropolitan Life Tower** sits just to the east of the park, lit up in lovely hues at night.

Church of the Transfiguration

1 E 29th St between 5th and Madison Av, **T** 1-212 684 6770, www.littlechurch.org *Subway N, R to 28th St. Map 3, B6, p264*

Known as the Little Church around the Corner, this tiny, immaculate Gothic structure with a charming garden is an anomaly in the otherwise busy rug district of Lower Midtown. Built in 1849, the church is noteworthy for its close association with the theatre. The Episcopalian Actors' Guild was established here in 1923 and, in 1973, the church was made a US landmark because of its work with the dramatic community. The St Faith stained-glass window is from a 14th-century Belgian church destoyed during the Napoleonic Wars.

Museum of Sex

233 Fifth Avenue at 27th St, **T** 1-212 689 6337, www.museumofsex.com *Sun-Fri 1100-1830, Sat 1100-2000. $14.50. Subway N, R, 6 to 28th St. Map 3, B6, p264*

Less risqué than the name suggests, this museum explores New York's sexual past from the mid-1800s to the present. From illegal abortion clinics and the Stonewall riots in Greenwich Village to prostitution and cross-dressing, the museum provides cursory coverage of the city's sex life.

Midtown

*Midtown is the crossroads of Manhattan, the bustling business and commercial centre of the city, sitting smack in the middle of the island. Hordes of tourists mix with workers in business suits during the day and, by night, the neon blitz of **Broadway** puts on a show. Midtown can seem flashy, austere and impersonal, but it's also home to some*

★ **Viewpoints**

B e s t

• **Observatory** at the Empire State Building, p69
• **Rainbow Room** at the Rockefeller Center, p78
• **Tram to Roosevelt Island**, p81
• **Star Bar** at the Shelburne Hotel, p177
• **Top of the Tower** at the Beekman Tower, p177

of the most eye-catching buildings of the last century, including the **Chrysler Building**, *the* **Empire State Building**, **Grand Central Terminal** *and the* **New York Public Library**.

These architectural icons are dotted between 59th Street and legendary **42nd Street**, *where Broadway stars have been born overnight. In winter, this area is particularly festive, with sparkly lights, ice-skaters at the* **Rockefeller Center** *and elaborate window displays adorning fancy department stores. The streets in this area contain some of the world's ritziest restaurants and hotels, not to mention the magnetic pull of* **Fifth Avenue** *shops and the tourist razzle-dazzle of* **Times Square**. *Further east is sophisticated* **Sutton Place** *and west is lively* **Hell's Kitchen**, *residential areas where many New Yorkers make their home. Discovering Midtown's charm among its imposing façades and gargantuan buildings is all part of the fun.*

▸▸ *See Sleeping p125, Eating and drinking p153, Bars and clubs p176*

◉ Sights

Empire State Building

5th Av at 34th St, www.esbnyc.com   *Daily 0930-2400, last elevator 2315. $11, $6 children. Subway B, D, V to 34th St-Herald Sq. Map 3, A5, p264*

Built in the record-breaking time of 14 months during the Great Depression, this icon of art deco is once again the tallest building in the city at 1250 feet (381 metres) – or 1472 feet if you include the antenna. Only the Sears Tower in Chicago and Petronas Towers in Kuala Lumpur are taller. Its construction was considered a spectacular work of modern engineering and efficient management, employing 3500 workers who, at one point, were able to complete 14 storeys in a mere 10 days. The building was completed for $45 million but struggled to get occupants, resulting in near-bankruptcy and the nickname the 'Empty State'. In 1945, on a foggy day, a B-25 bomber crashed into the 79th floor, killing 14 but only causing minimal damage to the building.

The building has 85 floors of commercial and office space plus an observation deck and its refined vertical lines make it the most noticeable building on the entire Manhattan skyline. It featured in the film *King Kong* and has also played a starring role in *An Affair to Remember*, with Cary Grant and Deborah Kerr, and in *Sleepless in Seattle*, with Tom Hanks and Meg Ryan. The view certainly has cinematic potential, despite the long line of tourists elbowing their way to the top. Every year more than three million make the trip up to the 86th-floor observatory for the best 360-degree panorama in New York. The tower is lit up at night, with different coloured lights used to denote a particular holiday or event. On Valentine's Day the chapel on the 80th floor hosts a giant wedding for allcomers and, in February, the New York City Roadrunners Club organizes the **Annual Run-Up**, a competition in which runners try to jog up the 1,860 steps in under 11 minutes.

The rather dusty and tourist-laden streets around the Empire State Building offer a soaring perspective of the skyscraper from below. Head north for more Midtown sights, east to Third Avenue for lively eateries, or south to 32nd Street between Broadway and Fifth Avenue, where all-night restaurants and a few good-spirited cafés form the heart of **Little Korea**.

Garment District

between 6th Av and 7th Av. *Subway 1, 9, to 28th St.*
Map 3, B4, p264

The rather tatty area west of the Empire State Building between
Sixth and Seventh Avenues is the centre of the city's clothing
industry. Designers work in the grungy warehouse buildings and
discount-hungry shoppers come to buy fashion jewellery, wigs, hats,
imported clothes, lingerie, luggage, beads, headwraps and toiletries
of all sorts. Here, too is the **Fashion Institute of Technology** (*7th
Av at 27th St, T 1-212 217 7999, www.fitnyc.suny.edu, Tue-Fri
1200-2000, Sat 1000-1700, free*), which has an excellent museum
featuring costumes and textiles from around the world.

At the east end of the district, **Herald Square** is the location of
the world's largest department store. **Macy's** takes up an entire
block of this otherwise shabby area (see p206). Opposite Macy's
Seventh Avenue entrance is **Madison Square Garden**, an arena
that's famous for its concerts and New York Knicks basketball games
(see p218). Gloomy **Penn Station** below Madison Square Garden
was formerly a beautiful iron-and-glass beaux arts structure but was
torn down in the 1960s. There are tentative plans to convert the
nearby **General Post Office** (8th Av, between 31st St and 33rd St)
into a new Penn Station, budgets permitting.

★ Grand Central Terminal

87 E 42nd St between Park Av and Lexington Av, **T** 1 212 340 2583,
tour information 1-212 935 3960, www.grandcentralterminal.com
*Trains run daily 0530-0130. Tours Wed 1230. Free. Subway 4, 5, 6, 7 at
42nd St-Grand Central. Map 4, G7, p267*

New York's original Grand Central Depot was an iron-and-glass
train shed that opened on this site in 1871. The arrival of electric
locomotives in the early 1900s demanded the construction of a
new station. A competition to design the station was won by

The energy, the brutality, the scale,
the contrast, the tension, the rapid change
and the permanent congestion are what the
New Yorker misses when he leaves the city.

'New York Panorama'
p203 of Architecture, (1938), Random House *.*

Whitney Warren, who created a beaux arts palace that's a must-see sight whether or not you intend to board a train. In 1960, the station came under threat from commercial developers, who wanted to build a bigger structure complete with a bowling alley and shops. Fortunately, locals saved it from the wrecking ball by fighting for its protection as a landmark building.

Approaching Grand Central from Park Avenue, you'll glimpse the impressive triple archway and sculptures above the entrance, including statues of Minerva, Mercury and Hercules that represent contemplation, speed and strength. In between is the station clock made from inch-thick Tiffany glass. On entering the main concourse, the scale and beauty of the design is likely to take your breath away. Light pours in through arched windows onto the airy central hall, which is 375 feet (114 metres) long and125 feet (38 metres) high. Above is a beautiful baroque-style ceiling, which sparkles like a starlit winter sky thanks to a massive renovation project in 1998 that cleaned away the grunge.

The grandeur of the structure is best admired from one of the balcony's restaurants or bars, where you can soak up the atmosphere and watch commuters rushing about below. Tucked away in the southwest corner is **Campbell Apartment**, a hideaway bar that's popular with locals who relax in its library-like surroundings.

The **Municipal Arts Society** gives insightful guided tours of the station every Wednesday at 1230, starting from the information booth in the centre of the main concourse.

● *Across the street at 120 Park Avenue is the small* **Whitney Gallery**, *a branch of the larger Whitney Museum Uptown. Its sculpture garden is a relaxing place to sit and is open daily from 1100 to 1800 (until 1930 on Thursdays). Admission is free.*

★ Chrysler Building
405 Lexington Av, **T** 1-212 682 3070. *Subway 4, 5, 6 to 42nd St-Grand Central. Map 4, G8, p267*

As soon as you catch a glimpse of the Chrysler Building, it's easy to understand why this is most New Yorkers' favourite skyscraper and why it has featured in so many photos and movies. The elegant, art deco 77-storey structure is topped by a triangular crown that shoots skywards. The distinctive spire is designed to look like a car radiator and is surrounded by gargoyles that point down at onlookers in a playful manner.

Built in 1930 during the golden age of skyscrapers, the Chrysler was the first building to exceed the height of the Eiffel Tower. In the race to build the world's tallest structure, architect William Van Alen kept his seven-storey spire secret until the very last moment by constructing it inside the building. However, rival architects trumped his efforts after only few months, with the unveiling of the Empire State Building. Though a ride to the top is impossible, be sure to admire the Chrysler both from afar and from up close; it's truly one of the most majestic sights on Manhattan's skyline.

★ New York Public Library and Bryant Park
5th Av and 42nd St, **T** 1-212 930 0830, www.nypl.org *Tue-Thu 1100-1930, Fri and Sat 1000-1800. Tours Tue-Sat 1100 ,1400. Free. Subway B, D, V to 42nd St. Map 4, G6, p266*

This dramatic beaux arts library, with its sweeping staircases, elaborate ceiling paintings and acres of gold leaf was built in 1911 as the world's largest research library. The highlight is the ornate, chandeliered reading room on the third floor, an enormous decadent space where diligent workers peer at weighty tomes. Throughout the library is displayed a selection of its most prized literary artefacts, including manuscripts of TS Eliot's *The Waste Land*, the diaries of Virginia Woolf, Herman Melville's letters to his family and Charlotte Brontë's portable writing desk. There are also worthwhile temporary exhibitions. Free walking tours begin at the information desk in Astor Hall, where you enter the building.

The museum café and an outdoor reading room – complete with newspapers, books and tables – overlooks **Bryant Park**, which, on a sunny day especially, is one of the loveliest settings in New York. This area, fashioned in French classical style, is a popular backdrop for Monday night free film screenings in summer. Note the dramatic Gothic, gold-tipped American Standard Building on the south side of the park.

● *Northeast of Bryant Park, photography enthusiasts should stop at the* **International Center of Photography** *(www.icp.org) at 43rd Street and Sixth Avenue. This is where photographers and photojournalists show their work in thought-provoking exhibits.*

Times Square
42nd St to 48th St between 6th Av and 9th Av. *Subway N, Q, R, S, W, 1, 2, 3, 7 to 42nd St-Times Sq.   Map 4, F-G5, p266*

The area defined as Times Square started life in the 1830s as the heart of the silk-stocking industry run by the famous Astor family. By the early 1900s *The New York Times* had moved in to give the area a new name. Soon afterwards, the arrival of the subway caused the city's theatres to relocate north to Times Square from the Bowery and lower Broadway, so that by the 1920s this part of Midtown was filled with theatres and flashing signs. More recently the square became known as 'Sin Street', having degenerated into a dangerous and dirty stretch, characterized by prostitutes, porn shops and drug-dealers. However, Mayor Rudolph Giuliani got his hands on it in the 1990s; sleaze moved out and Disney moved in. Today, the only harassment you're likely to experience comes from the other tourists elbowing you out of their way.

Locals abandon the place when they can, leaving Times Square to the tourists and the teenagers, who holler up at MTV's studio. Tacky

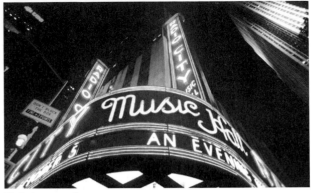

Lighting-up time
Radio City Music Hall puts on a show.

shops rub shoulders with expensive delis catering to the Broadway crowds and faux goods of all sorts are sold from the streets around. Although Times Square can seem obnoxious and gaudy, the bright lights and cheekiness of all those billboards make for an experience that everyone should have once, albeit briefly. Times Square's most famous event is the **New Year's Eve Ball-Drop**, when a million people converge on the area to watch long-time host Dick Clark enact a tradition that began on 31 December 1906.

● *The half-price theatre ticket booth TKTS is located on the centre island at 47th Street and Broadway and is one way of getting cheap tickets for Broadway shows.*

Rockefeller Center

48th St–51st St between 5th and 6th Av, **T** 1-212 332 6868, www.rockefellercenter.com *Subway B, D, F, V to 47th-50th Sts/Rockefeller Center, E, F to 5th Av-53rd St. Map 4, F6, p266*

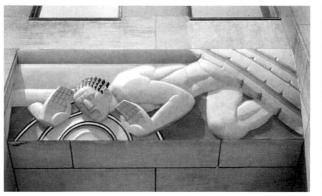

Listen here
Entertainment and business combine at the Rockefeller Center

The Rockefeller Center went up somewhat miraculously during the Great Depression thanks to John Rockefeller's dogged determination to keep the project rolling after many developers had to back out. Now, this handsome, bustling centre of business, entertainment, tourism and shopping is considered by many New Yorkers to be one of the best examples of modern architecture in the city and was declared a national historic landmark in 1988. Nineteen buildings, including the GE Building, the International Building, NBC Studios and the Associated Press Building create an art deco 'city-within-a-city' that combines commercialism and office space in an elegant manner. Artworks are displayed

! In 1932 the Mexican artist Diego Rivera was commissioned by Rockefeller to paint a mural inside the lobby of the GE Building. However, the completed artwork was destroyed after Rivera refused to remove his depiction of Lenin.

throughout the complex and the Channel Gardens fill the walkway leading to Fifth Avenue. **NBC Studios** offer tours of the network's operations from the lobby at 30 Rockefeller Plaza or you can catch air time at the live recording of the *Today Show* in the plaza every weekday morning from 0700. The crowd is full of enthusiastic out-of-towners from all over the country with signs saying "Hi Mom!" and "We're from Elkhart, Illinois".

Cafés, restaurants, bars and an underground shopping concourse surround the seasonal **ice-skating rink** in the centre of the plaza, open from October to April. Winter visitors can also marvel at the gigantic Christmas tree which is lit up from Thanksgiving to January each year. At other times, sip away on an expensive drink in the **Rainbow Room** on the 65th floor of the GE Building for one of the best views of Manhattan.

Radio City Music Hall

50th St at 6th Av, T 1-212 247 4777, www.radiocity.com *Tours daily 1000-1800. $15, children $9. Subway B, D, F, V to 47th-50th Sts/Rockefeller Center. Map 4, E6, p266*

Part of the Rockefeller Center complex, this art deco cinema was the largest in the world when it was built in 1932. Now it's the home of the leggy Rockettes during the annual Christmas spectacular, as well as hosting concerts and music events, including the MTV Music Awards. A renovation in 1999 has restored the original lavish decor to ensure a luxurious velvety experience but you'll have to pay to see it. Admire the famous sign outside at least.

St Patrick's Cathedral

50th St and 5th Av, **T** 1-212 753 2261, www.ny-archdiocese.org *Services daily; call for details. Subway B, D, F to 47-50th Sts-Rockefeller Ctr. Map 4, E7, p267*

Duck into this French Gothic, white-washed cathedral when the guilt of Fifth Avenue shopping gets too much. Built in 1878, St Patrick's is the largest Catholic cathedral in the USA but although it has its own architectural integrity, it sits oddly in the midst of skyscrapers and expensive stores. Nor does it offer any quiet reprieve from the busy streets outside, since camera-toting tourists flock around all sides of the church. Having said that, the Lady Chapel behind the altar and the stained-glass Rose Window above the organ are beautiful details, not to be missed.

Museum of Modern Art

11 W 53rd St, **T** 1-212 708 9400, www.moma.org *Due to reopen in early 2005. Subway E, V to 5th Av-53rd St. Map 4, E6, p266*

MOMA is currently being transformed to reopen with over twice the gallery space and an airy, glass-encased atrium in early 2005. The original museum, which opened just 10 days after the stock market crash in 1929, has a superb permanent collection, including important works by the post-Impressionists Cezanne, Gaugin, Seurat and Van Gogh, the Cubists Braque and Picasso and the contemporary American artists Wyeth and Hopper. During renovations, a portion of the museum's collection is on show at MOMAQNS (see p113).

Dahesh Museum of Art

580 Madison Av at 56th St, **T** 1-212 759 0606, www.daheshmuseum.org *Tue-Sun 1100-1800, 1st Thu each month 1100-2100. $9, $4 students and seniors; free 1st Thu each month 1800-2100. Subway B, D, F, V to 47th-50th St. Map 4, D7, p267*

This stunning anthology of European paintings, sculptures, prints and photographs from the 19th and early 20th centuries was collected by Salim Moussa Achi, a Lebanese writer and guru, with the nickname of Dr Dahesh. To New Yorkers, the museum has always been a treasured secret. However, it looks set to attract legions of new fans since moving from its former tiny space to a new spacious, modern building in 2003.

Fifth Avenue
59th St to 42nd St. *Subway E, F to 5th Av.* *Map 4, F6-G6, p266*

Museums, shops and more shops make up this glitzy stretch of Fifth Avenue from 59th Street down to around 42nd Street. Adopt an Uptown attitude and strut down the avenue where all the high-end designers vie for commercial space.

Start at the corner of Fifth Avenue and Central Park, where you'll notice the Grand Army Plaza and the **Plaza Hotel**. This is one of the most frequently filmed strips of Manhattan and acts as the gateway to the Upper East Side. Toy lovers will enjoy **FAO Schwarz** across the street at 59th Street. Head down to **Bergdorf Goodman**, the most chi chi of all the city's department stores, and then cross 57th Street to enter a particularly indulgent strip of designer shops, including **Tiffany's**, Cartier, Gucci, Henri Bendel and, eventually, **Saks Fifth Avenue** at 50th Street. Further down Fifth Avenue the shops become more mainstream and affordable.

● *Tiffany's has been at the corner of 57th Street and Fifth Avenue since 1940. To see why Audrey Hepburn felt so happy here, wander in and admire the elegant store full of tourists, hoping for a blue box.*

Museum of Television and Radio
25 W 52nd St, between 5th and 6th Av, **T** 1-212 621 6600.
Tue-Wed, Sun 1200-1800, Thu 1200-2000, Fri 1200-2100. $10.
Subway E,V to 5th Av-53rd St, B, D, F, V to 47-50th Sts-Rockefeller Ctr.
Map 4, E6, p266

Come to watch one of 150,000 television and radio programmes from American broadcast history, ranging from the Kennedy assassination to *The Jetsons* to *The Love Boat*, in the screening room or the self-selected library. Great for a rainy day, or for those yearning for that particular episode of a favourite show.

American Folk Art Museum

45 W 53rd St, *T* 1-212 265 1040, www.folkartmuseum.org
Wed, Thu, Sat and Sun 1030-1730; Fri 1030-1930. $9, $7 students and seniors; free Fri 1730-1930. Subway E,V to 5th Av/53rd St. Map 4, E6, p266

This airy five-storey building displays American folk art – quilts, weathervanes, pottery and paintings – and a smattering of work from anonymous artists. The museum's aim is to show how everyday traditions and crafts are worthy of recognition. The Museum of Arts & Design, formerly the American Craft Museum, is just across the street, in another roomy space full of 20th-century crafts made of metal, wood and ceramics.

Roosevelt Island

East River. *Tram runs Mon-Fri 0600-0230, Sat and Sun 0600-0330. $2 each way. Maps 4 and 5, p267 and p269*

Formerly called Welfare Island and once the location of the city's smallpox hospital, whose ruins are still visible on the southern tip, Roosevelt Island is now a rather drab residential complex. Nevertheless, despite the island's dreariness, it's worth visiting for the views. Take the 'tram' (actually a cable car) to the island from Second Avenue at the 59th Street Bridge for a great vista of Midtown and then stroll through the riverside park along the island's west side.

Upper East Side

The opulent Upper East Side stretches between 59th Street and 96th Street and is dominated by the decidedly upper-crust reaches of **Fifth Avenue** *and* **Park Avenue**, *with pricey designer shops and fancy brasseries lining Madison Avenue in the 70s and up. If the poodles and the plastic surgery don't put you off, there's more to this area than money and mansions. Although this part of Manhattan is regarded by many locals as a sterile part of the city, there's nothing dull about the paintings, sculptures, historical artefacts and other wonders found in the area's world-class museums.*

Art lovers could spend days exploring **Museum Mile**, *which stretches along Central Park's eastern border. The cultural line-up kicks off at 104th Street with a colourful Latino display at the Puerto Rican-based* **Museo del Barrio** *and historical toys, ships and furniture at the lively* **Museum of the City of New York**. *Moving down to 92nd Street is the* **Jewish Museum**, *followed by the* **Cooper-Hewitt National Design Museum** *and its stunning garden. A distinctive spiral structure by Frank Lloyd Wright announces the presence of the* **Guggenheim Museum**, *a few blocks down at 88th Street, while the stately* **Neue Galerie** *sits on the corner of 86th Street. At 82nd Street is the unmissable* **Metropolitan Museum of Art**, *whose stairways and galleries swarm with hundreds of daily visitors. Just down the street and one block east is the* **Whitney Museum of American Art** *at 75th Street and Madison Avenue, which houses contemporary art in a Bauhaus structure, while the* **Frick Collection** *further down at 70th Street is an attractive mansion filled with classical art.*

The Upper East Side is also home to its a fair share of rowdy bars and post-college crowds, perfect if you're craving a bit of fraternity-style drinking after all that culture.

▸▸ *See Sleeping p130, Eating and drinking p155, Bars and clubs p177*

▶ Making the most of the Museum Mile

It would be impossible to see all the museums along this stretch of Fifth Avenue in one day – even a week would be pushing it – so concentrate on those that particularly spark your interest.

If you want to avoid the crowds, note that a handful of the key museums stay open later on Friday evenings. The Metropolitan Museum of Art, Frick Collection, Whitney Museum, Neue Galerie and Cooper-Hewitt are open until 2100; the Guggenheim stays open until 2000.

Budget-concious visitors should also time their visit to coincide with the museum's free admission policy. The Jewish Museum is free every Thursday after 1700; the Museum of Modern Art every Friday after 1630; the Guggenheim and the Whitney every Friday after1800; and the Dahesh on the first Thursday of the month from 1800.

◉ Sights

★ Metropolitan Museum of Art

1000 Fifth Av at 82nd St, **T** 1-212 879 5500, www.metmuseum.org   *Tue-Thu 0930-1730, Fri and Sat 0930-2100, Sun 0930-1730; for times of guided tours ask at the information desk. $12 suggested donation, $7 donation for students and seniors (includes The Cloisters and a guided tour). Subway 4, 5, 6 to 86th St. Map 5, G6, p268*

The Met houses one of the world's most impressive collections of paintings, sculpture, objets d'art, artefacts, photographs and more. A complete tour would take several days but it is also possible to enjoy the museum's riches on a shorter and more focused visit.

With over two million objects to choose from, it would be difficult not to find something of interest among the costumes, furniture, Renaissance and modern art, photographs and antiquities.

The original museum was set up in 1870 in a small, red-brick, neo-Gothic building as a cultural enrichment centre for workers and grew rapidly in the late 1800s thanks to many well-heeled benefactors. Asian porcelains, European paintings, decorative arts and American arts were added to the collection in the following decades and, by the 1920s, a larger building had been erected. The Met has since been expanded and altered numerous times, making the vast space somewhat difficult to negotiate despite the fact that it is broken down into the seven different collections.

Enter the spacious, handsome **Great Hall** to pick up maps and get tour information. Behind the Great Hall is the medieval art collection but most visitors head first to the **Greek and Roman** halls to the left. This section was recently overhauled and provides a suitably grand introduction to the museum's collections. The Cypriot gallery on the upper floor leads on to exhibitions of **African**, **Oceanic** and **American** art, including ceremonial African wooden masks and Mayan sculptures.

Beyond are two floors of **modern art** including Picasso's *Portrait of Gertrude Stein* and works by Hopper, Pollock, Modigliani, Warhol, O'Keefe and others. The stunning **European art** galleries, encompassing works from the Renaissance right through to post-Impressionism, are housed on the upper level. This is the most visited part of the museum and it's easy to see why. Visitors flock here to see Renaissance works by Vermeer, El Greco, Rembrandt and Raphael – including his *Madonna and Child Enthroned with Saints* – and the 19th/20th-century art of Cezanne, Gaugin, Manet, Picasso, Renoir and Rodin.

The **American Wing** is tucked away on two floors at the museum's northwest corner and contains a fascinating display of paintings by Cassatt, Homer and Cole, plus Shaker furniture, Tiffany stained-glass and, downstairs, an indoor garden court with a café.

The northeast section of the upper floor is given over to **Asian art**, encompassing impressive pieces of Islamic art, as well as work from Japan, India and Southeast Asia. Don't miss the wonderfully soothing Astor Court in the Chinese section, a perfectly recreated Ming garden, with a pagoda, waterfall and goldfish pool. At ground level, meanwhile, the ancient wall paintings and mummies of the **Egyptian art** collection surround the breathtaking Temple of Dendur, which is fronted by a serene pool of water. The temple dates from 15 BC and was offered as a gift to the USA by the Egyptian authorities in 1965.

A variety of special exhibitions are on display in the museum throughout the year and, from May to October, the Cantor Roof Garden offers one of the best views of Central Park and the Midtown skyline.

● *The museum is open until 2100 on Friday and Saturday, with live classical music, cocktails and appetizers served on the balcony of the Great Hall; it's one of the most civilized ways to spend an evening in New York.*

Frick Collection
1 East 70th St at 5th Av, **T** 1-212 288 0700, www.frick.org
Tue-Thu and Sat 1000-1800, Fri 1000-2100, Sun 1300-1800. $12, $8 seniors, $5 students; price includes audio tour. Subway 6 to 68th St. Map 4, A7, p267

The delightful and lavish former home of the steel tycoon Henry Clay Frick is arguably the most pleasing destination on Museum Mile. Despite his reputation as a ruthless businessman, Frick bequeathed his house and its contents to the city. The mansion houses European artwork, porcelain and sculpture, mostly dating from the Renaissance to the end of the 19th century, including pieces by Van Dyck, Vermeer, Renoir, Gainsborough, Ingres and Goya. It became a museum in 1935 but its 18th-century furniture and intimate atmosphere mean that you'll feel like you're entering

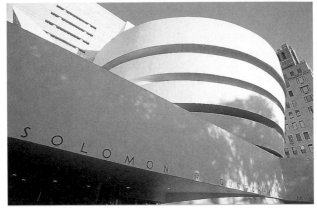

Do the Wright thing
The Guggenheim makes its mark on Museum Mile.

a wealthy friend's country estate. Sit calmly in the West Gallery to
admire Rembrandt under a glass ceiling or retire to the Garden
Court, with its playful fountain if you fancy a moment of peace.

Solomon R Guggenheim Museum

1071 Fifth Av at 89th St, *T* 1-212 423 3500, www.guggenheim.org
Sat-Wed 1000-1745, Fri 1000-2000. $15, $10 seniors and students.
Subway 6 to 86th St. Map 5, E6, p268

Frank Lloyd Wright's striking funnel-shaped building opened in 1959
and its curvy form is still sure to catch your eye amid the stately
upright homes of Fifth Avenue. Although the outside is a bit tattered
and chipped these days, the Guggenheim remains one of the most
noteworthy buildings in the city. It houses the art collection of
business tycoon Solomon Guggenheim, who amassed important

works by major 20th-century artists including Picasso, Kandinsky, Klee, Braque, Giacometti and Chagall as well as fine Impressionist and Post-Impressionist pieces by Cezanne, Gauguin, Van Gogh and others. Photographs by Robert Mapplethorpe, spanning the artist's career are located in a dedicated gallery on the fourth floor.

Wright planned for visitors to see the museum from the top down, so catch an elevator to the uppermost floor of the rotunda and weave your way down through the temporary exhibits, wandering into the rooms on each level to explore the permanent collections. Redevelopment work in 1992 resulted in the opening of a ten-storey adjacent tower complete with café, sculpture gallery and exceptional views of Central Park.

Cooper-Hewitt National Design Museum   ~~Jan 2005~~
2 E 91st St at 5th Av, **T** 1-212 849 8400, www.si.edu/ndm *Tue-Thu 1000-1700, Fri 1000-2100, Sat 1000-1800, Sun 1200-1800. $8, $5 seniors and students. Subway 6 to 96th St.   Map 5, D6, p268*

Quite apart from the fabulous array of pieces from the Smithsonian design collection, this museum deserves a visit simply for its art nouveau entrance, sumptuous Georgian interior and breathtaking garden with a café. Formerly the home of Andrew Carnegie, the two floors feature changing exhibitions that display some of the most avant-garde designs in the fields of fashion, packaging, technology, film, fabrics, ecological inventions and more. Even in the museum-rich surroundings of the Upper East Side, the Cooper-Hewitt is a highlight; take an hour or so to be inspired here.

Neue Galerie New York
1048 Fifth Av at 86th St, **T** 1-212 628 6200, www.neuegalerie.org *Sat-Mon 1100-1800, Fri 1100-2100. $10, $7 seniors and students. Subway 6 to 86th St.   Map 5, E6, p268*

Opened to the public in 2001, the elegant former home of Mrs Cornelius Vanderbilt III exhibits 20th-century work by German and Austrian artists and designers, including members of the Bauhaus and Expressionist movements. Works by Klimt, Schiele and Beckman are on permanent display, plus changing exhibits by the likes of Klee, Dix and Breuer (some are on loan from the Museum of Modern Art). Perhaps the best part of a visit is the chance to pause in the Viennese **Café Sabarsky**, where authentic Austrian pastries are served alongside the tastiest hot chocolate in the city (see p157).

Whitney Museum of American Art

945 Madison Av at 75th St, **T** 1-800 WHITNEY, www.whitney.org
Tue-Thu, Sat and Sun 1100-1800, Fri 0100-2100. $12, $9.50 seniors and students. Subway 6 to 77th St. Map 5, H7, p269

When the Whitney opened in 1966, it fulfilled the desire of its founder, Gertrude Vanderbilt Whitney, who wished to showcase the work of emerging American artists in avant-garde surroundings. The museum's maverick personality is exemplified by its harsh but effective concrete structure, which was designed to look like an upside-down staircase. Andy Warhol had his first museum show here and others, including Pollock, de Kooning and Jasper Johns, all got a boost by displaying work at the Whitney. This was also the first museum to present video and the Internet as valid art forms. The permanent exhibit includes many Hopper and O'Keefe paintings.

● *For brunch, visit **Sarabeth's** in the Whitney's Sculpture Court, which is open during museum hours (see p157).*

Jewish Museum

1109 Fifth Av at 92nd St, **T** 1-212 423 3200,
www.jewishmuseum.org *Sun-Wed 1100-1745, Thu 1100-2000, Fri 1100-1500. $10, $7.50 students and seniors, free children under 12; pay as you wish on Thu 1700-2000.* Map 5, D6, p268

> ★ **Museum cafés**
>
> **Best**
> - **Cantor Roof Garden** at the Metropolitan Museum of Art, p83
> - **Garden cafés** at the Cooper-Hewitt Design Museum, p87
> - **Café Sabarsky** at the Neue Galerie, p87
> - **Café Weissman** at the Jewish Museum, p88
> - **Sarabeth's** at the Whitney Museum, p88

A 1908 Warburg mansion houses the largest museum of Judaica outside Israel. The permanent exhibit traces the Jewish cultural experience and explores religious traditions dating back over 4,000 years through a vast and interesting collection of art, artefacts and media installations, many of which were rescued from Europe before World War II. Café Weissman downstairs is an excellent spot to sit and rest.

Museo del Barrio

1230 Fifth Av at 104th St. **T** 1-212 831 7272, www.elmuseo.org
Wed-Sun 1100-1700. $5 suggested donation, $3 students and seniors, free for children under 12. Subway 6 to 103rd St. Map 5, B6, p268

Opened in 1969 as a tribute to Puerto Rican artists, the museum has grown to include some Caribbean and Latin American art alongside its displays of crafts and paintings. Housed in part of a school building, the colourful exhibitions aim to enlighten visitors on the social issues surrounding Latin cultures. The museum is a good place to start an exploration either of Museum Mile to the south or nearby **Spanish Harlem**, east of Fifth Avenue, where Latin music and food can be enjoyed from 96th Street up to 116th Street.

Museum of the City of New York
1220 Fifth Av at 103rd St, **T** 1-212 534 1672, www.mcny.org
*Wed-Sat 1000-1700, Sun 1200-1700, suggested contributions $7
adults, $4 for seniors, students and children, $12 for families.
Subway 6 to 103rd St.   Map 5, B6, p268*

History buffs and toy enthusiasts will enjoy this spacious museum,
which has varied displays relating to New York, past and present.
Shipping vessels and city art through the ages surround an huge
statue of Robert Fulton, while the museum bookshop has a great
collection of educational toys and trinkets to take home.

Central Park and the Upper West Side

*With 58 miles of scenic pathways, a six-mile perimeter, 26,000 trees
and 25 million annual visitors, **Central Park** is the city's emerald-
green backyard. New Yorkers use their park to the full and are fiercely
proud of it. From peaceful flowers and fountains to frisbee-throwing
spaces, this park has something for everyone.*

*The **Upper West Side** is defined by its proximity to Central Park
and is inhabited by bohemian intellectuals and yuppies, who can
afford its pricey real estate. Rows of beautiful brownstones are
interspersed with famous apartment buildings, including the Dakota,
where John Lennon lived, on Central Park West. Here, too, is the
American Museum of National History and its enormous
collection of artefacts.*

*The busy intersection of **Columbus Circle** on Broadway from 58th
Street to 60th Street is the gateway to the Upper West Side. Once the
site of tenements and poverty-stricken immigrants, it is now being
transformed by the arrival of the glossy two-towered Time Warner
building. Beyond the cultural axis of the **Lincoln Center**, **Broadway**
becomes the quintessential New York food shopping street, with
famous grocers such as Zabar's, Fairway and Citarella, located*

alongside all-night diners and a weekend flea market at 77th Street. Further north, Columbus and Amsterdam Avenues are home to countless bars, restaurants catering for the students from **Columbia University**, *where a more laidback atmosphere prevails. Nearby, is the lofty but unfinished* **Cathedral of St John the Divine**.

Stretching right the way along the western side of the district is **Riverside Park**, *characterized by opulent apartment buildings, statues and sinuous paths.*

▶▶ *See Sleeping p132, Eating and drinking p157, Bars and clubs p178*

◉ Sights

★ Central Park

59th St to 110th St between 5th Av and Central Park West, **T** 1-212 360 3456, www.centralpark.org   *Daily 0600 0100. Subway (West Side): A, C, D, 1, 9 to 59th St-Columbus Circle or C to 72nd St-110th St; (East side) 4, 5, 6, N, R to 59th St or 6 to 68th St-110th St. Maps 4 and 5, p266 and p268*

Conceived by Frederick Law Olmsted and Calvert Vaux in the English pastoral tradition, America's first public park was designed as a place where people of all social backgrounds could mingle. It was intended to help change the city's hectic image and to provide a public space that could rival Europe's urban parks. The first section opened in 1853 and over the next 15 years more than four million trees, shrubs and vines were planted. Olmsted wrote that "every foot of the park's surface, every tree and bush, as well as every arch, roadway, and walk has been fixed where it is with a purpose."

Most New Yorkers insist that Central Park is the finest planned urban space in the world. You will see plenty of them jogging, rollerblading, cycling, boating, picnicking, playing baseball and badminton and, of course, people-watching within its borders. If you're visiting in summertime, there's also likely to be a concert, play or some other event taking place here. Check on the park website or in one of the weekly listings magazines to find out what's on throughout the year.

The entrance at 65th Street on the east side provides access to the **Wildlife Conservation Center** and the **Children's Zoo**, which is home to polar bears, sea lions and a rain forest. Further west is the **Carousel**, a folk-art merry-go-round from Coney Island. The original carousel was built in 1871 and was turned by horses but had to be replaced after two fires. **The Mall**, a wide promenade sheltered by a line of glorious American elm trees, stretches north of here. Every weekend it becomes a mecca for inline- and rollerskaters, who turn up to show off their skills and skate around to the tunes. To the east is the **Sheep Meadow**, an expanse of parkland that's perfect for ball games or sun bathing.

Close to the north end of the Mall is **Bethesda Terrace**, a stunning piazza and angel-themed fountain that provides the setting for many wedding photos. To the west is **Strawberry Fields**, a small and quiet spot at 72nd Street, which honours the late Beatle, John Lennon, who was shot outside the Dakota Building across the street (see box p95). The triangular memorial is decorated with a mosaic of inlaid stones and at its centre is Lennon's famous plea, 'Imagine'.

On the east side of the Lake is **Loeb Boathouse**, where you can rent a rowing boat, take a gondola ride, enjoy a relaxing cocktail or dine at the Boathouse Café. Smaller **Conservatory Water** (also known as Sailboat Lake) lies further to the east, just off Fifth Avenue. Here, ducks share the water with remote-controlled model boats, kids scramble over the *Alice in Wonderland* statue and birdwatchers scan for birds of prey, which nest on the nearby buildings. Other birds to be found in the park include herons, egrets and cormorants.

North of the Lake is **Belvedere Castle**, formerly the home of the city's weather station. It now contains educational exhibits and weather-monitoring instruments and offers a stunning view from the top. Beyond 79th Street, the **Delacorte Theater**, on the

Winter wonderland
Even in the snow, Central Park's appeal is undeniable.

shores of Belvedere Lake, offers performances of Shakespeare during the summer, often with a star-studded cast (see p197). Above 86th Street is the **Jacqueline Kennedy Onassis Reservoir**, where the former First Lady used to enjoy jogging.

Hidden in the northeastern corner, near Harlem Meer, is one of Central Park's secret treasures. The **Conservatory Gardens** are often overlooked but the flowers, fountains and hedges here form one of the prettiest spots in the city and a peaceful escape from the noisy streets. The statue, depicting *The Secret Garden* by Frances Burnett, was erected during the Great Depression as a tribute to children.

● *Tavern on the Green, near 67th Street on the west side, is Central Park's best-known restaurant. First used as a sheepfold in the 1870s, it reputedly turns more tables than any other restaurant in America, raking in a whopping $30 million every year. Come to see the lights and manmade snow, but not for the food.*

Central Park West
Subway B, C to 72nd St, 81st St or 86th St.   Map 5, A-H4, p268

Some consider the buildings along Central Park West to be the finest architecture in the city, particularly the large art deco apartment blocks from the late 1920s and early 1930s. Two of the finest examples of the streamlined architecture of the period include the twin-towered **Majestic** at 72nd Street and the **San Remo** at 74th Street. The towering **Century** at 62nd Street and the three-crowned **Beresford** at 81st Street (across from the American Museum of Natural History) are also worth seeing. The first luxury apartment building in the city, however, was the **Dakota** at 72nd Street, which was built in 1884 and is most famous as the last residence of John Lennon (see box p95).

American Museum of Natural History
Central Park West at 79th St, *T* 1-212 769 5200, www.amnh.org
Sun-Thu 1000-1745, Fri and Sat 1000-2045. Suggested donation $12, $7 children, $9 students and seniors; the IMAX and Hayden Planetarium cost extra. Subway B, C to 81st-Central Park West. Map 5, G3, p268

The whales, dinosaurs, butterflies and model planets that make up this expansive and interactive museum are sure to please adults and children alike. Most popular among the more than 30 million artefacts is the **Dinosaur Exhibit** on the fourth floor. It's the largest in the world, with more than 600 specimens on display. Visitors are encouraged to touch the spiny Barosaurus and to get up close and personal with a Tyrannosaurus Rex. The world's largest blue sapphire, the Star of India, sparkles in the **Hall of Gems and Minerals**, while the recently opened **Hall of Planet Earth**, in the Rose Center for Earth and Space, takes you on a journey following the earth's rotation. Also here is a planetarium and an IMAX theatre.

▶ Death of Lennon

John Lennon and Yoko Ono moved to New York in the early 1970s from Ascot in England, hoping to leave behind the Beatles' legacy and kick-start Lennon's new solo career. Lennon said he came to New York to find the centre, the place where everything was happening.

In 1980, Lennon returned from a recording session, buoyed by the release of *Double Fantasy*, his first album in five years. As he walked from his limo to his home in the Dakota Building, he was shot to death by a crazed fan. To the shock of admirers around the world, Lennon was dead at the age of 40.

The museum's original beaux arts structure opened in 1877 and the various halls, floors and rooms have been added piecemeal ever since, so the layout is slightly confusing. Pinpoint the galleries you want to see with a map on the way in and, if you're a real natural history fan, consider buying one of the special passes that will allow entry into all 42 exhibition halls, plus the Rose Garden and the planetarium. A Starry Nights jazz evening is held on the first Friday of every month in the Rose Center and is a sophisticated and fun way to explore outer space, while sipping wine.

Lincoln Center for the Performing Arts
62nd St to 66th St and Broadway, **T** 1-212 875 5456.
www.linconlcenter.org *Subway 1, 2 to 66th St Lincoln Center.*
Map 5, C3, p268 See also p183, p187 and p191

The white, 1960s concrete structures that make up the Lincoln Center could easily be tired and outdated by now but instead they are abuzz with some of New York's finest ballet, opera, music and film. Formerly the site of tenement houses and slums – the inspiration for the hit musical *West Side Story* – the Lincoln Center was built as part of a massive urban renewal project and is an airy space with fountains, art and eclectic crowds. As home to the American Ballet Company, the New York Philharmonic, the Metropolitan Opera House and the Walter E Reade Theater, which hosts the New York Film Festival, the complex draws in scores of New York's cultural elite. If you are attending a performance at any of the seven buildings venues, make sure to peer in to the Metropolitan Opera House to see the two enormous Marc Chagall tapestries hanging in the front windows. The atmosphere at night is glamorous and, in the summertime, free concerts and dance events take place around the sprawling complex.

Riverside Park

from 72nd St to 159th St. *Subway 1, 2 to 72nd St, 79th St or 86th St, 3 to 72nd St. Map 5, E1, p268*

Upper West Siders are known for their elitist yet laidback attitude, which may have something to do with the fact that they have green space on both sides of them. Riverside Park borders the Hudson River from 72nd Street right up to 159th Street. This certified scenic landmark is dotted with sumptuous homes, beaux arts buildings, statues and monuments, with some industrial landscapes at its northern end. Joggers, cyclists and rollerbladers are attracted to the trails that snake through the park.

Start your exploration of the park at the 72nd Street entrance, watched over by a statue of Eleanor Roosevelt or, on a summer evening, join locals at the **79th Street Boat Basin** to enjoy sunset over the Hudson River accompanied by a burger and a beer. Further north on Riverside Drive at 89th Street is the **Soldiers and Sailors Monument**, built in 1902 for those who died in the Civil War. At 93rd Street is the **Joan of Arc Park**, complete with a statue of the Maid of Orleans atop her horse in full armour. The bronze sculpture contains stones from both Rheims cathedral and the tower at Rouen, where Joan was imprisoned. At 120th Street is the **Riverside Church**, built by the Rockefeller family in 1930. The Gothic church has a 355-foot tower that can be climbed in good weather for views across the river. The huge, bombastic granite dome that serves as **General Grant's Tomb** is impossible to miss, perched on a hill at 122nd Street. Ulysses S Grant was a Unionist hero, who is given much of the credit for the defeat of Confederate forces in the American Civil War. The 1897 memorial has four rooms and statues honouring Grant's life from childhood up until his presidency.

● *If you're short on time but keen to see a few of the sights and leafy streets of the Upper West Side, take the M5 bus from Sixth Avenue. It drives right past Columbus Circle, the Lincoln Center and up scenic Riverside Drive, taking in many of the monuments mentioned above, before winding its way up to Harlem.*

Cathedral of St John the Divine

1047 Amsterdam Av at 112th St, T 1-212 316 7540, www.stjohndivine.org Mon-Sat 0730-1800, Sun 0700-1900. Services Mon-Sat 0800, 1215, 1730; Sun 0800, 0900, 0930, 1100, 1800. Tours, Tue-Sat 1100, Sun 1300. $5, $4 students and seniors. Subway B, C, 1 to 110th St. Map 6, H3, p270

Far from going up in a New York minute, the largest cathedral in the USA has yet to be completed, although construction began way back in 1892. A style change from Romanesque to Gothic, not to mention bankruptcy in 1994 and a fire in 2001 has meant years of architectural reworking with the completion date now scheduled for around 2050. Stunning in size, the church holds a number of treasures including beautiful stained-glass windows, Raphael-inspired tapestries and a silver triptych in the shape of a Russian icon created by Keith Haring just before his death in 1990. As you walk around inside the church the combination of Gothic and Romanesque architecture becomes apparent. The sanctuary and the choir are the most significant examples of the original Romanesque design commissioned by the bishop in 1891, while the nave demonstrates the Gothic style introduced by the architect Ralph Adams Cram in the first half of the 20th century. The floor at Poet's Corner is inscribed with quotations by great American writers, while the poetic offerings of current visitors are displayed on the surrounding wall. Kids will enjoy the playful Children's Sculpture Park outside.

● *After visiting the cathedral, be sure to nip across the street to the* **Hungarian Pastry Shop** *for some delicious hazelnut and chocolate cake, see p160.*

Harlem

Harlem spreads north of Central Park between 110th and 145th Streets. Since the 1920s, this neighbourhood has been the centre of black culture in New York, producing some of the best in music, art, dance and politics. Tucked into a sizeable and lively area are some lovely homes, gospel churches, local art, great soul food and, of course, the sound of jazz and blues.

Harlem was first developed in the 18th century as an agricultural retreat from the city but, during the mid-1800s, the land became unproductive and the farmers left to be replaced by Irish and German immigrants. In the early 1900s, brownstone tenements were constructed in the area, attracting another wave of immigrants from the Lower East Side, including a significant black community, who settled in the neighbourhood around 135th Street to find better housing and to escape the racism and violence that affected other parts of the city. Black churches moved to Harlem or were formed here and powerful black fraternal lodges and social clubs sprang up. By the 1920s, black Americans from the southern states were also flocking to participate in Harlem's economic opportunities and cultural life. Jazz developed throughout the early 20th century, attracting crowds from all over the city. Art, theatre, dance and comedy thrived and writers such as Langston Hughes, Countee Cullen and Zora Neale Hurston launched the **Harlem Renaissance** literary movement. Harlem, at its peak, was a symbol of independent black cultural success.

The area's current revival follows many years of unrest, starting in the 1960s, when heavy rioting led to fires that ravaged the area. The influx of drugs combined with economic hardship hit the neighbourhood hard and, by the 1970s and '80s, Harlem was regarded as an impoverished and dangerous ghetto. The area's recent regeneration, which has seen not only the arrival of Starbucks but also the opening of Bill Clinton's office space on 125th Street, can be traced to a 1996 initiative that aimed to redevelop the area economically.

▸▸ *See Eating p160, Bars and clubs p 179*

Abyssinian Baptist Church
132 W 138th St, **T** 1-212 862 7474. *Services Sun 0900 and 1100. Subway 2, 3 to 135th St.   Map 6, B5, p270*

The debate continues whether or not it's appropriate to recommend churchgoing in Harlem as part of a sightseeing itinerary. To locals, this is a way of life and not a tourist stop. However, the gospel music of Harlem is among the best in the country and many locals appreciate an audience. The Abyssinian is the best-known church in the neighbourhood so you're less likely to be a surprise visitor here and, even when there's no service, this pretty Gothic church is worth a visit. In the 1930s the church was presided over by Reverend Adam Clayton Powell Jr whose activism helped black Americans win economic rights. He also established the country's minimum wage laws during his time in Congress.

● *If it's standing room only at the Abyssinian, you won't have to look far to find another place of worship with a gospel choir. Alternatively, **Sugar Hill Bistro** at 458 W 145th Street serves a gospel brunch every weekend. This lovely brownstone also doubles as an art gallery and restaurant, with classic jazz every night, p160.*

Studio Museum in Harlem

144 W 125th St between Lenox Av and Adam Clayton Powell Jr Blvd, **T** 1-212 864 4500, www.studiomuseum.org *Wed-Fri, Sun 1200-1800, Sat 1000-1800. $7, $3 students and seniors, free children. Free admission for all on 1st Sat of every month. Subway A, B, C, D, 2, 3, to 125th St. Map 6, E5, p270*

Set up as a working studio for black artists in the 1970s, the museum has a wonderful display of art and has recently added a performance schedule for musicians, poets and others. Paintings, photography and sculpture dating from the Harlem Renaissance of the 1920s and 1930s are on display, as well as work by many contemporary artists.

Striver's Row

138 St and 139 St. *Subway B, C to 135th St. Map 6, B6, p270*

This elegant group of rowhouses on 138th and 139th Streets was commissioned in 1891 as an example of ideal urban living. When the black community moved into the neighbourhood after World War I, the streets become home to famous entertainers, including ragtime pianist Eubie Blake, composer WC Handy and comedian Stepin Fetchit. The beautiful brownstone homes, many of them designed by Stanford White, have now become popular tourist sights, but some locals complain that gentrification has robbed the area of its community feel.

Museums and galleries

- **American Folk Art Museum** Displays of American crafts, p81
- **American Museum of National History** Family-friendly museum featuring dinosaur exhibits and a planetarium, p94
- **Children's Museum of Manhattan** Plenty of hands-on fun for younger kids, p228
- **Children's Museum of the Arts** Interactive museum that encourages creative expression in many forms, p228
- **The Cloisters** Medieval artefacts in a magical setting, p105
- **Cooper-Hewitt National Design Museum** The Smithsonian collection displayed in beautiful Georgian surroundings, p87
- **Dahesh Museum of Art** A new modern setting for this glorious collection of European art, p79
- **Dia Center for the Arts** Chelsea's pioneering art space, p60
- **Fraunces Tavern Museum** George Washington's base during the war against the British, p39
- **Frick Collection** Choice pieces of European art, p85
- **International Center of Photography** Thought-provoking photography exhibitions, p75
- **Intrepid Sea-Air-Space Museum** A World War II exhibit based around the *USS Intrepid*, p228
- **Jewish Museum** The largest museum of Jewish culture outside Israel, p88
- **Lower East Side Tenement Museum** A fascinating insight into the history of the Lower East Side, p62
- **MoMAQNS** MoMA's outpost in Queens, p113
- **Museo del Barrio** A vibrant introduction to New York's Latin culture, p89
- **Museum at the FIT** International costumes and fashion, p71
- **Museum of African Art** African art and culture on display in Queens, p114
- **Museum of Arts & Design** 20th-century crafts, p81

Listings

⊙ Museums and galleries

- **Museum of Chinese in the Americas** The roots of Chinatown's burgeoning community, p48
- **Museum of Immigration** Exhibition about the thousands of people who entered the USA through Ellis Island, p36
- **Museum of Jewish Heritage** Holocaust memorial, p45
- **Museum of Modern Art** Showcase for international modern art; closed for redevelopment until 2005, p79
- **Museum of Sex** Exhibits exploring sex in the city, p68
- **Museum of Television & Radio** An archive of old wireless and screen favourites, p80
- **Museum of the City of New York** Eclectic New York objects, p90
- **National Museum of the American Indian** Artefacts from nearly every tribe in the USA, p38
- **Neue Galerie New York** German and Austrian artists, p87
- **New Museum of Contemporary Art** SoHo art space at the forefront of the contemporary art scene, p53
- **New York Public Library** Beaux arts library building with interesting literary artefacts, p74
- **Pierogi 2000** One of the city's most respected galleries, p112
- **PS1 Contemporary Art Center** Sought-after contemporary art space in Queens, p113
- **Solomon R Guggenheim Museum** Late 19th- and 20th-century art in a striking Frank Lloyd Wright building, p86
- **South Street Seaport Museum** The history of the port, p41
- **Studio Museum in Harlem** Local art and artefacts from the Harlem Renaissance and the present day, p100
- **Metropolitan Museum of Art** The big one. Historical art and artefacts from around the world, p83
- **Whitney Gallery** The Whitney Museum's smaller sibling, p73
- **Whitney Museum of American Art** 20th-century avant-garde American art, p88

奉献石燈籠 二基

武刕東叡山

Although first-time visitors may feel spellbound by Manhattan, the outer boroughs provide a quick escape if the city centre grind leaves you dizzy. Tucked into these neighbourhoods are parks, museums, interesting architecture, some great views of the city and undoubtedly the most genuine New York accents. Leaving Manhattan, the bridges over the Hudson and East Rivers provide unique perspectives on the city skyline.

North Manhattan and the Bronx 105 From the northern tip of Manhattan the city hustle seems miles away. Across the Harlem River, the Bronx welcomes zoo lovers and baseball fans.

Brooklyn 106 Home to roughly 2.5 million New Yorkers, this borough encompasses both the boisterous, tacky charm of Coney Island and the cutting-edge culture of Williamsburg.

Queens 112 The international mix of people here makes for great food and a growing art scene

Staten Island 114 A large residential area that's home to hard-working New Yorkers. It's best seen by taking the Staten Island Ferry.

North Manhattan and the Bronx

*Venture up to northern corner of Manhattan Island to enjoy the leafy tranquillity of **Fort Tryon Park** and the timeless medieval spirit of **The Cloisters**. The park looks out over the Hudson River to the Palisades in New Jersey and is one of the most peaceful and romantic settings in the city, with stone-walled gardens and beautiful flowers.*

*Across the Harlem River, the **Bronx** is the only part of New York City that's attached to the US mainland. Home to the Yankees baseball team, not to mention numerous rap stars, this borough also has an impressive collection of large parks and beautiful architecture, including Gothic-style Fordham University and the elegant mansions of Riverdale, which overlook the Hudson River.*

◉ Sights

★ The Cloisters
Fort Tryon Park at 190th St, **T** 1-212 923 3700, www.metmuseum.org
Mar-Oct, Tue-Sun 0930-1715; Nov-Feb, Tue-Sun 0930-1645. $12 suggested donation, $7 students and seniors, includes same-day admission to the Metropolitan Museum of Art. Subway A to 190th/Dyckman St, bus M4 to The Cloisters. Map 1, C5, p260

John Rockefeller donated land and money for a French 12th-century chapter house, the Spanish Fuentaduena Chapel and other Gothic and Romanesque chapels to be reassembled on this site in the 1930s. Now, shadowy, vaulted passageways and Gregorian chant set the mood for a collection of enchanting artefacts drawn from monastic cloisters in France and Spain. The paintings, tapestries and frescos are taken from the Metropolitan Museum of Art's medieval collection. Of particular interest are the Unicorn tapestries, manuscripts of Jean, Duke of Berry, the Annunciation Triptych by Robert Campin, stained glass and the flower and herb gardens.

● *A medieval festival takes place at the Cloisters in September every year, bringing to life the customs and spirit of the Middle Ages. Performers, jugglers, magicians and knights on horseback are part of a 20-year tradition that attracts a share of eccentric New Yorkers.*

New York Botanical Garden

Bronx River Parkway at Fordham Rd, **T** 1-718 817 8700, www.nybg.org *Apr-Oct Tue-Sun 1000-1800, Nov-Mar Tue-Sun 1000-1700. Admission $6, $3 seniors, $2 students, $1 children, free under-2s. Subway B, D to Bedford Pk Blvd, then bus Bx26 or Metro North from Grand Central Terminal to New York Botanical Garden. Map 1, C6, p260*

Two hundred and fifty acres of gardens and plants provide the perfect antidote to city madness. The Enid A Haupt Conservatory transports you through a mixture of eco-environments in a striking Victorian landmark building. Across the road, the **Bronx Zoo** is a big hit with visiting kids. See p227.

Brooklyn

Brooklyn was once called the city of homes and churches, due to a large influx of immigrants in the 1800s. By the mid-19th century it was the third-largest city in the USA but following the invention of the first passenger elevator in Manhattan in 1857, Brooklyn fell out of favour as developers opted to build tall city apartment buildings. The borough wasn't incorporated into New York City until 1898.

*Still regarded as independent and self-sufficient, Brooklyn has a cultural scene that rivals Manhattan, plus enough leafy parks and charming townhouses to ensure its inhabitants have little reason to cross over iconic **Brooklyn Bridge**.*

▸▸ *See Eating and drinking p161, Bars and clubs p179*

Sights

★ Brooklyn Bridge

walkway begins at Centre St opposite City Hall. *Subway 4, 5, 6 to Brooklyn Bridge-City Hall. Map 2, E8, p263*

The magical structure of the Brooklyn Bridge, with its twin Gothic towers and cathedral-like arches, rises gracefully 83 m above the East River. New Yorkers are fiercely proud of the bridge, which has inspired generations of poets, writers and engineers. The bridge was intended to replace the ferries between Brooklyn and Manhattan Island but it was several years before the plans of chief engineer John Roebling were approved and, even when construction began in 1867, it took almost 15 years to complete in the face of enormous difficulties. Two years into the project, Roebling's foot was smashed into a pier by a passing ferry. The engineer died of gangrene as a result. Roebling's son Washington took over the project but suffered, along with several other workers who were operating underwater, from decompression sickness, which left him crippled. His wife, Elizabeth, had to step in to keep the project rolling. In total, 27 people lost their lives building what was the world's longest suspension bridge at the time.

Walking across the bridge between Manhattan and Brooklyn is, for many, the perfect Sunday afternoon activity. A promenade for pedestrians, cyclists and roller-bladers runs from Centre Street's City Hall to leafy Brooklyn Heights, about a 40-minute jaunt by foot. The views of the Manhattan skyline are breathtaking and, at night, the backdrop of New York twinkles with candy-like appeal against the bridge.

● *From Brooklyn Heights the 'Promenade' leads along the waterfront, with jaw-dropping views of Manhattan and the harbour, to leafy, village-like Montague Street, where there are plenty of relaxed cafés and restaurants.*

Last exit to Brooklyn?
Escape Manhattan by crossing the mighty Brooklyn Bridge but don't forget to look back at the view.

Brooklyn Museum of Art

200 Eastern Pkway at Washington Av, Prospect Heights, **T** 1-718 638 5000 *Wed-Fri 1000-1700, Sat and Sun 1100-1800 or 1100-2300 on the 1st Sat of the month. $6, $3 students and seniors, free under-12s. Subway 1, 2 to Eastern Pkwy-Brooklyn Museum. Map 1, I5, p261*

The second-largest museum in the country has an excellent, broad-ranging collection of traditional and contemporary art. The beautiful beaux arts building holds over 1.5 million artefacts, covering everything from Native American art and American paintings to Rodin sculptures and ancient Egyptian objects.

Brooklyn Botanic Garden

1000 Washington Av, Prospect Heights, **T** 1-718 623 7200. *Oct-Mar Tue-Fri 0800-1630, Sat, Sun and holidays 1000-1630; Apr-Sept Tue-Fri 0800-1800, Sat and Sun 1000-1800. $3, $1.50 students and seniors, free under-16s. Admission free on Tue. Subway 1, 2 to Eastern Pkwy-Brooklyn Museum. Map 1, I5, p261*

Right next to the Museum of Art, 52 acres display thousands of pretty plants and an impressive bonsai tree collection. The garden holds an annual cherry blossom festival in April and even has its own star walk, the Celebrity Path, which shows off famous Brooklyn residents.

Prospect Park

T 1-718 965 8951. *Daily 0500-0100. Subway 1, 2 to Grand Army Plaza, Q, S to Prospect Park, F to 15th St-Prospect Park Map 1, I4-5, p261*

Brooklyn's answer to Central Park, this lovely, sprawling spread of 526 acres was designed by Olmsted and Vaux in 1866. A carousel, small zoo, ice rink, and outdoor summer concerts make it a great place to spend an afternoon.

Coney Island

1208 Surf Av, **T** 1-718 265 3400, www.coneyislandusa.com *Most rides and sights open May-Sep. Subway F, Q, W to Coney Island-Stillwell Av.* Map 1, K-L4, p261

For some good-humoured tackiness and seaside fun, travel out to Coney Island, a slice of Americana and a boisterous younger sibling to the more sedate holiday venues on Long Island. Fun-spirited and seedy, Coney Island revels in its cheeky, blue-collar atmosphere, turns up its nose at 21st-century social mores and parties like the good old days.

Situated at the base of Brooklyn, only 12 miles from Manhattan, this has been a holiday destination since the 1920s, when it was the site of a world-famous amusement park. The beach here is enticing as long as you're not expecting the clean strands of the Hamptons and, from Memorial Day to Labor Day, Coney Island is still abuzz with visitors who come here to enjoy the neon lights, stuffed animal prize booths, video arcades, souvenir shops, bumper cars and roller coasters. The most famous and heart-stopping ride is the Astroland **Cyclone**, a 75-year old wooden rollercoaster that careers along at up to 60 miles an hour.

Separating the fairground rides from the beach is the **Boardwalk**, where palm readers, peep shows and $1 tat stores ply their trade. Stroll east along it to reach the **New York Aquarium** (see p230) and **Brighton Beach**, home to a large Russian population and known as Little Odessa after the film that was made here. Flashy clothing and plenty of vodka make for a festive, kitschy atmosphere in the busy restaurants on Brighton Beach Avenue.

●*Nathan's Famous, next to the subway on Surf Avenue, is the official birthplace of the Coney Island dog, now known as the hot dog. Since 1916 it has held a stomach-busting hot-dog eating competition every Fourth of July. For the perfect Coney Island experience, buy your dog from the other branch of Nathan's on the Boardwalk and enjoy it, complete with sauerkraut and sautéed onions, right on the beach.*

Williamsburg

Brooklyn. *Subway L to Bedford Av.   Map 1, H5-6, p261*

Jungle-pop-electro-punk-retrodance is what the flyer says outside
the subway in Williamsburg. It pretty much sums up this artistic
haven around Bedford Avenue. If you're not into trendsetters with
green knee-socks, punk hairdos, body art and piercings, then
Williamsburg may not be your bag but if you want a taste of the
most thriving arts and music scene in New York, then this eclectic,
edgy, still grungy area is the place for you. No less than 10,000
artists live in Williamsburg, the highest density of anywhere in New
York, supplemented by self-conscious young hipsters, who fill the
streets around Bedford Avenue and N Sixth Street. One of the city's
most respected art galleries is the **Pierogi 2000** at 177 N Ninth
Street (*T 1-718 599 2144, www.pierogi2000.com, open Sep-Jul
Mon-Fri 1200-1800 and by appointment*), which shows
contemporary work by Brooklyn artists. The migration of
struggling artists, writers and musicians to Williamsburg for its
cheaper rents and loftier spaces gives the whole area a
campus-like feel. Restaurants, bookstores, art galleries, cafés and
bars have sprung up, making it a fun destination for a night out.
However, Williamsburg also maintains its original Latino vibe and
working-class spirit and is home to an Orthodox Jewish
population, just a few blocks away.

Queens

*Queens' charm lies in its many faces, foods and languages. A huge
variety of ethnic groups – Irish, Greek, Korean, Chinese, Cuban, Irish,
Brazilian, Vietnamese – call this borough home, so that a visit here
feels like a trip around the world. Take the Number 7 subway out,
dubbed the **National Historic Trail** by the government, to experience
the multicultural atmosphere.*

Queens is going through something of a revival these days, especially around the formerly industrial area of Long Island City, with enough culture moving into the area to make even Brooklynites sit up and take notice.

Sights

PS1 Contemporary Art Center

22-25 Jackson Av at 46th Av, Long Island City, **T** 1-718 784 2084, www.ps1.org *Thu-Mon 1200-1800. $5, $2 students. Subway E, F to 23rd St/Ely Av, 7 to 45 Rd-Court House Sq, G to Court Sq. Map 1, F5, p260*

This is the only Queens venue where avant-garde Manhattanites will happily queue up around the block on a Saturday afternoon to get in. Founded in 1971 and now part of MOMA, PS1 is dedicated solely to contemporary art and draws in a wide array of exhibits to its former school building. In addition to the galleries, PS1 offers a family jam series, called 'Warmup', in summer, complete with beach, outdoor dance floor, cheap beer and a first-rate view of Manhattan.

MoMAQNS

33rd St at Queens Blvd, **T** 1-212 708 9400, www.moma.org *Mon-Thu 1000-1700, Fri 1000-1945, Sat and Sun 1000-1700. $12, $8.50 students and seniors, children free. Subway 7 to 33rd St. Map 1, G5, p261*

The warehouse space of MOMAQNS, though easily accessible from the 7 train, houses only a portion of the normal MOMA collection and sits in a rather grim section of Long Island City on a busy street with little charm around. Unless you're a complete modern art junkie, consider waiting to see the artistic treats until MoMa in Midtown reopens in 2005 (see p79).

Museum of African Art
36-01 43rd Av, 3rd Flr, Long Island City, **T** 1-718 784 7700. *Mon, Thu, Fri 1000-1700, Sat and Sun 1100-1700. $6, $3 students, seniors and children. Subway 7 to 33rd St.   Map 1, F5, p260*

This museum relocated to Queens from SoHo but will eventually move to the Museum Mile at 110th Street. It houses a variety of interesting African art and culture, including textiles, photographs, masks and paintings. In the same building is a temporary space displaying a handful pieces by the Japanese-American sculptor and designer, **Isamu Noguchi** (*T 1-718 204 7088, Wed-Fri 1000-1700, Sat and Sun 1100-1800, $5, $2.50 students and seniors*).

Staten Island

*The leafy streets and big parks of Staten Island make many locals want to keep their slice of the city independent from other boroughs' problems and have even voted to secede the city in past years. While most short-term visitors don't make this primarily residential borough a high-priority on their must-see list, Staten Island takes pride in its status as a historical landmark, as one of the first places that Giovanni da Verrazano stopped in 1524. The **Verrazano Bridge** links the island with Brooklyn and, at 4,260 feet (1,311 metres) is one of the world's longest suspension bridges but most visitors choose to hop on the **Staten Island ferry** for stunning views of the city (see p29).*

Accommodation in New York can take up a big chunk your budget but, if money is no issue, then the selection and quality of the city's hotels are astounding. There are Uptown hotels for suited types, Downtown hotels for style-savvy hipsters and just about everything in between, from small boutiques to large chains, bed and breakfasts to studio rentals. Finding a cheap sleep in New York may seem impossible at first but a handful of moderately priced hotels and hostels, not to mention the trustworthy YMCAs, ensure that even the most budget-conscious visitors should find somewhere to lay their heads. Having friends in New York can help but, usually, their pint-sized apartments won't accommodate visitors for long.

The swanky, classic hotels featured in so many New York films are abundant in Midtown, along with identikit hotel chains and branches of the YMCA, while quirkier boutiques seem to have cropped up everywhere, especially in SoHo and around Gramercy Park and Union Square. Most hostels are clustered around the Upper West Side.

$ Price Sleeping codes

AL	$400 and over	**C**	$100-179
A	$250-399	**D**	$50-99
B	$180-249	**E**	$49 and under

Prices are for a double room in high season. They do not include breakfast unless otherwise stated

Accommodation prices vary drastically depending on the time of year, so you may get lucky if visiting out of high season. Eventhen, hotels may offer special deals and discounts, with room prices often reduced enormously at the last minute. Visit the official tourist site (www.nycvisit.com), which has links to hotel specials offered by the big chains, or consult www.hotres.com for details of $99 room deals in the city.

It's worth noting that hotel rooms in New York City are usually much, much smaller than those available elsewhere in the United States, so if you're visiting for a week or longer and want more space, consider either an apartment swap (see www.craigslist.org) or a short-term rental (www.affordablenewyorkcity.com). **Metro Home** (*247 W 35th St, T 1-212 965 1102, F 1-212 965 1149, www.metro-home.com*) has furnished studios and apartments to rent for a variety of price ranges and time periods – some studios are available for less than $100 a night depending on the season.

Hostels with dorm beds for as little as $25 per person are the cheapest option. Visit www.hostelhandbook.com/usa/nynyc.htm for further information. YMCAs may have a somewhat institutional feel, but they offer safe single and double private rooms.

Finally, when calculating your accommodation budget, remember that hotel tax of 13.25% plus a $2 per night occupancy charge will be added to your bill.

Sleeping

★ **Places to stay without breaking the bank**

Best

- **Maritime Hotel** The essence of Meatpacking style, p120
- **Abingdon Guest House** Cosy and romantic, p120
- **Larchmont Hotel** A great location at a good price , p121
- **Carlton Arms Hotel** Funky, arty and affordable, p125
- **Jazz on the Town** Clean new hostel with added extras, p130

Lower Manhattan

Hotels

AL Ritz-Carlton New York, Battery Park, 2 West St, **T** 1-212 344 0800, **F** 1-212 344 3801, www.ritz-carlton.com *Subway 4, 5 to Bowling Green. Map 7, G1, p272* Perched on the tip of Manhattan overlooking New York Harbour, the Ritz-Carlton has a view that few hotels in New York can rival. Even if you can't afford to stay here, it's worth venturing up to the stunning indoor/outdoor bar on the 14th floor to enjoy the panorama of the Statue of Liberty and Ellis Island. Few hotels can match the amenities here, either, including a water sommelier and telescopes in the bedrooms so that you can peer out at the boats and bridges. Although it's not the most buzzing area of town for nightlife, the nautical views and the proximity of Battery Park outside are enough compensation.

B-C The Holiday Inn Wall Street, 15 Gold St at Platt St, **T** 1-212 232 7700, 1-800 HOLIDAY, **F** 1-212 425 0330, www.HolidayInnWSD.com *Subway A, C to Broadway-Nassau St, J, M, Z, 1, 2, 4, 5 to Fulton St. Map 7, D4, p272* As far as the Financial District goes, this is a better deal than many of the upscale banker hangouts, with good offers, especially at the weekends. The rooms are quite small, but it's spanking clean, friendly and safe.

SoHo and Tribeca

Hotels

AL 60 Thompson, 60 Thompson St, **T** 1-212 431 0400, 1-877 431 0400, **F** 1-212 431 0200, www.Thompsonhotels.com *Subway C, E to Spring St. Map 2, A4, p262* One of Downtown's hippest hotels, 60 Thompson takes pride in its unmarked entrance, designer decor, down duvets and fancy toiletries. There's no shortage of beautifully dressed men and women in this neutral-toned minimalist hotel. You'll find them hanging out in the hotel's ultra-cool Thom's Bar (see p168). Part of the swanky hotel scene that became popular a few years ago, 60 Thompson is one of those places where you can pretend to be a happening New Yorker, as long as you're prepared to part with some serious cash.

AL SoHo Grand Hotel, 310 West Broadway, **T** 1-212 965 3000, 1-800-965-3000, **F** 1-212 965 3244, www.sohogrand.com *Subway A, C, E, 1, 2 to Canal St. Map 2, B4, p262* The dramatic cast-iron entry leads to a sumptuous flash bar and enormous clock in the lobby. The models, rock stars and media types who stay here enjoy the cool, minimalist decor and the photography from nearby galleries.

C Cosmopolitan, 95 West Broadway at Chambers St, **T** 1-212 566 1900, 1-888 895 9400, **F** 1-212 566 6909, www.cosmohotel.com *Subway A, C, 1, 2 to Chambers St. Map 7, A1, p272* This seven-storey hotel in an old loft building in Tribeca is one of the few affordable places to stay Downtown. It's not the Ritz by any means, but every room has its own bathroom and desk and the owners pride themselves in keeping everything very spick and span. Popular with European guests, the Cosmopolitan is within easy walking distance of SoHo and Chinatown and is just down the street from Bubby's, one of the best brunch places in the city (see p141).

Greenwich Village and Chelsea

Hotels

B Maritime Hotel, 363 W 16th St, **T** 1-212 242 4300. *Subway A, C, E to 14th St. Map 3, E2, p264* The former headquarters of the US Maritime Union, this tall, portholed building was an eyesore on a dusty stretch of Ninth Avenue until some stylish hoteliers came to the rescue. Perfectly poised on the edge of the Meatpacking District, this is an ultra-cool hotel, where pretty young things stay for much cheaper prices than the equivalent in SoHo. The design honours the building's past by maintaining the nautical theme throughout the rooms but the outdoor 'lounge' is a soothing surprise, a patch of greenery in an otherwise urban locale.

B-C Abingdon Guest House, 13 Eighth Av, **T** 1-212 243 5384, **F** 1-212 807 7473, www.abingdonguesthouse.com *Subway A, C, E, L to 14th St. Map 3, F3, p264* Two 1850s townhouses combine to create this classy guesthouse in the heart of the West Village. Its terribly romantic and cosy and, for the location, it's really a bargain. The nine rooms have names such as Ambassador, Essex and Landau, plus four-poster beds and fireplaces to make you feel properly at home. The laidback, friendly Brewbar café is just below, perfect for a morning coffee before a strolling around the neighbourhood. Party-goers should look elsewhere, however: the Abingdon is quiet and wants to stay that way.

B-C Chelsea Hotel, 222 W 23rd St, **T** 1-212 243 3700, **F** 1-212 675 5531, www.chelseahotel.com *Subway C, E, 1, 2 to 23rd St. Map 3, C3, p264* Built as one of New York's first co-operative apartments in 1884, the characterful Chelsea Hotel has been home to many writers and artists over the years, including Dylan Thomas, Mark Twain, Tennessee Williams and Arthur Miller, many of whom

Sleeping

lived here long term. The hotel has also been the setting for many films but it is most famous as the place where Sid Vicious of the Sex Pistols murdered Nancy Spungen. Don't let that fact put you off enjoying its bohemian atmosphere. It's a bit tattered these days but still retains its lively and artsy persona. The lobby and rooms are filled with interesting artwork and the velvety, candle-lit Serena bar lures cocktail-drinkers downstairs.

C Washington Square Hotel, 103 Waverly Pl, **T** 1-212 777 9515, 1-800 222 0418, **F** 1-212 979 8373, www.washingtonsquare hotel.com *Subway A, C, E, F, V, S to W 4th St. Map 3, G5, p264* Bob Dylan lived here for some time when he sang for a pittance in the adjacent square. Though it's had a renovation since, the rooms are still average and very small. Size doesn't matter, though, when you're in the heart of the Village, right on Washington Square Park and an easy stroll from some of the city's best cafés. Breakfast is included and so is Tuesday night at bistro C3 next door.

C-D Chelsea Lodge, 318 W 20th St, **T** 1-212 243 4499, www.chelsealodge.com *Subway C, E to 23rd St. Map 3, D3, p264* This beautiful brownstone on a leafy Chelsea street was converted in the late 1990s into a hotel, suitable for budget travellers. The 22 rooms and four suites fill up quickly but this is one of the most inviting and friendly places to stay, so it's worth booking early. Rooms come with shared or private bathrooms, while the suites have kitchenettes.

D Larchmont Hotel, 27 W 11th St, **T** 1-212 989 9333, **F** 1-212 989 9496, www.larchmonthotel.com *Subway F, V to 14th St, L to Sixth Av. Map 3, F4, p264* One of the better bargains in the city is located on one of the prettiest streets in Greenwich Village, near Washington Square Park. It's a beaux arts building that looks and feels like a proper New York apartment block. The clean, sparse rooms share facilities but the hotel provides robes and slippers in case you need to pop to the bathroom in the middle of the night. Breakfast is included in the price, but you may prefer to nip out for coffee at one of many nearby cafés along Sixth Avenue or University Place.

Hostels

E Chelsea Center, 313 W 29th St, **T** 1-212 643 0214, **F** 1-212 473 3945, www.chelseacenterhostel.com *Subway A, C, E to 34th St-Penn Station. Map 3, B3, p264* Located close to the Garment District, this hostel is friendly and clean with a student-like feel, and even has a little garden out back. A dorm bed costs $30 per night (cash only), including breakfast, tax, bedding and good conversation – according to the owner. Consult the website for details of the East Village branch.

Lower East Side and East Village

Hotels

A Surface Hotel, 107 Rivington St, **T** 1-212 475 2600. *Subway F, J, M, Z to Delancey-Essex Sts. Map 2, A8, p263* Owned in part by *Surface*, the San Francisco-based design magazine, this hotel is hoping to attract style-hungry professionals. The glassy, modern highrise serves as an interactive space for designers of all sorts, who can afford its steep prices and don't mind the grittiness of the surrounding area. An anomalous newcomer to the Lower East Side, the Surface Hotel is a sure sign of change in this traditionally working-class neighbourhood.

C Off-SoHo Suites Hotel, 11 Rivington St between Bowery and Chrystie St, **T** 1-212 979 9808, 1-800 633 7646, **F** 1-212 979 9801, www.offsoho.com *Subway F, V to Lower East Side/2nd Av, J, M to*

Bowery, S to Grand St. Map 2, A7, p263 Off-SoHo sits smack in the middle of New York's trendy, rowdy, bar-hopping, boutique-shopping Lower East Side. Close to Downtown's cool bars, restaurants, clubs and shops, and definitely edgier at night than hotel-heavy Midtown, this is a good choice for those who plan to spend most of their time out and about. The spacious wood-floor rooms are clean and each has a working kitchenette, but the decor is a bit on the tacky side.

C-D Second Home on Second Avenue, 221 Second Av, **T** 1-212 677 3161, www.secondhomecitysearch.com, secondh@aol.com *Subway F, V to Lower East Side/2nd Av. Map 3, E8, p265* This home away from home is run by the friendly Carlos, who will make you feel welcome in his tidy seven-room bed and breakfast. It's a favourite with European travellers and a rare find in the East Village. A few rooms have their own bath but they are significantly more expensive than those without. There's a small, shared kitchen, too. Call a month ahead to save your place.

Hostels

E Bowery's Whitehouse Hotel of New York, 340 Bowery between 2nd St and 3rd St, **T** 1-212 477 5623, **F** 1-212 473 3150, www.whitehousehotelofny.com *Subway F, V, S to Broadway-Lafayette St, 6 to Bleecker St. Map 3, H8, p265* Certainly not posh, this hostel is home to some permanent residents as well as visitors. It's safe though, and for its Downtown location, there isn't a cheaper place in sight. The slightly seedy air and the shoebox-sized rooms are quickly overcome by the friendly locals, students and European backpackers who work and stay here.

Flatiron District and around

Hotels

AL Inn at Irving Place, 56 Irving Pl, **T** 1-212 533 4600,
www.innatirving.com *Subway L, N, Q, R, W, 4, 5, 6 to 14th St-Union
Sq. Map 3, D7, p265* This discreet 12-room Victorian brownstone
is a decadent choice for those who want antiques, fireplaces and
the personal touch. Luxurious and peaceful, the high price includes
robes, maid service and continental breakfast on one of New York's
loveliest streets near Gramercy Park.

A W Union Square, 201 Park Av South, **T** 1-212 253 9119,
F 1-212 253 9229, www.whotels.com *Subway L, N, Q, R, W, 4, 5,
6 to 14th St–Union Sq. Map 3, E7, p265* This chic chain is ideal for
visitors with a big budget who like to feel part of the scene. The
branch at Union Square is probably the most popular due to its
central location, lounge area, luxurious spa and hotel restaurant,
Olives, which serves up a lovely breakfast. Rooms have large desks
and fluffy pillows, offset by the W's trademark minimalist decor.
Check the website for details of other branches.

B Gramercy Park Hotel, 2 Lexington Av, **T** 1-212 475 4320,
1-800 221 4083, **F** 1-212 505 0535, www.gramercyparkhotel.com
Subway 6 to 23rd St. Map 3, D8, p265 Built in 1831, this hotel is
where 11-year-old John F Kennedy lived with his parents, where
27-year old Humphrey Bogart got married (again) and, most
recently, where Cameron Crowe filmed some of the scenes of
Almost Famous. It's a long-standing favourite with European
visitors and rock bands, who are drawn to the relaxed rooftop bar
and the dimly-lit, romantic bar and lounge. What the somewhat
raggedy rooms lack in comfort they make up for in charm. Staying
here allows you the special key to New York's only private park.

Sleeping

D Carlton Arms Hotel, 160 E 25th St at 3rd Av, **T** 1-212 679 0680, www.carltonarms.com *Subway 6 to 23rd St. Map 3, C7, p265* Basic is how the friendly owner describes his small, clean, cheerful hotel, located in a residential area bordering Gramercy Park. The 52 rooms are all painted differently by various artists. Many Europeans stay here for its budget price, convenient central location and laidback yet safe atmosphere, so book early. Rates vary depending on whether you opt for a shared or a private bathroom and there are online discounts for students and overseas visitors.

D Hotel 17, 225 E 17th St between 2nd Av and 3rd Av, **T** 1-212 475 2845, **F** 1-212 677 8178, www.hotel17.citysearch.com *Subway N, Q, R, W, 4, 5, 6 to 14th St–Union Sq, L to 3rd Av. Map 3, E8, p265* This brownstone overlooking leafy Stuyvesant Square offers a good glimpse of residential New York life. The hotel is popular with artists and musicians and was used as the location in Woody Allen's *Manhattan Murder Mystery*; it's even claimed that Madonna once stayed here. The slightly tattered, bohemian feel extends to the guest rooms, which have fireplaces, high ceilings, dilapidated wallpaper and shared bathrooms. Come with cash and travellers' checks as credit cards aren't accepted.

Midtown

Hotels

AL Waldorf-Astoria, 301 Park Av at 50th St, **T** 1-212 355 3000, 1-800 924 3673, www.waldorf.com *Subway E, V to Lexington Av-53rd St, 6 to 51st St. Map 4, F7, p267* Rub shoulders with visiting diplomats and expense-account guests at this luxurious, restored art deco hotel. It has been accommodating the rich and famous since 1931, including the likes of Cary Grant, Princess Grace of Monaco and numerous American Presidents. Despite the grandeur, the hotel run specials if it's not fully booked, so it's worth checking out if you fancy a night or so of royal treatment.

AL-A Le Parker Meridien, 118 W 57th St, **T** 1-212 245 5000, 1-800 543 4300, **F** 1-212 708 7471, www.parkermeridien.com *Subway F, N, Q, R, W to 57th St.   Map 4, D5, p266* The refurbished rooms, wonderful brunch at Norma's on the ground floor and the rooftop pool keep monied guests and business travellers coming back to the Parker Meridien. Its Midtown location is perfect for those who want to be close to Central Park and don't mind taking a cab to reach Downtown. Don't miss the lobby artwork by Damien Hirst and Charles Long.

AL-A Plaza Hotel, 768 Fifth Av, **T** 1-212 759 3000, 1-800 759 3000, **F** 1-212 759 3167, www.fairmont.com *Subway N, R, W to 5th Av-60th St.   Map 4, D6-7, p266* This 1907 deluxe joint has been in more films than almost any other hotel in town. What makes it so special is its location, just across the street from Central Park and bordering Fifth Avenue's ritzy shops. Most famous is Frank Lloyd Wright's former suite at number 223 and the wooden Oak Room Bar with its elegant smoky feel. The Palm Court off the lobby is a decadent spot to have tea amongst gold-leafed, over-the-top decor. Despite its glitz, the Plaza is still one of the most romantic hotels anywhere.

A The Bryant Park, 40 W 40th St, **T** 1-212 642 2200, **F** 1-212 869 4446, www.thebryantpark.net *Subway B, D, F, V to 42nd St.   Map 4, H6, p266* Set in the glamorous American Standard Building overlooking Bryant Park, this modern, chic boutique hotel has been featured in numerous design magazines. It draws a crowd of flashy urban types, who appreciate the leafy outlook and the stylish rooms. The Cellar Bar gets rave reviews as a top drinking spot but dress up if you want to blend in with its sophisticated clientele. Room rates vary depending on the time of year, so check online for discounts.

A-B Casablanca Hotel, 147 W 43rd St, **T** 1-212 869 1212,
F 1-212 391 7585, www.casablancahotel.com *Subway N, Q, R, W, S,
1, 2, 3, 7 to 42nd St-Times Sq, B, D, F, V to 42nd St. Map 4, G5, p266*
If being central is important (read, right in the middle of all that
razzle dazzle), this Moroccan-themed hotel is a standout in the
Theater District. Rick's Café inside serves complimentary breakfast,
daytimes snacks and wine, cheese and champagne in the evening
and every reservation includes free membership of a nearby gym
and Internet access in every room.

A-B The Majestic Hotel, 210 W 55th St, **T** 1-212 247 2000, 1-800
336 4110, reservations@themajesticny.com *Subway B, D, E to
Seventh Av. Map 4, D5, p266* This plush hotel is housed in a
historic building with a French Riviera feel and offers guests a
choice of decor in each room, ranging from opulent gold and
purple to more soothing earth tones. For those who like to be in
the midst of everything and don't mind spending a few bucks for
a great view (ask when you book) this place is great. The Ava
Lounge on the penthouse level is one of New York's hippest hotel
bars (see p176).

A-B Shelburne Murray Hill, 303 Lexington Av, **T** 1-212 689
5200, **F** 1-212 779 7068, www.affinia.com *Subway 6 to 33rd St.
Map 4, H8, p267* The apartments and suites here are an affordable
way for visitors to enjoy boutique chic without the attitude. The
location is convenient, without being right in the rowdy hubbub of
Midtown, and the sleek, recently refurbished rooms come in a
range of sizes and prices, with good deals depending on the date.
What's more, the Star Bar (see p177) at the top of the building has
one of the best rooftop views in the city.

B-C Hotel Metro, 45 W 35th St between 5th Av and 6th Av,
T 1-800 356 3870, **F** 1-212 279 1310, www.hotelmetronyc.com
Subway B, D, F, V, N, Q, R, W to 34th St-Herald Sq. Map 3, A5, p264

Although it's situated in a rather shabby area near the Empire State Building, this hotel is really good value for Manhattan. The typically small rooms are clean, the lobby does its best to seem upscale, breakfast is included in the price and there's even a free small gym – overall, considering the central location, it's a bargain. There's also a fantastic view from the rooftop bar in summer.

B-C Roger Williams Hotel, 131 Madison Av, **T** 1-212 448 7000, **F** 1-212 448 7007, www.therogerwilliamshotel.com *Subway 6 to 33rd St.   Map 3, B6, p264* Contemporary decor and a candlelit lobby makes this boutique hotel a surprising find in the otherwise gloomy rug district of Midtown. Trendy and affordable, it's popular with business people and anyone looking for a stylish bargain. Perks include champagne at check-in, free continental breakfast and a fitness centre, plus small terraces in some rooms. Of course, its bargain status means it fills up quickly, so book well in advance.

C Red Roof Inn, 6 W 32nd St, **T** 1-212 643 7100, 1-800 RED ROOF **F** 1-212 643 7101. *Subway B, D, F, V, N, Q, R, W to 34th St-Herald Sq, 6 to 33rd St. Map 3, A4, p264* The Red Roof is a surprisingly chic chain hotel, refurbished in a modern, neutral-toned, New York style for savvy visitors who want quality at a great price. Although it sits right next to rather gloomy Herald Square, the hotel is surrounded by Little Korea, which is full of foodie surprises, with the bargain shops of the Garment District conveniently close by. Extra offerings include a fitness center and web TV.

C ThirtyThirty New York City, 30 E 30th St, **T** 1-212 689 1900, **F** 1-212 689 0023, www.3030nyc.com *Subway 6 to 28th St. Map 3, B6, p264* The stark, clean, designer decor consistently makes this one of the most popular budget boutiques in the city. Despite its location in the rug district, it's within easy walking distance of Union Square, Downtown or Midtown. You'd have to spend a great deal more for the same style elsewhere.

C-D Broadway Inn, 264 W 46th St at 8th Av, **T** 1-212 997 9200, 1-800 826 6300, **F** 1-212 768 2807, www.broadwayinn.com *Subway A, C, E to 42nd St-Port Authority. Map 4, F4, p266* T his 40-room basic bed and breakfast is on the fringes of Times Square, perfect for those who plan to spend time at Broadway theatres but want something more original than a huge Marriott. Exposed-brick, books for all to share, enthusiastic staff and breakfast on the house are a few of its charms. Like many true New York homes, though, it's a 'walk-up', meaning there is no elevator.

C-D Pickwick Arms, 230 E 51st St, **T** 1-212 355 0300, 1-800 742 5945, **F** 1-212 755 5029, www.pickwickarms.com *Subway E, V to Lexington Av-53rd St, 6 to 51st St. Map 4, E8, p267* True budget travellers won't mind the small, uncomplicated, very clean rooms, most of which have their own bathroom. The Pickwick has two restaurants and a rooftop garden for lounging and its convenient Midtown location means you are close to many of the sights. The neighbourhood has many good restaurants and the nearby United Nations adds an international flavour.

D Habitat Hotel, 130 E 57th St at Lexington Av, **T** 1-212 753 8841, 1-800 255 0482, **F** 1-212 829 9605, www.stayinny.com *Subway N, R, W to Lexington Av-59th St, 4, 5, 6 to 59th St. Map 4, D8, p267* This upscale budget hotel has been given a fresh coat of paint, which makes it feel like a prize discovery for the traveller who wants everything at a good price. Black-and-white photos adorn the walls, all rooms have sinks and breakfast is included in the price. Just outside are the shops and attractions of fashionable 57th Street and Central Park is just two blocks away. Book ahead, or try your luck last minute.

D-E Gershwin Hotel, 7 E 27th St, **T** 1-212 545 8000, **F** 1-212 684 5546, www.gershwinhotel.com *Subway N, R, 6 to 28th St. Map 3, B7, p265* This funky, artsy place seems more like an upscale hostel than a hotel, with its eclectic furniture and red façade. Tucked into the otherwise unremarkable rug district of lower Midtown, this is a bargain with a central location, just off Fifth Avenue, and an alternative feel. The variety of rooms and dorms are all at the affordable end of the scale.

Hostels

D-E YMCA Vanderbilt, 224 E 47th St, **T** 1-212 756 9600, **F** 1-212 752 0210, www.ymcanyc.org *Subway S, 4, 5, 6, 7 to 42nd St-Grand Central. Map 4, F8, p267* Slightly pricier than the average hostel, the clean, collegiate-style Vanderbilt has upbeat rooms with sinks and suites with private baths. Despite hundreds of rooms, it books up surprisingly quickly, so call ahead. Facilities include a luggage room, laundry and access to a fitness centre.

E Jazz on the Town, 130 E 57th St, **T** 1-212 932 1600, www.jazzonthepark.com *Subway 4, 5, 6 to 59 St. Map 4, D8, p267* This newly opened sibling of the longtime hostel Uptown (see p134) offers beds in brightly-coloured, clean dorm rooms for as little as $23 a night including breakfast. The 24-hour reception, Internet access and free tickets to the Ricki Lake show are just three of the perks in this friendly hostel with a lively feel. You're sure to meet some other adventurous travellers here.

Upper East Side

Hotels

AL The Carlyle Hotel, 35 E 76th St, **T** 1-212 744 1600, 1-800 227 5737, **F** 1-212 717 4682, www.thecarlyle.com *Subway 6 to 77th St. Map 5, H7, p269* If you want to splash out in every sense, the Carlyle is one of the best places to do it. Surrounded by the exclusive shops and high culture of the Upper East Side, this hushed, posh hotel has been home to many famous visitors, including The Beatles. Woody Allen plays jazz here weekly and other performers put on a regular cabaret in the Café Carlyle. If you can't afford to stay here, have a drink at Bemelmans Bar, named after the artist Ludwig Bemelmans who painted the murals on the walls when he resided in the hotel in the 1940s.

B-C The Bentley, 500 E 62nd St, **T** 1-212 644 6000, www.nychotels.com *Subway F to Lexingon Av/63rd St, 4, 5, 6 to 59th St/Lexington Av. Map 4, C10, p267* The Bentley is a charming, sleek hotel, situated off the beaten track near York Avenue. The rooftop bar and restaurant and the south-facing guestrooms all enjoy some breathtaking views of the East River, the 59th Street Bridge and Manhattan and there's easy access to the Upper East Side's shops and museums. It feels like a well-priced boutique hotel, thanks to its chic decor, but it actually has 197 rooms, so booking a few days ahead is usually sufficient. Breakfast included.

Hostels

D-E YMHA de Hirsch Residence at the 92nd Street Y, 1395 Lexington Av, **T** 1-212 415 5650, 1-800 858 4692, **F** 1-212 415 5578. *Subway 6 to 96th St. Map 5, D8, p269* Run by the Young Men's Hebrew Association, the 92nd Street Y is as close to an intellectual hostel as one might find, with lectures, performances, readings and other events taking place every week. The dorm rooms are clean, spacious, safe and good value. Visitors also have use of a fitness centre.

Upper West Side

Hotels

B Empire Hotel, 44 W 63rd St, **T** 1-212 265 7400, 1-888 822 3555, **F** 1-212 315 0349, www.empirehotel.com *Subway 1, 2 to 66th St-Lincoln Center. Map 4, C3, p266* One of the few affordable hotels near the Lincoln Center, the Empire draws in cultural types to its velvety lobby and frayed rooms. A slightly dilapidated feel and eccentric guests make this one of a kind in the area. The 381 rooms are tiny and decorated with all sorts of patterns and kitschy florals but the hotel is proud of its old-fashioned charm.

C Hotel Beacon, 2130 Broadway between 74th and 75th Sts, **T** 1-212 787 1100, 1-800 572 4969, **F** 1-212 787 8119, www.beaconhotel.com *Subway 1, 2, 3 to 72nd St.   Map 5, H2, p268* Right smack in the heart of the Upper West Side shopping district, this is a good choice for those who want to be close to Central Park and the bustle of Broadway. Some rooms have kitchenettes, so you can make the most of all the desirable food shops nearby (Zabar's, Fairway, Citarella). The large rooms in this tall, renovated building fill with sunshine; ask for a window overlooking Broadway to watch all the action from above.

C-D Malibu Studios Hotel, 2688 Broadway at 103rd St, **T** 1-212 222 2954, 1-800 647 2227, **F** 1-212 678 6842, www.malibuhotelnyc.com *Subway 1 to 103rd St.   Map 5, B2, p268* Set near peaceful Riverside Park and close to Columbia University, the Malibu is a decent and affordable choice but is far away from anything Downtown. Recent remodelling has spruced up the rather lacklustre rooms, adding black-and-white photos to the clean decor. Come here if actually getting some sleep on a budget is a priority. Cash and travellers' checks only.

Hostels

D YMCA West Side, 5 W 63rd St, **T** 1-212 875 4100, **F** 1-212 875 1334, www.ymcanyc.org *Subway A, C, B, D, 1, 2 to 59th St/ Columbus Circle. Map 4, C4, p266* This enormous 500-room hostel fills up quickly due to its wonderful location, close to Central Park, Midtown and the Lincoln Center. The clean and simple rooms are run with astounding efficiency and some have their own bathrooms for a bit more money. There's a cafeteria, fitness area and laundry here, too.

E Central Park Hostel, 19 W 103rd St at Central Park West, **T** 1-212 678 0491, www.centralparkhostel.com *Subway B, C to 103rd St. Map 5, B4, p268* This clean, remodelled hostel sits in a brownstone on an attractive street, just off Central Park. Although it's quite a trek away from the centre of town, its brightly coloured, sunny rooms and cheap prices will keep you cheerful. Cash or travellers' checks only.

C-E International House, 500 Riverside Dr at 125th St, **T** 1-212 316 8473, 1-212 316 8436 (summer only), **F** 1-212 316 1827, www.ihouse-nyc.org *Subway 1 to 125th St. Map 6, D1, p270* Foreign students and touring scholars fill the halls of this large, pretty, old building during the school season, but in the vacations its provides quiet, charming visitor accommodation near Harlem and Columbia University. Rates drop in summer for dorm-style rooms, with regular hotel rooms available for slightly more. The cafeteria is a good place to eat cheaply.

E Hostelling International New York, 891 Amsterdam Av at 103rd St, **T** 1-212 932 2300, **F** 1-212 932 2574, www.hinewyork.org *Subway 1 to 103rd St. Map 5, B2, p268* The hostel was formerly a residence for elderly women and its huge, redbrick form covers a whole city block on the broad sweep of Amsterdam Avenue, near Columbia University. It feels rather institutional, but it's cheap, very clean and has helpful staff who offer plentiful information and city tours. Book a week or two ahead for a room.

E Jazz on the Park, 36 W 106th St at Central Park West, **T** 1-212 932 1600, **F** 1-212 932 1700, www.jazzonthepark.com *Subway B, C to 103rd St. Map 5, A4, p268* This long-serving hostel is inviting and friendly, despite the miniscule rooms. A beer lounge in the basement hosts a variety of hip-hop and jazz acts and the summer barbecues are a fun slice of Americana. The price includes a private locker and breakfast. Internet access is available and bikes or roller-blades can be rented here, too.

New York's restaurant scene, fickle as it may be, holds on to its reputation as one of the most extensive and innovative in the world. Fashionable restaurants are at the centre of New York social life, and they can come and go very quickly if they don't pass muster with the city's discerning diners. The selection and quality of food is mind-boggling, the chefs are world-renowned and the service can be impeccable. However, it's not necessary to spend a fortune for a mouth-watering meal. Many locals prefer the 60-year-old kosher diner or the hidden Italian trattoria to the glitzy, hyped hotspots.

A culinary tour of New York will take you to all corners of the city, so keep your tastebuds primed for all sorts of gastronomic delights. Every style of cuisine can be found here: Greek and Lebanese, Japanese and Korean, Indian and Vietnamese, Ethiopian and French, Italian and Caribbean. Downtown eateries tend to attract a young, laidback clientele, while Uptown restaurants are more upscale in appearance and price. Reserve tables in advance, or be prepared to wait during busy periods.

Lower Manhattan

Restaurants

$$$ American Park at the Battery, Battery Park, opp 17 State St at Pearl St, **T** 1-212 809 5508. *Mon-Sat 1130-1500 and 1700-2100, Sun 1100-1500. Subway N, R, W to Whitehall St, 1, 9 to South Ferry. Map 7, H3, p272* One of countless restaurants offering hefty Financial District fare: sirloin, lamb and a raw bar. It's worth the expense for the astounding view of New York Harbour.

$$$ 14 Wall Street, 14 Wall St, 31st Floor, **T** 1-212 233 2780. *Mon-Fri 0700-0930, 1200-1500 and 1700-2000. Subway 4, 5 to Wall St. Map 7, F4, p272* It's worth the cost of eating at this bistro to enjoy the incredible views of Downtown. Enjoy filet mignon and foie gras with banker types. The building was formerly JP Morgan's library (and the apartment he kept for his mistress).

$$ Cassis, 52 Stone St, **T** 1-212 425 3663. *Mon-Sat 1200-2200, Subway N, R, W to Whitehall St. Map 7, G4, p272* Hearty, French-inspired salads, seafood and steak on one of the most delightfully renovated streets in the otherwise staid Financial District. Summer seats on the cobbles out front are enchanting.

$$ Harry's Hanover Square, 1 Hanover Sq, **T** 1-212 425 3412.
Mon-Fri 1200-2230. Subway 2, 3 to Wall St. Map 7, F4, p272 The Wall
Street crowd indulges in steak and veal chops but you can have a
burger at the bar for an affordable taste of the financial scene.

$ Seh Ja Meh, 26 John St, **T** 1-212 766 5825. *Mon-Fri 1130-2100,
Subway A, C to Broadway-Nassau St. Map 7, D4, p272* Cheap and
cheerful. Sample Korean dumplings and various concoctions of
rice, meat and vegetables at a fair price.

Chinatown, Little Italy and Nolita

Restaurants

$$$$ Capitale, 130 Bowery, **T** 1-212 334 5500. *Mon-Sat
1730-2200. Subway J, M, Z to Bowery. Map 2, B6, p262* The most
exquisite dining in town takes place in in the former Bowery
Savings Bank. This elegant, gilded setting is an anomaly in an
otherwise raucous area. The food is Americana deluxe: spring lamb
and borscht with a twist.

$$ Café Gitane, 242 Mott St, **T** 1-212 334 9552. *Daily 0900-2400.
Subway 6 to Bleecker St or Spring St. Map 2, A6, p262* This cool
joint oozes with Moroccan-French-inspired charm. Local hipsters
and visitors will find it a delightful place for breakfast, salad,
couscous and citron pressé any time of day.

$$ Café Lebowitz, 14 Spring St, **T** 1-212 219 2399. *Daily
0930-0200. Subway 6 to Spring St. Map 2, A6, p262* An excellent
place for brunch and Sunday papers or an evening glass of wine
with sumptuous halibut and roasted chicken. The bar is as chic as
the people.

$$ Lombardi's, 32 Spring St. **T** 1-212 941 7994. *Mon-Thu 1130-2300, Fri and Sat 1130-2400, Sun 1130-1000. Map 2, A6, p262* An institution since 1905 and consistently voted New Yorkers' favourite pizza place. Come here for a pizza and some Chianti.

$ Café Habana, 17 Prince St, **T** 1-212 625 2001. *Daily 0900-2400. Subway 6 to Spring St. Map 2, A6, p262* Hipsters of the Nolita set descend to this buzzy Cuban café for its cilantro-infused salsa, chipotle chilli, delectable empanadas and cool vibe.

$ Joe's Shanghai, 9 Pell St, **T** 1-212 233 8888. *Sun-Thu 1100-2300, Fri and Sat 1100-2400. Subway J, M, Z, N, R, Q, W, 6 to Canal St. Map 2, C7, p263* There's always a queue at this timeless Chinatown favourite. Brothy dumplings and Peking Duck are worth waiting for, so don't balk at the plain decor.

$ New Green Bo Restaurant, E 66 Bayard St, **T** 1-212 625 2359. *Daily 1100-2300. Subway J, M, Z, N, R, Q, W, 6 to Canal St. Map 2, C6, p262* Delicious dumplings, noodles and classic Szechwan dishes are served in sparse surroundings to a mostly Chinese crowd. Communal tables, tasty food and cheap prices.

$ Peking Duck House, 28 Mott St, **T** 1-212 227 1810. *Sun-Thu 1130 2230, Fri and Sat 1130-2330. Subway J, M, Z, N, R, Q, W, 6 to Canal St. Map 2, C6, p262* Crispy duck and pancakes continue to please customers in this long-running Chinatown institution.

$ Sweet-n-Tart Restaurant, 20 Mott St, **T** 1-212 964 0380. *Mon-Thu 1000-2400, Fri-Sun 1000-2400, Subway J, M, Z, N, R, Q, W, 6 to Canal St. Map 2, C6, p262* Kitschy in a fun, fluorescent, Formica way. Stick around for dim sum and fruity milk shakes brought to you by an electric dumb waiter.

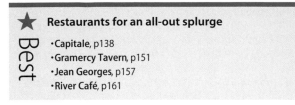

★ **Restaurants for an all-out splurge**

Best
•**Capitale**, p138
•**Gramercy Tavern**, p151
•**Jean Georges**, p157
•**River Café**, p161

Cafés

$ Ciao Bella, 285 Mott St, **T** 1-212 431 3591. *Daily 1100-2200. Subway 6 to Bleecker St. Map 2, C6, p262* A fine gelato is perfect after your meal or as you stroll around the boutiques. Savour New York's answer to Italian ice cream.

$ Tea & Tea, 51 Mott St, **T** 1-212 766 9889. *Mon-Fri 1100-2330, Sat and Sun 1100-2400. Subway J, M, Z, N, R, Q, W, 6 to Canal St. Map 2, C6, p262* Every kind of green tea and lychee-inspired beverage is on the menu. A civilized place to pause in these chaotic streets.

SoHo and Tribeca

$$$ Balthazar, 80 Spring St, **T** 1-212 965 1414. *Mon-Thu 0730-1200, Fri and Sun 0730-0200. Subway N, R, W to Prince St, 6 to Spring St. Map 2, A5, p262* The trendy scene and mouth-watering bread make this one of the hippest brunches in town. Dinner is good too, with French-style seafood, but tables are hard to come by.

$$$ The Mercer Kitchen, 99 Prince St, **T** 1-212 966 5454. *Mon-Thu 0700-2400, Fri-Sun 0700-0100. Subway N, R, W to Prince St. Map 2, A5, p262* Come here to star spot while eating spring rolls, fancy pizzas and creative American treats. If it's booked up, have a drink in the comfy lounge instead.

$$$ The Odeon, 145 W Broadway, **T** 1-212 233 0507. *Mon-Fri 1130-0200, Sat, Sun 1100-0200, Subway A, C to Chambers St.* Map 7, B2, p272 One of the chicest brasseries in New York. It's always full of nice-looking folks and always open late for burgers, salad and wine.

$$ Blue Ribbon Sushi, 119 Sullivan St, **T** 1-212 343 0404. *Daily 1200-0200. Subway C, E to Spring St.* Map 2, A4, p262 A stylish place to eat sushi. Come for the atmosphere, the gardens and the hip crowd rather than the rolls.

$$ Bubby's, 120 Hudson St, **T** 1-212 219 0666. *Mon-Thu 0800-2300, Sat 0900-2400, Sun 0900-2200.Subway 1, 9 to Franklin St.* Map 7, A1, p272 For lovers of comfort food, this places serves the best macaroni and cheese in the city. The enormous portions and lively atmosphere make this a kid-friendly place for brunch.

$$ Café Noir, 32 Grand St, **T** 1-212 431 7910. *Daily 1200-0400. Subway A, C, E, 1, 9 to Canal St.* Map 2, B4, p262 Come to this sexy candlelit spot for late-night munchies, tapas, music and a Mojito.

$$ Felix, 340 W Broadway, **T** 1-212 431 0021. *Mon-Fri 1200-2400, Sat 1130-2400, Sun 1130-2230. Subway A, C, E, 1, 9 to Canal St.* Map 2, B5, p262 For many New Yorkers this is the ultimate brunch place. Patrons pour onto the sidewalk in the summer to sample French fare in a shabby chic setting and to spot supermodels.

$$ Jerry's, 101 Prince St, **T** 1-212 966 9464. *Daily 0830-2300. Subway N, R, W to Prince St.* Map 2, A5, p262 This upscale diner serves a fine brunch and is a welcome resting point in the SoHo strip, with unpretentious red booths and a tasty American menu.

$$ Pfiff, 35 Grand St, **T** 1-212 334 6841. *Daily 1800-2400. Subway A, C, E, 1, 9 to Canal St.* Map 2, B5, p262 In late 2003, New Yorkers were hailing Pfiff as one of the best new restaurants around. It's a

Eating and drinking

★ **Tables for star-spotting**

Best

·**Balthazar**, p140
·**Mercer Kitchen**, p140
·**Felix**, p141
·**Raoul's**, p142

romantic and laidback spot, where tropical seafood is served against a background of relaxed Cuban tunes.

$$ Pravda, 281 Lafayette St, **T** 1-212 226 4944. *Mon-Wed 1700-0100, Thu 1700-0230, Fri and Sat 1700-0330, Sun 1800-0100. Subway F, V to Broadway-Lafayette St. Map 3, G7, p265* Despite its late-90s status, scenesters still frequent this buzzing Russian cave to indulge in tasty tapas-style treats, while sipping on lethal vodkas.

$$ Raoul's, 180 Prince St, **T** 1-212 966 3518. *Daily 1730-0200. Subway C, E to Spring St. Map 2, A4, p262* Francophiles in New York agree that this place serves the city's best pommes frites but otherwise it's more about the cool SoHo scene than the food.

$$ Salt, 58 MacDougal St, **T** 1-212 674 4968. *Mon-Fri 1800-2300, Sat and Sun 1130-0530, 1800-2300. Subway C, E to Spring St, 1, 9 to Houston St. Map 3, H5, p264* A treasured neighbourhood eaterie, with an American menu. The popular prix-fixe option includes a main dish plus two sides for $20.50.

$$ 66, 241 Church St, **T** 1-212 925 0202. *Mon-Sat 1130-1500, 1800-2400, Sun 1130-1500, 1800-2230. Subway 1, 9 to Franklin St. Map 2, C4, p262* Tasty, high-class Chinese food, communal tables and upbeat music make this new arrival a hot spot in Tribeca.

★ **Best**

Brunch spots

- **Café Gitane**, p138
- **Balthazar**, p140
- **Bubby's**, p141
- **Kitcheonette**, p143
- **Cornelia St Café**, p147

$$ Zutto, 77 Hudson St, **T** 1-212 233 3287. *Daily 1145-1430, 1730-2300. Subway 1, 9 to Franklin St. Map 2, D4, p262* Skip expensive Nobu and head down the street to this place instead. Excellent sushi, 'kamikaze' rolls and scrumptious salted beef slices are served in well-lit and serene surroundings.

$ Kitcheonette, 80 W Broadway, **T** 1-212 267 6740. *Mon-Fri 0730-2200, Sat-Sun 0900-2200, Subway 1, 2, 3, 9 to Chambers St. Map 7, B1, p272* A buzzing Tribeca country kitchen, where newspapers and coffee complement the homemade grits, French toast and turkey sausage.

$ Lunchbox Food Co, 357 West St, **T** 1-646 230 9466. *Mon-Fri 0600-2300, Sat 0800-0200, Sun 0800-2300. Subway 1, 9 to Houston St. Map 2, A1, p262* This cute diner has an outdoor garden space and offers an innovative twist on organic burgers and sandwiches. Test some of the lip-smacking chocolatey desserts and doughnuts.

$ Ñ, 33 Crosby St, **T** 1-212 219 8856. *Sun-Thu 1700-0200, Fri and Sat 1700-0400. Subway 6 to Spring St. Map 2, A5, p262* This tiny, wonderful tapas spot bursts with flavour and even hosts a flamenco band on Wednesday nights. *Oct 2003 visit.*

$ Pepe Rosso To Go, E 149 Sullivan St, **T** 1-212 677 4555. *Mon-Sat 1100-2300, Sun 0400-2300. Subway C, E to Spring St. Map 2, A4, p262* Delicious paninis, pear and gorgonzola salads, and pastas made by true Italians whose prices are right.

Cafés

$ 12 Chairs Café, 56 MacDougal St, **T** 1-212 254 8640. *Sun-Fri 0800-2300 Map 3, H5, p262* This small, unpretentious café is a gem in the bustle of SoHo streets. Breakfast is served all day, or try some blintzes and pirogis.

Greenwich Village and Chelsea

Restaurants

$$$ Grange Hall, 50 Commerce St, **T** 1-212 924 5246. *Mon-Fri 1200-1500, 1800-2330, Sat and Sun 1000-1600, 1800-2330. Subway 1, 9 to Christopher St. Map 3, H4, p264* A beautiful art deco bar and restaurant is hidden on one of the West Village's prettiest corners. A slice of heavenly Americana.

$$$ Pastis, 9 Ninth Av, **T** 1-212 929 4844. *Sun-Thu 0900-0200, Fri and Sat 0900-0300. Subway A, C, E to 14th St. Map 3, F2, p264* One of Keith McNally's many successful restaurants, Pastis buzzes at all hours of the night with handsome New Yorkers looking to indulge themselves. Tasty bar food includes frites and oysters.

$$$ Red Cat, 227 10th Av, **T** 1-212 242 1122. *Mon-Thu 1730-2300, Fri and Sat 1730-2400, Sun 1700-2200. Subway C, E to 23rd St. Map 3, C1, p264* Clapboard chic and New England flair are invoked at this Chelsea favourite. Tasty seafood and vegetable appetizers are well worth the expense.

Bellavitae 24 Minetta Lane
212 473 5121
Jan 05.
Brilliant!

$$ Cafeteria, 119 Seventh Av, **T** 1-212 414 1717. *Daily 24 hrs. Subway 1, 9 to 18th St. Map 3, E4, p264* Buzzing all day and night with a techno vibe, this white minimalist restaurant serves satisfying sandwiches, salads and meat loaf.

$$ Cowgirl Hall of Fame, 519 Hudson St, **T** 1-212 633 1133. *Daily 1130-2300. Subway 1, 9 to Christopher St Map 3, G3, p264* Come to this lively bar and restaurant to whoop it up Western-style with Southern/Mexican fare, including enchiladas, frito pies and lethal Margaritas in mason jars.

$$ Florent, 69 Gansevoort St, **T** 1-212 989 5779. *Mon-Wed 0900-0500, Thu-Sun 24 hrs. Subway A, C, E to 14th St. Map 3, F2, p264* This classic diner, the backdrop to many films, is the place to be seen eating burgers, muffins and steak frites in the small hours.

$$ Hue, 91 Charles St, **T** 1-212 691 4170. *Mon-Sat 1800-2400, Sun 1800-2200. Subway 1,9 to Christopher St-Sheridan Sq. Map 3, G3, p264* This French-Vietnamese lounge/restaurant has a hip, Zen-like quality, helped in no small measure by plum sake and shrimp on sugar cane sticks. A waterfall and skylight contribute to the dreamy atmosphere.

$$ Markt, 401 W 14th St, **T** 1-212 727 3314. *Daily 1130-2400. Subway A, C, E to 14th St. Map 3, E2, p264* Markt has enough Belgian beer to make you giddy plus delicious moules/frites combos or oysters if you're feeling particulary flamboyant.

$$ Mary's Fish Camp, 64 Charles St, **T** 1-646 486 2185. *Mon-Sat 1200-1500, 1800-2300. Subway 1, 9 to Christopher St Map 3, G4, p264* A charming find in the Village, this informal seafood hut offers some of the freshest tilapia, snapper and lobsters anywhere.

★ Best

○
Ｂ
ｅ
ｓ
ｔ

Burgers

·Corner Bistro, p147
·Trailer Park, p147
·McHale's, p154
·Island Burgers and Shakes, p155
·JG Melon, p156

$$ Negril Village, 362 W 23rd St, 1st floor, **T** 1-212 807-6411. *Daily 1200-2400. Subway C, E, 1, 9 to 23rd St. Map 3, C3, p264* Palm trees and reggae complement Caribbean delights like jerk chicken, pineapple salsa and fruity drinks.

$$ O Mai, 158 Ninth Av, **T** 1-212 633 0550. *Sun-Thu 1730-2300, Fri and Sat 2400. Subway C, E to 23rd St. Map 3, D2, p264* Vietnamese food at its best, including spicy beef and chilli-lime red snapper, served in a minimalist Chelsea hangout.

*excellent
weightless
pizza
Jau/05*

$$ Otto, 1 Fifth Av, **T** 1-212 674 2044. *Daily 0900-2330. Subway A, C, E, F, V to W 4th St. Map 3, G6, p264* Recently opened by celebrity chef Mario Batali, Otto is popular thanks to its delicious posh pizza and extensive, 500-bottle wine list.

$$ Piadina, 57 W 10th St, **T** 1-212 460 8017. *Daily 1800-2330. Subway F, V to 14th St, L to Sixth Av. Map 3, F5, p264* Charming Italian waiters, candlelight, delicious bread and pasta make this tiny, brick basement a timeless locals' favourite. The hand-written menu includes excellent seafood and pasta specials.

$$ Sapore, 55 Greenwich Av, **T** 1-212 229 0551. *Daily 1200-2300. Subway 1, 2, 3, 9 to 14th St, Map 3, F4, p264* A tiny trattoria that serves some of the tastiest fettucine in town. It's easy on the wallet, atmospheric and fun.

$$ Westville, 210 W 10th St, **T** 1-212 741 7971. *Daily 1200-2400. Subway 1, 9 to Christopher St.   Map 3, F4, p264*   The down-on-the-farm American food always attracts a queue. Come early for corn-on-the-cob, macaroni, burgers or cobbler.

$-$$ Da Andrea, 557 Hudson St, **T** 1-212 367 1979. *Daily 1730-2230. Subway 1, 9 to Christopher St-Sheridan Sq. Map 3, G3, p264*   Affordable Northern Italian food, such as taglioni, gnocchi and mussels, make this a good spot for a casual meal.

Mainly for breaky

$ Cornelia St Café, 29 Cornelia St, **T** 1-212 989 9319. *Sun-Thu 1000-0100, Fri, Sat 1000-0200. Subway A, C, E, F, V to W 4th St. Map 3, G5, p264*   The exposed brick, wooden chairs and jazz performances at night are part of the charm but the lovely and affordable brunches are still the best reason to visit.

$ Corner Bistro, 331 W 4th St, **T** 1-212 242 9502. *Daily 1400-0330. Subway A, C, E to 14th St. Map 3, F3, p264*   This no-frills spot serves one of the best burgers in town. It's a heavenly greasy affair at a cheap price. The queue moves quickly so don't let it deter you.

$ Moustache, 90 Bedford St, **T** 1-212 229 2220. *Daily 1200-2300. Subway 1, 9 to Christopher St. Map 3, H4, p264*   Tiny, unpretentious and surprisingly cheap, this Middle Eastern restaurant serves lamb, couscous and mint tea.

$ Trailer Park, 271 W 23rd St, **T** 1-212 463-8000. *Daily 1200-0100. Subway C, E to 23rd St. Map 3, C2, p264*   The velvet Elvises make this the perfect trashy environment for juicy burgers and BLTs served in plastic baskets.

Cafés

$ Caffe Rafaella, 134 Seventh Av, **T** 1-212 929 7247. *Daily 1100-0200. Subway 1, 9 to Christopher St. Map 3, F4, p264* Big, comfy chairs, heavenly desserts and a lazy wintry feel will keep you here longer than you'd planned.

$ Caffè Reggio, 119 MacDougal St, **T** 1-212 475 9557. *Daily 1000-0100. Subway A, C, E, F to W 4th St. Map 3, H5, p264* An ancient café with a fair amount of charm despite the tourist vibe outside.

$ Jack's, 138 W 10th St, **T** 1-212 929 0821. *Mon-Fri 0700-2100, Sat and Sun 0800-2000. Subway 1, 9 to Christopher St. Map 3, F4, p264* One of the most socially conscious and nicest coffeeshops in New York. Jack's sells fair trade coffee that is stir-brewed.

Lower East Side and East Village

Restaurants

$$$ Industry (Food), 509 E 6th St, **T** 1-212 777 5920. *Sun-Wed 1800-2400, Thu-Sat 1800-0100. Subway F, V to Lower East Side-2nd Av. Map 3, G11, p265* A sleek, wood-panelled restaurant. Don't let the pretentious hipsters at the bar cloud your vision of lobster bruschetta or ribs infused with a port-and-pomegranate sauce.

$$-$$$ Suba, 109 Ludlow St, **T** 1-212 982 5714. *Mon-Thu 1800-2230, Fri-Sun 0600-2330. Subway F to Delancey St, J, M, Z to Delancey-Essex St. Map 2, A8, p263* Tapas upstairs at the bar are fine, but don't miss the sexy restaurant downstairs, which sets the tone nicely for Spanish-Latino delights such as chipotle tuna and saffron duck.

$$ Epicerie/Café Charbon, 168-170 Orchard St, **T** 1-212 420 7520. *Sun-Thu 1130-0200, Fri and Sat 1130-0400. Subway F, V to Lower East Side-2nd Av. Map 2, A7, p263* Although it looks like a French grocery, this is a hip little bistro set smack in the middle of one of New York's trendiest streets. Sneak next door for live jazz at Café Charbon after a satisfying meal at the Epicerie.

$$ Esperanto, 145 Av C, **T** 1-212 505 6559. *Sun-Thu 1800-2400, Fri and Sat 1800-0200, Sun 1100-1600. Subway F to 2nd Ave, 6 at Astor Pl. Map 3, F11, p265* This eternally hopping Brazilian/Cuban restaurant features lively music and Mojitos as well as nicely seasoned Latin food.

$$ Five Points, 31 Great Jones St, **T** 1-212 253 5700. *Mon-Sat 1800-2400, Sun 1130-1530, 1800-2200. Subway F, V to Broadway-Lafayette. Map 3, G7, p265* A water fountain complements the duck, pork chops and scallops. Happy hour with $5 Martinis and $1 oysters is not to be missed.

$$ Jules Bistro, 65 St Mark's Pl, **T** 1-212 477 5560. *Mon-Fri 1130-0130, Sat and Sun 1130-0100. Subway 6 to Astor Pl. Map 3, F9, p265* Jazz resonates through this warm, inviting and lively French bistro. The hearty fare includes a tasty brunch served until late in the afternoon.

$$ Katz's Delicatessen, 205 E Houston St, **T** 1-212 254 2246. *Sun-Tue 0800-2200, Wed-Thu 0800-2300, Fri and Sat 0800-0300. Subway F, V to Lower East Side-Second Av. Map 3, H9, p265* The king of New York delis. Come here for corned beef and pastrami sandwiches big enough to feed a family. The systematic ordering makes for a raucous but entertaining event and you may spot some well-known New Yorkers in the queue.

$$ La Palapa, 77 St Mark's Pl, **T** 1-212 777 2537. *Mon-Fri 1200-2400, Sat and Sun 1100-2400. Subway 6 to Astor Pl. Map 3, F9, p265* Mexicans in New York say this earthy, relaxed restaurant does an excellent job of imitating the real deal from over the border. Mole sauce, spicy seafood and cinnamon turnovers keep locals happy.

$$ Mogador Café, 101 St Marks Pl, **T** 1-212 677 2226. *Sun-Thu 0900-1230, Fri and Sat 0900-0130. Subway 6 to Astor Pl. Map 3, F8, p265* Enjoy couscous and other Moroccan delicacies at sidewalk tables in the East Village.

$$ Schillers Liquor Bar, 131 Rivington St, **T** 1-212 260 4555. *Mon and Tue 0800-0200, Wed-Fri 0800-0300, Sat 1000-0300, Sun 1000-0200. Subway F to Delancey, J, M, Z to Essex St. Map 2, A8, p263* Keith McNally's latest venture is an affordable bistro, complete with antique mirrors, a doughnut machine, Cuban sandwiches and the usual cool faces who frequent the Lower East Side.

$$ Second Avenue Deli, 156 Second Av, **T** 1-212 677 0606. *Sun-Thu 0700-2400, Fri and Sat 0700-0300. Subway 6 to Astor Pl. Map 3, F8, p265* This kosher Eastern European institution has been around longer than any visitor and its blintzes, potato pancakes and hot corned beef sandwiches may be the best in New York. A three-decker sandwich will set you back $17 but it's easily large enough for two or more.

$ Great Jones Café, 54 Great Jones St, **T** 1-212 674 9304. *Mon-Thu 1700-2400, Fri 1700-0100, Sat 1130-0100, Sun 1130-2400. Subway 6 to Bleecker St. Map 3, H8, p265* Cajun comfort food, jambalaya, fried chicken, mashed potatoes and gravy, make this little, kitschy Elvis-inspired bar and restaurant a place of which even New Orleans would be proud.

$ **'Inoteca**, 98 Rivington St, **T** 1-212 614 0473. *Daily 1100-0300. Subway F, V to Lower East Side-2nd Av. Map 2, A8, p263* Paninis, cheese and wines galore. What more could you ask from this hip new addition to the Lower East Side?

$ **Supper**, 156 E 2nd St, **T** 1-212 477 7600. *Sun-Thu 1100-0100, Fri and Sat 1100-0200. Subway F, V to Lower East Side-2nd Av. Map 3, H10, p265* Rustic yet hip, this chandeliered Italian restaurant pleases locals with its 'priest stranglers' (tubes of pasta with ricotta, mozzarella and red sauce) and asparagus parmesan.

Cafés

$ **ChikaLicious Dessert Bar**, 203 E 10th St, **T** 1-212 995 9511. *Daily. Subway 6 to Astor Court. Map 3, F8, p265* New York's first dessert bar. Need we say more? I leaven.

$ **teany**, 90 Rivington St, **T** 1-212 475 9190. *Daily 0900-0100. Subway F, V to Lower East Side-2nd Av. Map 2, A8, p263* Musician Moby's welcoming tea shop has an enormous selection of teas, organic nibbles and desserts. — *good coffee + cakes Jan/05*

Flatiron District and around

Restaurants

If you're craving a curry, head to **Little India** (25th St to 30th St on Lexington Av), where you'll find a wide range of Indian restaurants and fast-food joints, plus sari shops and Bollywood rental stores.

$$$$ **Gramercy Tavern**, 42 E 20th St, **T** 1-212 477 0777. *Mon-Thu 1200-1430, 1730-2200, Fri 1200-1400, 1730-2300, Sat 1730-2300, Sun 1730-2200. Subway N, R, W, 6 to 23rd St. Map 3, D6, p264* If you

want to splash out just once, head for this classy American restaurant run by celebrity chef Tom Colicchio. For a slightly cheaper taste of the superlative cuisine, consider eating in the more casual bar area at the front.

$$-$$$ Kitchen22, 34 E 22nd St, **T** 1-212 228 4399. *Mon-Sat 1700-2230. Subway N, R, W, 6 to 23rd St. Map 3, D6, p264* Celebrity chef Charlie Palmer's three-course prix fixe menu is a bargain at $25; it includes beef carpaccio, port-glazed salmon and flourless chocolate cake. The young crowd and gigantic lampshades make the atmosphere pleasing and chic.

$$ Coffee Shop, 29 Union Square West, **T** 1-212 243 7969. *Sun and Mon 0800-0200, Tue 0800-0400, Wed-Sat 0800-0530. Subway L, N, Q, R, W, 4, 5, 6 to 14th St-Union Sq. Map 3, E6, p264* A fashionable, international clientele always crowds into this upscale American-Brazilian diner. The bar downstairs is an atmospheric, dark hideaway.

$$ L'Express, 249 Park Av South, **T** 1-212 254 5858. *Daily 24 hrs. Subway 6 to 23rd St. Map 3, D7, p264* This is one of those places that makes you want to be a New Yorker. It's not the fact that the burgers, salads and steak frites are good and the wine is abundant but rather that this is a beautiful bar with realistic prices and a buzzing atmosphere that stays open all night.

$ Republic, 37 Union Sq West, **T** 1-212 627 7168. *Sun-Wed 1130-2230, Thu-Sat 1130-2330. Subway L, N, Q, R, W, 4, 5, 6 to 14th St-Union Sq. Map 3, E6, p264* The noodles are cheap, tables are communal and it's noisy and bustling. Come here for a quick Pan-Asian meal.

$ Zen Palate, 34 Union Sq East, **T** 1-212 614 9291. *Daily 1130-1500, 1730-2230. Subway L, N, Q, R, W, 4, 5, 6 to 14th St-Union Sq.*

Map 3, E6, p264 The vegetarian menu at this busy Union Square student hangout has something for everyone, from burritos, pasta, spinach and crêpes, to delicious raspberry iced tea. Affordable prices and health-conscious flair.

Cafés

71 Irving Place, 71 Irving Pl, **T** 1-212 995 5252. *Daily 0700-2300. Subway L, N, Q, R, W, 4, 5, 6 to 14th St-Union Sq. Map 3, D7, p265*
One of those places you don't want everyone to find out about. Come here for coffee and muffins, to read the paper and observe New Yorkers snatching a moment of calm in this serene basement coffee shop with benches outside.

Midtown

Restaurants

$$$ Esca, 402 W 43rd St, **T** 1-212 564 7272. *Mon-Sat 1730-2230. Subway A, C, E to 42nd St-Port Authority. Map 4, G3, p266* Mario Batali's Italian seafood may be pricey but this is the best raw bar in the city.

$$-$$$ Café St Bart's, 109 E 50th St, **T** 1-212 888 2664. *Winter Mon-Fri 0800-1500; summer Mon-Fri 0800-2200, Sun 1130-1600. Subway 6 to 51st St. Map 4, E7, p267* Jutting out from handsome St Bartholomew's Church is terraced seating (with a tent in winter) where a Californian menu is served. Come for the unusual experience of dining on Park Avenue, with office buildings and the Waldorf-Astoria next door.

$$-$$$ Grand Central Oyster Bar & Restaurant, Grand Central Terminal, Lower Concourse, 42nd St at Park Av, **T** 1-212 490 6650.

Mon-Fri 1130-2130, Sat 1200-2130. Subway S, 4, 5, 6, 7 to 42nd St-Grand Central. Map 4, G7, p267 Oyster lovers shouldn't miss this 90-year-old landmark below the station. Sit at the counter for a good look at over 30 varieties of fresh oysters from the East Coast.

$$ Kum Gang San, 49 W 32nd St, **T** 1-212 967 0909. *Daily 24 hrs. Subway B, D, F, V, N, Q, R, W to 34th St-Herald Sq. Map 3, A5, p264* The most well-known of Little Korea's restaurants boasts a fake waterfall and the best bulgogi (marinated beef) or bibimbap (rice bowl with veggies and meat) on the strip.

$$ L'Entrecote, 1057 First Av, **T** 1-212 755 0080. *Mon-Sat 1800-2200. Subway N, R, W to Lexington Av-59th St. Map 4, D9, p267* Tiny family-run restaurant with ten tables that never disappoints. Hearty and delicious French food.

$$ Le Madeleine, 403 W 43rd St, **T** 1-212 246 2993. *Daily 1200-1500, 1700-2300. Subway A, C, E to 42nd St-Port Authority. Map 4, G3, p266* For theatre-goers, this French bistro and pretty garden are a welcome oasis among otherwise tacky tourist restaurants.

$$ McHale's, 750 Eighth Av, **T** 1-212 997 8885. *Mon-Sat 1200-0100, Sun 1600-2400. Subway A, C, E to 42nd St. Map 4, F4, p266* One of the best burgers in town is served at this 1950s-style wooden bar. It's also an excellent place for a pint or two.

$$ Ruby Foo's, 1626 Broadway, **T** 1-212 489 5600. *Daily 1130-2400. Subway C, E, 1, 9 to 50th St. Map 4, F5, p266* One of the few Times Square spots that actually deserves its popularity. The delicious Asian-fusion cuisine will leave you happy before or after your Broadway show. Call ahead for reservations.

$$ Sushi-Yasuda, 204 E 43rd St, **T** 1-212 972 1001. *Mon-Fri 1200-1415, 1800-2215. Sat 1800-2215. Subway S, 4, 5, 6, 7 to 42nd*

St-Grand Central Map 4, F8, p267 For the most decadent sushi in Manhattan join the Japanese ex-pats and tuck into salmon rolls, tuna and scallops.

$ Island Burgers & Shakes, 766 Ninth Av, **T** 1-212 307 7934. *Fri and Sat 1200-2330, Sun-Thu 1200-2230. Subway C, E to 50th St. Map 4, E3, p266* A laidback surfer feel and over 60 varieties of burger, including the Slick Willie. One of the best burger joints in town.

$ Nook, 746 Ninth Av, **T** 1-212 247 5500. *Daily 1100-2300. Subway C, E to 50th St. Map 4, E3, p266* This tiny, BYOB, cash-only world food joint has great goulash and $7 brunch items.

$ Pam Real Thai Food, 404 W 49th St, **T** 1-212 333 7500. *Daily 1130-2300. Subway C, E, 1, 9 to 50th St. Map 4, F4, p266* Pam is a Bangkok transplant and her food has the flavours to prove it. From duck to durian, this is genuine, affordable fare served in an unpretentious neighbourhood setting.

Upper East Side

Restaurants

$$$ La Goulue, 746 Madison Av, **T** 1-212 988 8169. *1200-2330 daily. Subway 6 to 68th St-Hunter College. Map 4, A7, p267* For a swish, lively, upscale meal, come to La Goulue where the tables pour out onto the sidewalk in summer. The sophisticated bistro fare is a treat after all that fancy shopping along Madison Avenue.

$$ Patsy's Pizzeria, 1312 Second Av, **T** 1-212 639 1000. *Daily 1130-2245. Subway 9 to 68th St. Map 4, A9, p267* This New York chain is 70 years old and popular all over town for its coal-oven pizzas done to cheesy, flavourful perfection.

Eating and drinking

$$ Rosa Mexicano's, 1063 First Av, **T** 1-212 753 7407. *Daily 1700-2400. Subway N, R, W to Lexington Ave-59th St. Map 4, C9, p267* A lively, reliable Mexican that has the best guacamole in town, not to mention powerful Margaritas and enough chilli and cilantro in its burritos and enchiladas to knock your socks off.

$$ Serafina's, 1022 Madison Av at 79th St, **T** 1-212 734 2676. *Sun-Thu 1200-2400. Fri and Sat 1200-0200. Subway 6 to 77th St. Map 5, G7, p269* Always packed, this buzzy Italian restaurant has a keen following for its thin-crust pizzas, fresh mozzarella and pastas. Ask to sit on the open-air top floor in the summertime.

$$ Ulrika's, 115 E 60th St, **T** 1-212 355 7069. *Mon-Fri 1130-1500, 1730-2230, Sat 1200-1600, 1730-2300, Sun 1200-1600, 1700-2130. Subway N, R, W to Lexington Av-59th St. Map 4, C7, p267* A little Swedish gem that's a welcome change in the boisterous district near Bloomingdale's. Try the herring plate or indulge in some *kottbullar* (Swedish meatballs).

$ JG Melon's, 1291 Third Av, **T** 1-212 744 0585. *Daily 1130-0230. Subway 6 to 77th St. Map 4, A8, p267* Unlike many of the stuffier restaurants on the Upper East Side, this is a friendly locals' joint serving truly fabulous burgers to a groovy jukebox soundtrack.

★ **Pizza**

Best

·**Lombardi's**, p139
·**Otto**, 146
·**Patsy's Pizzeria**, p155
·**Serafina's**, p156
·**Grimaldi's**, p162

Cafés

Don't miss **Café Sabarsky** at the Neue Galerie (see p87) for Viennese coffee, pastries and hot chocolate or even goulash, spargel and sauerkraut. Alternatively, try **Sarabeth's**, at the Whitney Museum (see p88). It's an ideal brunch spot after strolling along Museum Mile.

Serendipity 3, 225 E 60th St, **T** 1-212 838 3531. *Sun-Thu 1130-2400, Fri 1130-0100, Sat 1130-0200. Subway N, R, W to Lexington Av-59th St. Map 4, C9, p267* If shopping is too exhausting, put your feet up over a large, signature Frozen Hot Chocolate. Serendipity has a movie named after it but is even more famous for its delectable sweet treats and sandwiches.

Central Park and the Upper West Side

Restaurants

\$\$\$\$ Jean Georges, 1 Central Park W, Trump International Hotel, **T** 1-212 299 3900. *Mon-Fri 1200-1430, 1730-2300, Sat 1730-2300, Sun 1130-1430, 1730-2300. Subway A, C, D, 1, 9 to 59th St-Columbus Circle. Map 4, C4, p266* To really impress someone, bring them to

Eating and drinking

one of New York's most famous restaurants on Columbus Circle. Asian-inspired food in a minimalist beige restaurant. It's truly impressive – as it should be at these prices.

$$ Isabella's, 359 Columbus Av at 77th St, **T** 1-212 724 2100. *Mon-Thu 1130-2400, Fri and Sat 1130-0100, Sun 1000-2300. Subway 1, 9 to 79th St. Map 5, H3, p268* This is the most popular brunch spot on the Upper West, Side so come early or late for a sidewalk table to watch chic Uptown folk pass by.

$$ Josie's, 300 Amsterdam at 74th S), **T** 1-212 769 1212. *Mon-Wed 1200-2300, Thu and Fri 1200-2400, Sat 1130-2400, Sun 1100-2200. Subway B, C, 1, 2, 3, 9 to 72nd St. Map 5, H2, p268* Originally a vegetarian restaurant, Josie's serves scrumptious organic food of all sorts now, including meat dishes. It is always packed and friendly.

$ Boat Basin Café, W 79th St at the Hudson River. *Mid Apr-Oct Mon-Sat 1100-2330, Sun 1200-2230. Subway 1 to 79th St. Map 5, G1, p268* A picnic-like atmosphere pervades this riverside café. Lucky locals come for its relaxed vibe, beer, burgers, boats and romantic views.

$ Gennaro, 665 Amsterdam Av at 92nd St, **T** 1-212 665 5348. *Sun-Thu 1700-2230, Fri anc Sat 1700-2300. Subway 1, 2, 3, 9 to 96th St. Map 5, D2, p268* Excellent Mediterrean Italian food, including antipasto, bruschetta, Portobello mushrooms, pastas and tiramisu, is served at this cash-only neighbourhood restaurant.

$ H&H Bagel's, 2239 Broadway, **T** 1-212 595 8003. *Daily 24 hrs. Subway 1, 9 to 79th St. Map 5, G2, p268* When New Yorkers want a bagel, this is typically the first place that comes to mind. Fill up on cream cheese and lox before heading off to Central Park.

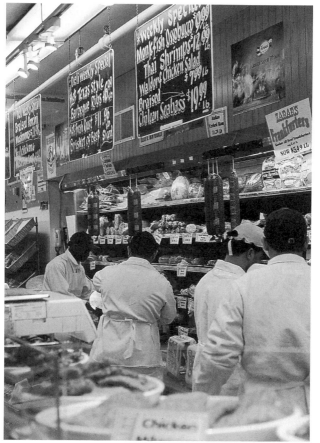

Deli delights
Zabar's is heaven for Uptown foodies.

$ Saigon Grill, 620 Amsterdam Av at 90th St, **T** 1-212 875 9072. *Daily 1100-2400. Subway 1, 9 to 86th St. Map 5, D2, p268* Locals who line up outside reckon this is the best Vietnamese in the city. Dumplings, noodles, seafood and coconut-tree decor.

Cafés

Alice's Tea Cup, 102 W 73rd St, **T** 1-212 799 3006. *Mon 1200-1700, Tue-Fri 1130-2000, Sat 1030-2200, Sun 1100-2000. Subway B, C 1, 2, 3, 9 to 72nd St Map 5, H3, p268* Over 100 tea selections, tasty brunch, sandwiches and desserts make this a must-visit. Go to the back room for calmer surroundings.

Café Lalo, 201 W 83rd St, **T** 1-212 496 6031. *Mon-Thu 0800-0200, Fri 0800-0400, Sat 0900-0400, Sun 0900-0200. Subway B, C to 81st St. Map 5, F2, p268* For coffee, sweets, sandwiches and a delightful cosy atmosphere, come to this perfect spot to take a break and people-watch.

Hungarian Pastry Shop, 1030 Amsterdam Av between 110th St and 111th St, **T** 1-212 866 4230. *Mon-Sat 0730-2330, Sun 0830-2230. Subway 1, 9 to 110th St. Map 6, H2, p270* If you've made it up this far, you'll probably need a break from sightseeing. One block south of the Cathedral of St John the Divine, this shop has been serving the best hazelnut and chocolate cake since 1961.

Harlem

Restaurants

$$ Sugar Hill Bistro, 458 W 145th St between Amsterdam Av and Convent Av, **T** 1-212 491 5505. *Mon-Fri 1700-2330, Sat 1100-2330, Sun 1100-2200. Subway A, C, B, D, 1, 9 to 145th St.*

Map 6, A3, p270 There's gospel brunch at the weekend and southern fried chicken every day at this jazzy Harlem spot.

$ Home Sweet Harlem Café, 270 W 135th St between Adam Clayton Powell Jr Blvd and Frederick Douglass Blvd, **T** 1-212 926 9619. *Mon-Fri 0730-1930, Sat 0900-1900, Sun 1000-1600. Subway B, C, 2, 3 to 135th St. Map 6, C4, p270* A tattered, comfortable café on a leafy street in Harlem's historic district. Soups of the day are made with care, breakfast is served all day (including delicious waffles), and there are also salads, sandwiches and cheese platters.

Brooklyn

Restaurants

$$$$ River Café, 1 Water St, **T** 1-718 522 5200. *Mon-Sat 1200-1500, 1730-2300, Sun 1130-1500, 1730-2300. Subway A, C to High St. Map 2, F9, p263* The most famous restaurant in Brooklyn is one of the most romantic in the city, with stellar views of Manhattan that help justify the expensive price. Fairy lights, flowers and all sorts of seafood are on offer from this barge under the Brooklyn Bridge.

$$ Patois, 255 Smith St, **T** 1-718 855 1535. *Tue-Thu 1730-2230, Fri and Sat 1800-2330, Sun 1100-1500, 1700-2200. Subway F, G to Carroll St. Map 1, H4, p261* The cosy, casual, exposed brick atmosphere always bring in local crowds to this well-respected restaurant. Aim for the outdoor garden if it's warm and don't miss the escargots and oysters.

$-$$ Pacifico, 269 Pacific St, **T** 1-718 935 9090. *Mon-Thu 1730-1100, Fri-Sat 1130-2330, Sun 1130-2300, Subway F, G to Bergen St. Map 1, H4, p261* Just off Smith Street is this heavenly Mexican hangout, with candles and a wooden patio. The guacamole, enchiladas, quesadillas and salsa won't disappoint.

$ Grimaldi's, 19 Old Fulton St, **T** 1-718 858 4300. *Mon-Fri 1130-2300, Sat 1200-2400, Sun 1200-2300. Subway A, C to High St-Brooklyn Bridge. Map 2, F9, p263* The thin-crust pizza, red-checkered tablecloths and Frank Sinatra tunes make for a fun, relaxed atmosphere at this consistently top-ranked pizza spot under the Brooklyn Bridge.

$ Carmaya, 139 North 6th St, **T** 1-718 302 4441. *Tue-Fri 1700-2400, Sat and Sun 1200-2400. Subway L to Bedford Av. Map 1, G5, p261* This surfboard-inspired place has a DJ, sand in its bar and, in the warmer months, a lovely outdoor space. The food is staple pasta, fish, clam chowder and a fairly decent brunch.

$ L-Café, 189 Bedford Av, **T** 1-718 302 2430, *Mon-Fri 0900-2400, Sat and Sun 1000-2400. Subway L to Bedford Av. Map 1, G5, p261* Fashion conscious hipsters fill this laidback, reasonably priced restaurant with an enormous garden. It serves a good brunch, with pancakes and omelettes, and American fare at night.

$ **Sea**, 114 North 6th St, **T** 1-718 384 8850. *Mon-Thu 1130-0100. Fri and Sat 1130-0230, Sun 1130-2200. Subway L to Bedford Av. Map 1, G5, p261* Williamsburg cool with a clubby Manhattan twist. This fun and funky Thai restaurant comes complete with swings, a shallow pool and a DJ. Excellent basil and chilli-infused food is served at reasonable prices and the Mojitos aren't bad either.

New York's nightlife comes in many forms and lasts from dusk till dawn. Although the bar-lounge-club combination continues to be popular, mixing music and cocktails with a mellow vibe, New York is also currently witnessing a revival in large-scale clubbing. Venues, where hundreds can dance, are opening in abandoned warehouses in Chelsea around 10th and 11th Avenues, with owners hoping to attract an older, more sophisticated clientele whose party spirit isn't fuelled by drugs.

Elsewhere, you'll find flashy designer hotel bars, peanut-tossing, beer-guzzling dive bars and low-key jazz lounges. Head to the Lower East Side and East Village for local DJs and live bands or to the Meatpacking District for everything from biker hangouts to wine bars. Uptown is generally quieter, but it does have some rowdy sports bars and a few chic clubs. Irish pubs, some of better quality than others, can be found nearly everywhere, with a concentration around Midtown.

Most bars and lounges open at 1000 and don't close until 0400, although some may call it a night at around 0200. Dedicated dance clubs open later, many around 2100-2200, but don't really get going until 2300 or so, when queues wrap around the block. Clubs charge anywhere from $5 to $30 for admission; Friday and Saturday are typically the most expensive nights but prices fluctuate depending on the DJ or live act.

Check local listings in *The Village Voice* or *Time Out New York* for up-to-the-minute information. For details of clubs offering live music, see Music p187. For details of gay and lesbian venues, see Gay and lesbian, p221. Finally, don't forget your ID card or passport, as most bars and clubs strictly card everyone regardless of age.

Lower Manhattan

Bars

Jeremy's Ale House, 254 Front St, at Dover St, **T** 1-212 964 3537. *Subway 2, 3, 4, 5, J, M, Z to Fulton St, A, C to Broadway-Nassau St. Map 7, C6, p272* Frat-boys from Wall Street drink huge beers served in styrofoam in this cavernous bar.

Rise, Ritz-Carlton New York, 2 West St, Battery Park, **T** 1-917 790 2626. *Subway 4, 5 to Bowling Green. Map 7, H2, p272* For one of the best views of the Statue of Liberty, have a drink in this romantic, sophisticated indoor/outdoor bar on the 14th floor.

Ulysses, 95 Pearl St, **T** 1-212 482 0400. *Subway J, M, Z to Broad St, 2, 3 to Wall St. Map 7, F4, p272* This large Irish pub attracts an after-work crowd who share buckets of beer on the cobbled pavement of Stone Street.

> ▶ **Party poopers**
>
> A city report in the 1920s noted that "when strangers come to New York, they want to run wild". In response Mayor Jimmy Walker enacted the 'cabaret law', or dance ban, in 1926, which outlawed dancing in the city's bars. Incredibly, this Prohibition-era ruling is still enforced: dancing is not permitted in bars and clubs unless they have a cabaret licence in addition to a liquor licence. Businesses complain that licences are hard to come by and are currently pushing for more liberal rules to be introduced, dependent on serious soundproofing and other restrictions. Meanwhile the city's party people were dealt another blow by Mayor Bloomberg, who introduced an anti-smoking law in early 2003.

Chinatown, Little Italy and Nolita

Bars

Ear Inn, 326 Spring St, **T** 1-212 226 9060. *Subway 1, 9 to Houston St. Map 2, A3, p262* This down-to-earth bar and crowd make beer-drinking very easy. The 'B' on the sign burnt out many years ago and the new name stuck.

Liquor Store Bar, 235 W Broadway at White St, **T** 1-212 226 7121. *Subway 1, 9 to Franklin St. Map 2, B4, p262* This cool, unpretentious locals' bar is respectably low-key. It's an excellent place to enjoy a beer and to people-watch by the large front windows on Broadway.

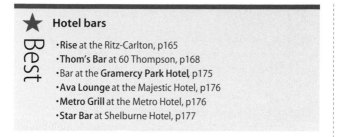

★ **Best**

Hotel bars

- **Rise** at the Ritz-Carlton, p165
- **Thom's Bar** at 60 Thompson, p168
- Bar at the **Gramercy Park Hotel**, p175
- **Ava Lounge** at the Majestic Hotel, p176
- **Metro Grill** at the Metro Hotel, p176
- **Star Bar** at Shelburne Hotel, p177

No Moore, 234 W Broadway, **T** 1-212 925 2595. *Subway 1, 9 to Franklin St. Map 2, B4, p262* This bi-level bar attracts a laidback after-work crowd who enjoy live music.

Onieal's, 174 Grand St, between Mulberry St and Centre St, **T** 1-212 941 9119. *Subway S to Grand St. Map 2, B6, p262* This upscale speakeasy seems lost in space in the midst of Chinatown and Little Italy. Sofas cushion the good-looking crowd of locals who discovered this anomaly long ago.

Red Bench, 107 Sullivan St between Prince and Spring Sts, **T** 1-212 274 9120. *Subway C, E to Spring St. Map 2, A4, p262* A very intimate, cosy, candlelit bar-lounge that locals want to keep secret.

Lounges and clubs

Don Hill's, 550 Greenwich St, at Spring St, **T** 1-212 334 1390. *Subway C, E to Spring St. Map 2, B2, p262* A no-frills bar/music venue serving up Brit-pop, '80s bands and heavy metal to an eclectic crowd.

Bars and clubs

Double Happiness, 173 Mott St, between Broome St and Grand St, **T** 1-212 941 1282. *Subway J, M, Z to Bowery, 6 to Spring St. Map 2, B6, p262* Without some inside information, you'd never find this hidden stone basement bar. It's dark, sexy and hip, with a DJ spinning clubby tunes and lots of corners for you to chill out in.

Knitting Factory, (see Arts and entertainment, p188). A variety of rooms and a couple bars, with great musical talent.

Merc Bar, 151 Mercer St, **T** 1-212 966 2727. *Subway N, R to Prince St. Map 3, H6, p264* This eternally hip bar-lounge draws a lively, pretty group to its couches and fancy cocktails.

Zinc Bar, (see Arts and entertainment, p189). Latin, Brazilian, Cuban jazz and more are on offer at this small, velvety spot tucked away belowstairs. The back room is romantic and roomier. $5 cover.

SoHo and Tribeca

Bars

Bar 89, 89 Mercer St, between Broome St and Spring St, **T** 1-212 274 0989. *Subway 6, C, E to Spring St. Map 2, B5, p262* This large space in SoHo pulls in a good-looking group of twentysomethings. The co-ed bathrooms are famous for their doors, which steam up when they're locked.

Thom's Bar, 60 Thompson St, **T** 1-212 219 2000. *Subway 6, C, E to Spring St. Map 2, B4, p262* Mojitos and Manolo Blahnik's mingle at this unmarked and ultra-hip SoHo hotel lounge-bar. Don't miss the terraced area in summer.

Greenwich Village and Chelsea

Bars

The Half King, 505 W 23rd St, **T** 1-212 462 4300. *Subway C, E to 23rd St. Map 3, C1, p264* This stylish pub has a back garden, useful for the literary folks who hang out here. It's owned by journalist Sebastian Junger, author of *The Perfect Storm*, and hosts regular poetry readings.

Open, 559 W 22nd St, at 11th Av, **T** 1-212 243 1851. *Subway C, E to 23rd St. Map 3, D1, p264* A sleek, industrial-style bar and café serving light food and cocktails, it makes an excellent stop off in Chelsea's gallery district.

The Otheroom, 143 Perry St, **T** 1-212 645 9758. *Subway 1, 9 to 14th St. Map 3, G3, p264* A low-key crowd and vast beer and wine selection mean it's worth wandering over to this chilled-out, candlelit bar tucked away on a quiet street.

Rhone, 63 Gansevoort St, between Greenwich St and Washington St, **T** 1-212 367 8440. *Subway A, C, E to 14th St, L to 8th Av. Map 3, F2, p264* An excellent selection of wine and some French attitude to go with it. Hip urban types mingle here every night of the week.

Shade, 241 Sullivan St, **T** 1212 982 6275. *Subway A, C, E, F, V, B, D to W 4th St. Map 3, G5, p264* Crêpes, wine and a dark atmosphere make this bar a surprising find off Washington Square's rather rowdy thoroughfare.

White Horse Tavern, 567 Hudson St, **T** 1-212 989 3956. *Subway A, C, E to 14th St. Map 3, G3, p264* A loud, charming neighbourhood favourite where Dylan Thomas drank himself to

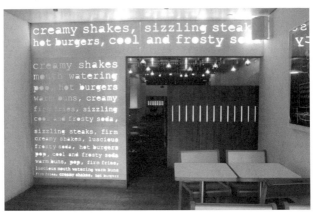

Poptastic
Burgers, shakes and pool tables: Pop Burger mixes it up.

death and where locals now sup beer until the wee hours. Sit outside if it's warm.

WXOU Radio, 558 Hudson St, **T** 1-212 206 0381. *Subway 1, 9 to Christopher St. Map 3, G3, p264* A low-key, non-descript neighbourhood bar with no pretensions. Come here when you want to get away from the scene.

Lounges and clubs

APT, 419 W 13th St, **T** 1-212 414 4245. *Subway A, C, E to 14th St, L to 8th Av. Map 3, E2, p264* Although it's not as exclusive now as during its heyday, this lounge-club still has attitude. The unmarked entry leads pretty twentysomethings in Jimmy Choo's to comfortable couches upstairs and DJs downstairs.

Avalon, 47 W 20th St, **T** 1-212 807 7780. *Subway F, V to 23rd St. Map 3, D5, p264* A former Episcopalian church is now a warren of dimly-lit bars and lounges leading to the chapel dance floor where DJs play electronica. The original Avalon was labelled a 'drug supermarket' and closed down after years of trouble, including a shooting, but the revamped club seems to have eschewed its dodgy past for a more innocent future with an anything-goes crowd.

Bungalow 8, 515 W 27th St, between 10th Av and 11th Av, **T** 1-212 629 3333. *Subway C, E to 23rd St. Map 3, B2, p264* Swanky lounge-bar-club serving fancy drinks to swishy crowds. It's worth the money for a more civilized clubby night out.

Cielo, 18 Little W 12th St, **T** 1-212 941 1540. *Subway A, C, E to 14th St, L to 8th Av. Map 3, F2, p264* Well-heeled dancers shake the night away in a former beef locker that's now a Euro-styled industrial club. The sunken dance floor and intimate feel are accompanied by pricey cocktails and champagne.

Coral Room, 512 W 29th St, between 10th Av and 11th Av, **T** 1-212 244 1965. *Subway 1, 9 to 28th St. Map 3, B2, p264* A mermaid swims in the club's pool and you can drink out of a fish bowl. A truly aquatic experience with faux coral and trendy New Yorkers.

Glass, 287 10th Av, between 26th St and 27th St, **T** 1-212 904 1580. *Subway 1, 9 to 28th St.. Map 3, C2, p264* Glass is a cool bar that seems like a gallery space, with jazz, Latin and lounge music in a sexy setting. Beware of the unisex loos: outsiders can watch while you preen in front of the mirror.

Kavehaz, 37 W 26th St, **T** 1-212 343 0612. *Subway 1, 9 to 28th St. Map 3, C5, p264* This coffeehouse-bar-lounge serves up jazz, chocolate fondue, food and drinks in an artistic, comfortable, funky Chelsea atmosphere.

Pop Burger, 60 Ninth Av, **T** 1-212 414 8686. *Subway A, C, E to 14th St, L to 8th Av. Map 3, E2, p264* A new futuristic lounge-diner-restaurant, Pop Burger suits hipsters who want a burger and milk shake followed by a game of pool.

Lower East Side and East Village

Bars

Ace Bar, 531 Fifth St, **T** 1-212 979 8476. *Subway L to 1st Av, 6 to Astor Pl. Map 3, G11, p265* Pool tables and dart boards make this a welcoming, anything-goes drinking dive in the East Village. The booths in the back are more relaxed.

Angel's Share, 8 Stuyvesant St, 2nd Flr, **T** 1-212 777 5415. *Subway 6 to Astor Pl. Map 3, F8, p265* Enter via an unassuming Japanese restaurant, through a door with a paper sign and discover the best kept secret in Manhattan. A friendly crowd sip Asian-themed cocktails under a faux fresco.

Bar Veloce, 175 Second Av, **T** 1-212 260 3200. *Subway L to 3rd Av. Map 3, F8, p265* This tiny, slick, narrow wine bar is the most sophisticated place to drink in the East Village. Come here to sample some wine, to romance a date or to eat one of the delicious paninis.

Fat Black Pussycat, 130 W 3rd St, between MacDougal and Sixth Av, **T** 1-212 533 4790. *Subway A, C, E, F, S, V to W 4th St. Map 3, G5, p264* A pub at the front and a lounge at the back make this carefree bar a local favourite for its diversity and happy-go lucky crowd of drinkers.

Il Posto Accanto, 190 E 2nd St, **T** 1-212 228 3562. *Subway F, V to Lower East Side-2nd Av. Map 3, H10, p265* This welcoming little wine bar will charm you with its selection of bottles and its friendly owner.

Marion's Continental Restaurant & Lounge, 354 Bowery, **T** 1-212 475 7621. *Subway 6 to Bleecker St. Map 3, H8, p265* Crazy tiki nights and fabulous Martinis make this old-world kitsch hangout better for its bar than its food.

McSorley's Old Ale House, 15 East 7th St, **T** 1-212 473 9148. *Subway N, R, W to 8th St, 6 to Astor Pl. Map 3, G8, p265* Spit and sawdust, down and dirty, check your pretensions at the door and don't dare to order a Martini. Opened in 1854, this is the oldest continually operational bar in New York and the only one that can claim 'Abraham Lincoln drank here'. Light or dark ales are served in a friendly but no-nonsense atmosphere.

Nuyorican Poets Café, 236 E 3rd St, **T** 1-212 780 9386. *Subway F, V to Lower East Side-2nd Av. Map 3, H10, p265* Talented wordsmiths slam poetry in this hippy-ish setting. Beginners shouldn't shy away from the microphone.

Perbacco, 234 E 4th St between Av A and B, **T** 1-212 253 2038. *Subway F, V to Lower East Side-2nd Av. Map 3, G10, p265* Lovely Italian wines are topped off with tapas, olives, mozzarella, focaccia and tomatoes in this tiny, delightful East Village gem.

Ruby Lounge, 186 E 2nd St, **T** 1-212 387-9400. *Subway F, V to Lower East Side-2nd Av. Map 3, H10, p265* The antiques and velvet drapes at this stylish newcomer create a sexy yet casual atmosphere. Mediterranean tapas complement the Caipirinhas.

Temple Bar, 332 Lafayette St, **T** 1-212 925 4242. *Subway 6 to Bleecker St. Map 3, H7, p265* New Yorkers take their cocktails seriously and this bar ranks as one of the best places for a 'killer' Martini. Dark, candlelit and stylish.

Lounges and clubs

Happy Ending, 302 Broome St, **T** 1-212 334 9676. *Subway F to Delancey St, J, M, Z to Delancey-Essex St. Map 2, B7, p263* This former brothel and massage parlour is a now a seductive bar-cum-lounge arranged over two floors, with wild cocktails and red lighting.

Pianos, 158 Ludlow St, between Stanton St and Rivington St, **T** 1-212 505 3733. *Subway F to Delancey St, J, M, Z to Delancey-Essex St. Map 2, A8, p263* There's great music at this bar-club-lounge: DJ's spin tunes upstairs and trendy Downtowners listen to music downstairs. One of the better bars on the Lower East Side.

Plant Bar, 217 E 3rd St, between Av B and Av C, **T** 1-212 375 9066. *Subway F at 2nd Av. Map 3, H10, p265* The cabaret laws prevented the return of the DJs, so this small, hip, den-like lounge reopened with a 6,000-album MP3 jukebox instead. Choose your own chilled-out tune for free.

Flatiron District and around

Bars

Bar at the Gramercy Park Hotel, 2 Lexington Av, **T** 1-212 475 4320. *Subway 6 to 23rd St. Map 3, D7, p265* This revamped classic neighbourhood bar is old school in the front and velvety, shabby-chic seductive in the candlelit back lounge area.

Beauty Bar, 1 E 14th St, **T** 1-212 539 1389. *Subway L to 3rd Av. Map 3, E8, p265* Cool, kitschy and usually packed, this bar, made out of a 1960s beauty parlour, has vintage hairdryers to sit under and you can get a manicure while you're having a drink.

Flatiron Lounge, 37 W 19th St, **T** 1-212 727 7741. *Subway 1, 9 to 18th St. Map 3, D5, p264* There are potent cocktails and a sophisticated vibe at this sexy art deco bar.

Jazz Standard, 116 E 27th St, **T** 1-212 576 2232. *Subway 6 to 28th St. Map 3, B7, p265* A great place to hear jazz. Wynton and Branford Marsalis play downstairs at the Blue Smoke barbecue restaurant but so do many lesser known talented musicians. Call ahead to reserve a table.

Molly's, 287 3rd Av, **T** 1-212 889 3361. *Subway 6 to 23rd St. Map 3, C7, p265* A neighbourhood pub with sawdust on the floor, friendly bartenders and jealous locals who prefer to keep Molly's all to themselves.

Old Town Bar, 45 E 18th St, **T** 1-212 529 6732. *Subway 4, 5, 6, L, N, R, Q, W to 14th St-Union Sq. Map 3, D6, p264* The Old Town Bar has literary history, wooden booths and enough flavour for a whole night's drinking, if the after-work drinkers don't crowd you out.

Park Bar, 15 E 15th St, **T** 1-212 367 9085. *Subway 4, 5, 6, L, N, R, Q, W to 14th St-Union Sq. Map 3, E7, p265* Candles and dark wood create a romantic vibe at this small, classy bar. A sophisticated Union Square stopping point.

Midtown

Bars

Ava Lounge, Majestic Hotel, 210 W 55th St, **T** 1-212 956 7020. *Subway N, Q, R, W to 57th St. Map 4, D5, p266* Inspired by Ava Gardner, this hotel bar is 1950s penthouse perfection and has a breezy outdoor area with views down to Times Square. Typically for a hotel bar, a gin and tonic will set you back at least $9.

Blue Fin, W Times Sq Hotel, 1567 Broadway, **T** 1-212 918 1400. *Subway N, R, W to 49th St, 1, 9 to 50th St. Map 4, E5, p266* One of the greatest people-watching spots in Times Square. Step off the sidewalk and sip fancy cocktails behind the glass windows with New Yorkers and tourists.

The Campbell Apartment, Grand Central Terminal, entrance at 15 Vanderbilt Av, **T** 1-212 953 0409. *Subway 4, 5, 6, 7, S to 42nd St-Grand Central. Map 4, G7, p267* Tucked away in Grand Central, men smoke cigars and professionals mingle in the wood-panelled former office of businessman John Campbell. Due to a peculiar legal loophole, the Campbell Apartment is one of the few bars where it's legal to smoke. Go to relish the 1940s vibe.

Metro Grill, Metro Hotel, 45 W 35th St, **T** 1-212 279 3535. *Subway B, D, F, N, R, Q, W to 34th St-Herald Sq. Map 3, A6, p264* Neck-cranking views of the Empire State Building makes this no-frills rooftop bar a must in the warmer months.

Royalton Lounge, Royalton Hotel, 44 W 44th St, **T** 1-212 869 4400. *Subway B, D, F, V to 42nd St-Bryant Pk. Map 4, G6, p266* This chi chi, upscale hotel bar draws in well-dressed city folk who can afford its cocktails and who know exactly where to go to feel sophisticated.

Star Bar, Shelburne Murray Hill Hotel, 303 Lexington Av at 37th St, **T** 1-212 689 5200. *Subway 4, 5, 6, 7, S to 42nd St-Grand Central Terminal. Map 4, H8, p267* The Star Bar offers perhaps the most stunning Midtown views of any hotel bar. Come here for chummy drinks in the warmer months as breathtaking skyscrapers twinkle above.

Top of the Tower, Beekman Hotel, 49th St and 1st Av, **T** 1-212 980 4796. *Subway 6, E, V to 51st St. Map 4, F9, p267* The elegant indoor/outdoor piano bar atop the Beekman Hotel has a great view of the Midtown skyline and an old-fashioned but ageless charm.

Villard, Palace Hotel, 24 E 51st St, **T** 1-212 303 7757. *Subway 6, E, V to 51st St-Lexington Av. Map 4, E7, p267* Plush, dark and opulent, this is a top place for a discreet secret agent rendezvous. Cuddle up among the swanky, expensive red velvet.

Upper East Side

Bars

The Auction House, 300 E 89th St, between 1st Av and 2nd Av, **T** 1-212 427 4458. *Subway 4, 5, 6 to 86th St. Map 5, E9, p269* Velvety drapes and antique furniture create a romantic, thrift-store chic at this relaxed neighbourhood bar.

Bar Harbour, 1470 First Av, between 76th St and 77th St, **T** 1-212 288 2188. *Subway 6 to 77th St. Map 5, H9, p269* Appropriately preppy Upper East Siders mingle in this bi-level nautical bar.

Bemelmans Bar, Carlyle Hotel, 35 E 76th St, **T** 1-212 744 1600. *Subway 6 to 77th St. Map 5, H7, p269* Playful Bemelman-esque murals fill the walls, piano music fills the air and swishy cocktails fill the glasses at this eye-popping Uptown bar.

Fondue, 303 E 80th St, between 1st Av and 2nd Av, **T** 1-212 772 2390. *Subway 6 to 79th St. Map 5, G9, p269* Tiny, trendy bar, with Moroccan-style couches, serving sake, beer and fondue (chocolate, caramel or cheese) till the small hours. Classic films and recent hits are screened here on Sunday nights.

Upper West Side

Bars

All State Café, 250 W 72nd St, between Broadway and West End Av, **T** 1-212 874 1883. *Subway 1, 2, 3, 9 to 72nd St. Map 4, A2, p266* This grungy basement bar on the Upper West Side serves cheap beers and tasty burgers, which suits the fun, anything-goes clientele just fine.

Shalel Lounge, 65 W 70th St, **T** 1-212 873 2300. *Subway B, C, 1, 2, 3, 9 to 72nd St. Map 4, A4, p266* This Downtown-meets-Uptown bar-lounge has Moroccan-themed decor and a seductive, romantic atmosphere. Paper-bag lanterns hang in a series of cave-like rooms and there's a secret waterfall to discover.

Lounges and clubs

Evelyn Lounge, 380 Columbus Av at 78th St, **T** 1-212 724 5145. *Subway 1, 9 to 79th St. Map 5, G2, p268* Shabby-chic velvety sofas pull in late-night pick-up crowds. Evelyn is one of the livelier Upper West Side lounge-clubs, spread over two floors with dancing downstairs.

MOD, 505 Columbus Av, **T** 1-212 989 3600. *Subway 1,9, B, C to 86th St. Map 5, F3, p268* Austin Powers meets the Upper West Side in this funky, psychedelic lounge-club.

Harlem

Lounges and clubs

Lenox Lounge, 288 Malcolm X Blvd between 124th St and 125th St, **T** 1-212 427 0253. *Subway 2, 3 to 125th St. Map 6, E6, p270* This well-known Harlem bar and lounge hosts some of the best jazz in the city for a mixed crowd of students and locals, who cram together in the zebra-inspired back room.

Brooklyn

Lounges and clubs

Halcyon, 227 Smith St, **T** 1-718 260 9299. *Subway F, G to Bergen St. Map 1, H4, p261* This hipster café incorporates a DJ area and a space-age, bachelor-pad furniture store. Locals come to munch on homemade cookies, buy records and hear music. It's perhaps cooler than anywhere in Manhattan.

Luxx, 256 Grand St between Driggs Av and Roebling St, Williamsburg, **T** 1-718 599 1000. *Subway L to Bedford Av. Map 1, G5, p261* Slightly away from the main Williamsburg strip is this edgy electro-clash bar-club where all sorts of punks, gay and lesbian, and colourful types come to hear cutting-edge music before it goes mainstream.

Although Broadway is likely to be the first thing that visitors associate with New York entertainment, it's only a slice of what the city has to offer. The sheer range of performances, shows, screenings, gigs and other arts events may leave you feeling euphoric or frustrated. Choose between opulent Broadway musicals and thought-provoking Off-Broadway plays; blockbusters and arthouse films; improv comedy or classical ballet; opera, salsa or hip-hop. No other city in the world hosts quite so much entertainment and you're going to need stamina to enjoy it to the full.

Cinema

Filmmakers just can't seem to get enough of New York and, with more than 250 movies shot here each year, it's no surprise that you'll recognize many sights from the big screen. When it comes to watching films, whether you're a fan of the big flashy Hollywood spectacles or prefer obscure foreign-language films with subtitles, New York has a moviehouse to suit, including a commendable number of independent and arthouse cinemas. Two significant film festivals take place in the city each year, the **New York Film Festival** in October and the **Tribeca Film Festival** in May. The latter was first organized by Robert De Niro and others to help boost Lower Manhattan after September 11th and has, so far, been a great success. There's also free, open-air cinema at the **HBO Bryant Park Summer Film Festival** in June and many other important film debuts, premieres and events throughout the year. Tickets for new releases should be bought in advance by calling **T** 1-212 777 FILM or by booking online at www.moviefone.com.

Angelika Film Center, 18 W Houston St, **T** 1-212 777 FILM. *Subway F, V to Grand St, N, R to Prince St, 6 to Bleecker St. Map 3, H7, p265* The local bastion of independent film screenings. Call ahead to buy your ticket in advance as it sells out many nights.

Film Forum, 209 W Houston between 6th Av and Varick St, **T** 1-212 727 8110. *Subway 1, 9 to Houston St. Map 3, H5, p264* This small venue hosts documentaries, silent comedies and well-known classics from some of the greatest American and international directors.

Landmark Sunshine Cinema, 143 E Houston St between 1st Av and 2nd Av, **T** 1-212 777 FILM. *Subway V to Lower East Side-2nd Av. Map 3, H9, p265* The recently opened Landmark features excellent independent and foreign films and has the comfiest seats in town.

Paris, 4 W 58th St at 5th Av, **T** 1-212 688 3800. *Subway F to 57th St, N, R, W to 5th Ave-59th St. Map 4, D6, p266* As seductive as its name suggests, the curvy Paris is the perfect place to see a film after rambling around Central Park or the Fifth Avenue shops.

Walter Reade Theater, 70 Lincoln Center Plaza at 65th St (above Alice Tully Hall), **T** 1-212 875 5600. *Subway 1, 2 to 66th St-Lincoln Center. Map 4, B3, p266* Housed in the atmospheric Lincoln Center, this is acoustically the best cinema in New York. Programming focuses on foreign films.

Comedy and cabaret

New York comedy has had a huge revival in recent years, with fringe performers now making a good showing at big venues and unconventional shows attracting local crowds to the smaller clubs. Check out the experimental comedians, musicians and performance artists at **Moonwork** and the unique brand of entertaining improvization offered by the **Upright Citizens' Brigade**. Cabaret is available in many forms from cosy, candlelit performances to elegant shows in expensive hotel bars. Note that most comedy shows charge a small admission and a two-drink minimum.

Café Carlyle, Carlyle Hotel, 35 E 76th St, **T** 1-212 570 7189. *Subway 6 to 77th St. Map 5, H7, p269* This chic 90-person cabaret venue is a perfect place to hear Woody Allen's Monday night jazz band or Bobby Short's Saturday night show. Phone a week ahead for your reservation.

Caroline's on Broadway, 1626 Broadway at 50th St, **T** 1-212 757 4100. *Subway N, R, W to 49th St. Map 4, E5, p266* This big and ritzy venue in Times Square features some well-known talent who often get filmed for televized comedy shows.

Comedy Cellar, 117 MacDougal St between Bleecker St and W 3rd St, **T** 1-212 254 3480. *Sun-Thu 2100, 2300; Fri 2100, 2245, 1230. $10-15 plus two-drink minimum. Subway A, C, E, F, V to W 4th St. Map 3, H5, p264* Many famous comics have made guest appearances in this intimate environment, including Jerry Seinfeld who filmed *Comedian* here.

Gotham Comedy Club, 34 W 22nd St, between 5th Av and 6th Av, **T** 1-212 367 9000. *$10-15 plus two-drink minimum. Subway, F, V, N, R, W to 23rd St. Map 3, D5, p264* It's usually easier to get a seat here than at many comedy clubs. Often has a talented line-up.

Moonwork, Greenwich Village Center, 219 Sullivan St, **T** 1-212 254 3074, www.moonwork.com   *Sat eve every 2 wks except in summer.   Subway A, C, E to W4 St.   Map 3, H5, p264*   Set in a Greenwich Village school, this unscripted show features original cabaret acts in a relaxed environment. The $15 cover charge includes all the beer you can drink.

The Supper Club, 240 W 47th St, **T** 1212 921 1940.   *Subway N, R, W, 1, 2, 3, 9, 7 to 42nd St-Times Sq.   Map 4, F4, p266*   This ornate, romantic cabaret space is a wonderful place to dine and dance to the tunes of respectable 12-piece bands.

Upright Citizens' Brigade, 307 W 26th St, **T** 1-212 366 9176, www.ucbtheatre.com   *Subway C, E at 23rd St.   Map 3, C3, p264*   One of the best places to see comedy in New York, with improv, sketches and solo acts every night at cheap prices ($5-7). 'Asssscat 3000' at 2130 on Sunday is free, but arrive early to get tickets.

Dance

Since Isadora Duncan introduced modern dance to New York in the early 1900s, New York has attracted a high calibre of choreographers and dancers, including the hugely influential Martha Graham, widely considered the mother of modern dance. The city now has five major dance companies, including the **American Ballet Theater** and the **New York City Ballet**, several modern troupes and handfuls of solo stars.

City Center Theater, 55th St between 6th Av and 7th Av, **T** 1-212 581 1212.   *Subway F, N, Q, R, W to 57th St.   Map 4, D5, p266*   The Dance Theater of Harlem and the Alvin Ailey are just two of the many famous troupes that perform in this fabulous Moorish-inspired setting.

▶ Learning Latin

The Latin culture of New York bursts in to life on the dancefloor. Here are a few Latin music events to help you get your groove on...

The Copacabana, 560 West 34th St at 11th Av, **T** 1-212 239 2672, www.salsanewyork.com *Tue, Fri and Sat 1800-0300. $10-15.* Come here to salsa the night away at one of the city's longest-serving Latin clubs.

Latin Sunday Party with Jimmy Anton, Dance Manhattan Studio, 39 West 19th St between 5th Av and 6th Av, 5th Floor, **T** 1-212 807 0802, www.dance-manhattan.com *1st and 3rd Sun of the month 1700-2100.* This is the longest-running mambo event in New York. Participants are advized to "dress to sweat".

Nell's Mambo Night, 246 W 14 St between 7th Av and 8th Av, **T** 1-212-675-1567, www.cubansoul.com *Wed 2100-2300.* Classic salsa downstairs and old-school Cuban music upstairs at this lively joint. Check for flyers offering reduced admission.

Joyce Theater, 175 Eighth Av at 19th St, **T** 1-212 242 0800. *Subway A, C, E to 23rd St. Map 3, D3, p264* Downtown's dance house hosts fabulous performances by touring modern dance companies in a welcoming and intimate setting.

Metropolitan Opera House, 65th at Columbus Av, **T** 1-212 362 6000. *Subway 1-9 to 66th St-Lincoln Center. Map 4, B3, p266* The American Ballet Theater puts on stunning traditional performances from May to July. International touring companies also perform here.

New York State Theater, 65th St at Columbus Av, **T** 1-212 870 5570. *Subway 1-9 to 66th St-Lincoln Center. Map 4, B3, p266* The New York City Ballet performs in winter and spring at this beautiful bejewelled venue at the Lincoln Center. It provides the setting for spectacular, romantic performances such as *Romeo and Juliet* or *Swan Lake*.

Music

This city has a much broader musical soundtrack than the endless round of hip-hop and rap hits pumping out of the radio stations might suggest. New York's music is as multi-faceted as its inhabitants. Jazz and blues are heard in dedicated venues from Harlem down to Greenwich Village, the **New York Philharmonic** performs at Carnegie Hall, while Brazilian breakbeats, Afro-pop and hip-hop fill the clubs. Rather than attending a live gig many New Yorkers choose to hangout in lounges to hear some of the latest electronica, hip-hop and funk-inspired tunes in cheaper, more inviting surroundings. Listings in the weekly magazines will direct you to countless venues on any night of the week. For occasional venues, see also Bars and clubs, p163. Don't miss Central Park's free summer concerts for rock, classical, opera, funk and more.

Rock, pop, hip-hop and techno

Apollo Theater, 5253 W 125th St at Frederick Douglass Blvd, **T** 1-212 531 5337. *Subway A, B, C, D to 125th St. Map 6, E4, p270* Opened in Harlem in 1914, the Apollo has hosted more music stars than anywhere else in New York over the years. From the 1930s to the 1970s, this was the pinnacle of black entertainment and was once said to have the most sophisticated and challenging audiences in the US. Duke Ellington, Billie Holiday and the Jackson Five all made their start here, and the weekly Wednesday amateur nights allowed Sarah Vaughan, Ella Fitzgerald and James Brown to get their break, too. A renovation in 2002 has brought the Apollo back to its feet, and the famous amateur nights still fill up the house, though the performances tend to lean more towards hip-hop and comedy shows these days.

Arlene Grocery, 95 Stanton St, **T** 1-212 473 9831. *Subway F to Second Ave. Map 3, H9, p265* Indie bands and folksy rockers debut at this hip little Lower East Side spot. Monday nights feature metal and punk karaoke.

Bowery Ballroom, 6 Delancey St, **T** 1-212 533 2111. *Subway 6 to Spring St. Map 2, A7, p263* Big rock and pop acts want to play here because of its excellent ambience and great bar.

Irving Plaza, 17 Irving Plaza at 15th St, **T** 1-212 777 6800. *Subway L, N, R, 4, 5, 6 to 14 St-Union Sq. Map 3, E7, p265* It's standing-room only for the respected rock, electronica and techno acts who play in this large venue.

The Knitting Factory, 74 Leonard St, **T** 1-212 219 3055. *Subway 1, 2 to Franklin St. Map 2, C4, p262* Big name rockers, jazz groups and folk acts fill this avant-garde multi-roomed house of music.

Madison Square Garden (see Sports, p218)

Radio City Music Hall (see Sights, p78)

SOB's, 204 Varick St, **T** 1-212 243 4940. *Subway 1, 9 to Houston St. Map 3, H4, p264* After midnight Brazilian funk, R&B, Afro-pop and all sorts of hip-hop acts help the punters dance the night away in this bamboo hut-inspired club.

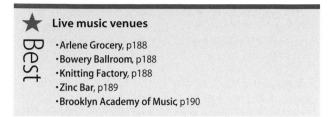

★ **Live music venues**

Best

- Arlene Grocery, p188
- Bowery Ballroom, p188
- Knitting Factory, p188
- Zinc Bar, p189
- Brooklyn Academy of Music, p190

Jazz

Birdland, 315 W 44th St, **T** 1-212 581 3080. *Subway A, C, E to 42nd St-Port Authority.* *Map 4, G4, p266* This established jazz club hosts nightly shows at 2100 and 2300. The steep cover, from $20 plus a $10 drink minimum, is worth it for the select talent on show.

Blue Note, 131 W 3rd St, **T** 1-212 475 8592. *Subway A, C, E, F to W 4th St.* *Map 3, G5, p264* The long-running Village jazz stalwart is touristy and expensive but the line-up rarely disappoints.

Red Blazer, 32 W 37th St, **T** 1-212 947 6428. *Subway B, D, F, N, R to 34th St-Herald Sq.* *Map 4, H6, p266* Old-time swing bands make an evening at Red Blazer an offbeat but memorable experience.

Village Vanguard, 178 Seventh Ave, **T** 1-212 255 4037. *Subway 1, 2 to Christopher St-Sheridan Sq.* *Map 3, F4, p264* All the greats play in this basement in the West Village. It's regarded by many as the best jazz venue in the city.

Zinc Bar, 90 W Houston, **T** 1-212 477 8337. *Subway A, C, B, D to W 4th St.* *Map 3, H6, p264* This cool and cosy candlelit jazz joint also hosts Brazilian, Latin, African and other world music.

Arts and entertainment

▶ **Broadway on the cheap**

'Rush' tickets for Broadway and Off-Broadway shows are available from the venue for as little as $10 on the day of the performance. Call each venue in advance to check its policy: some sell rush tickets in the morning, while others wait until one hour before show time.

Otherwise, head for the **TKTS** booth in Times Square at 47th Street and Broadway (Mon-Sat 1500-2000; Wed and Sat 1000-1400; Sun 1100-1900), where same-day tickets are sold for a variety of performances. Be prepared for a long wait, as the queue can be dreadful.

Classical and opera

Classical music and opera tend to focus around the Lincoln Center and Carnegie Hall but it's worth looking out for classical and choral performances at the city's churches, especially around Christmas.

Brooklyn Academy of Music, 30 Lafayette Av, Brooklyn, **T** 1-718 636 4100. *Subway M, N, Q, R, W, 1, 2, 4 to Atlantic Av. Map 1, H4, p261* The oldest concert hall in the country has at been the cultural heart of Brooklyn life since 1861. BAM has its own orchestra and hosts well-respected opera performances. It also stages a variety of experimental dance, music and theatre groups.

Carnegie Hall, 154 W 57th St, **T** 1-212 247 7800, www.carnegiehall.org. *Subway A, C, B, D, 1, 9 to 59th St-Columbus Circle, N, R, Q, W to 57th St. Map 4, D5, p266* One of the world's premier concert venues, Carnegie Hall was built in 1891 and still promises superb acoustics and a beautiful setting. Tchaikovsky conducted on opening night and, since then, the world's most talented performers have taken to the stage here.

Lincoln Center, 66th St-Lincoln Center, **T** 1-212 875 5456.
www.linconlcenter.org *Subway 1, 2 to 66th St-Lincoln Center.*
Map 5, C3, p268 See also p95 Classicists heaven: elegant Alice Tully
Hall showcases chamber music, while the lavish Metropolitan
Opera House is in full operatic mode from September to May. The
New York State Theater houses the New York City Opera and the
Avery Fisher Hall is home to the New York Philharmonic.

Theatre

Choose from the large, well-funded Broadway shows staged in
ornate theatres or the offbeat and cosier Off Broadway and
Off-Off Broadway venues, where audiences are much smaller
but productions are of high quality. The location of the theatre,
commercial factors and the number of seats dictate whether or
not a production is designated as 'Broadway', 'Off Broadway' or
'Off-Off Broadway'. Some of the best performances aren't
necessarily the big ones, so check local listings if you're looking
for a less mainstream show. Tickets for big hits on Broadway and
long-running productions can cost between $35 and $200. Less
commercial performances usually cost much less, $15 to $50, say.
For Shakespearean enthusiasts, the free outdoor productions in
Central Park usually showcase fine talent.

Broadway theatres

Shuffle down to 42nd Street where the choice of spectaculars will
dazzle you. A few Broadway theatre buildings are so beautiful that
the actual performance may seem secondary. Particularly
noteworthy is Broadway's oldest theatre, the **Lyceum** (149 W 45th
St, **T** 1-212 239 6300), built in 1903, with an ornate lobby and
staircase. The done-up **New Amsterdam** (214 W 42nd St, **T** 1-212
282 2900) has a fairytale appeal thanks to its elaborate murals and
balconies, while the **Music Box** (239 W 45th St, **T** 1-212 239 6200),
built in 1921 by Irving Berlin, is an intimate jewel box of a theatre.

American Airlines Theater, 229 W 42nd St, **T** 1-212 719 1300. *Subway A, C, E to 42nd St. Map 4, G4, p266* The Roundabout Theater Company, one of the most audacious groups in town, performs in this great old theatre on 42nd Street.

Circle in the Square Theater, 1633 Broadway at 50th St, **T** 1-212 307 2705. *Subway 1, 2 to 50th St, N, R, W to 49th St. Map 4, E5, p266* This unpretentious Off-Broadway theatre hosts some of Broadway's best plays in an unassuming circular space.

Ford Center for the Performing Arts, 214 W 43rd St, **T** 1-212 307 4100. *Subway 1, 2, 3, 9, 7, B, D, N, R, W to 42nd St-Times Sq. Map 4, G4, p266* The toe-tapping, Tony award-winning production of *42nd Street* at this attractive theatre looks set to run and run.

Performance Space 122, 150 First Av, **T** 1-212 477 5288. *Subway L to 1st Av. Map 3, F9, p265* Experimental theatre, dance, music, film and video take place in this former school that's now a no-frills Off-Off Broadway venue. Many talented performers made their start at PS 122.

Theater Row Theater, 424 W 42nd St, **T** 1-212 332 0027. *Subway A, C, E to 42nd St. Map 4, G3, p266* This complex of five theatres, formerly burlesque houses and immigrant homes, showcases some excellent Off Broadway talent.

New Yorkers like to celebrate and rarely need to look far for an excuse to party, so it's probable that visitors will come across some type of event or festival at any time of year. Parades – from the wacky Mermaid Parade at Coney Island to the wild Hallowe'en parade in Greenwich Village – are a particularly popular way for the city to let its collective hair down, with 50-plus organized events taking place every year. In addition, cultural festivals, open-air film screenings, Fashion Week, art fairs and food festivals fill the streets, cinemas and restaurants year-round.

The web site www.nycvisit.com and weekly magazines such as *Time Out New York*, the *New Yorker* and the free *Village Voice*, will keep you abreast of events in this happening city.

January

Three Kings Parade The Museo del Barrio hosts this Latin celebration each 5 January, complete with children, camels and donkeys strutting their way up Fifth Avenue as far as 116th Street in Spanish Harlem.

Chinese New Year Parade Dragon parades and fireworks add even more life and colour to the irrepressible atmosphere of Chinatown for Chinese New Year, which takes place on the first full moon between 21 January and 19 February. Consult www.nycvisit.com for the exact dates each year.

Winter Antiques Show (www.winterantiquesshow.com) The premier antiques show in the US is held in mid January each year at the Seventh Regiment Armory on Park Avenue and 67th Street.

February

Twenty-four-hour Marriage Marathon If you want to tie the knot on Valentine's Day, join the fifty or so couples who get married each year atop the Empire State Building.

March

St Patrick's Day Parade The Irish have been parading down Fifth Avenue on 17 March for 200 years, sporting all kinds of green attire. A boozy party in Irish pubs all over town follows.

April

Easter Parade Another parade makes its way down Fifth Avenue in late March or April, complete with bonnets and Easter baskets.

May

Tribeca Film Festival (www.tribecafilmfestival.org) Since 2002, founder Robert De Niro (and more recently Martin Scorsese) has promoted the importance of New York's film industry by showing foreign, American and independent films in support of the recovery of Lower Manhattan post September 11th.

Ninth Avenue International Food Festival Every May the streets along Ninth Avenue in Hell's Kitchen, are filled with ethnic foods from around the world.

June

Mermaid Parade On the first Saturday of June all sorts of eccentric New Yorkers flock out to Coney Island to show off their mermaid-inspired garb and celebrate summer at one of New York's wackiest street parties.

Puerto Rican Day Parade This rowdy Latin party is one of the biggest and most notorious parades in town. It parties down Fifth Avenue on the first Sunday in June with floats, music and food.

Metropolitan Opera Parks Concerts (www.metopera.org/parks.html) Free open-air operas in Central Park are one of the city's most romantic attractions in June. Bring a bottle of wine and a blanket and chill out with the locals as you listen to Puccini's *Turandot* or Donizetti's *Lucia di Lammermoor*.

HBO Bryant Park Summer Film Festival Classic films are shown outdoors every Monday between June and August. Nudge your blanket into the green space of Bryant Park and arrive early to stake your spot and have a picnic.

Central Park Summer Stage (www.summerstage.org) Many top international performers play jazz, funk, rock, blues and more at Rumsey Playfield in Central Park (enter at Fifth Avenue and 69th Street) from June until August. The concerts are often free.

New York Shakespeare Festival (**T** 1-212 539 8750, www.shakespeareincentralpark.org) The Delacorte Theater at 81st Street hosts big name productions of the Bard from late June to late August. Free tickets, maximum two per person, are distributed on a first-come-first-served basis from 1300 on the day of the event. Be prepared to queue.

Restaurant Week (www.nycvisit.com) Participating restaurants offer three-course prix-fixe menus to coincide with the year ($20.04 in 2004) plus great lunch and dinner specials at a fraction of the normal price.

Museum Mile Festival (www.museummile.org) Take in some culture on the cheap as the stretch of museums from 86th to 104th Streets open their doors for free on the second Tuesday of June.

JVC Jazz Festival (www.festivalproductions.net/jvcjazz/newyork.htm) For two weeks towards the end of June various venues around town host all sorts of jazz performances.

Lesbian and Gay Pride Week (www.nycpride.org) A huge and spirited parade down Fifth Avenue to Greenwich Village is followed by a street fair in the last week of June.

Fleet Week Thousands of white-dressed sailors adorn the docks and streets of the city for this annual naval reunion at the end of June. Visit some of the ships at Pier 86.

July

Fourth of July Macy's puts on a spectacular display of fireworks each year at 2100. Go to a rooftop, Battery Park or the East River for the best views.

Washington Square Music Festival Chamber music, jazz and big bands bring the square to life on Tuesdays in July and August.

August

Harlem Month The music, food, dance and entertainment at this lively street festival on Fifth Avenue between 125th and 135th Streets make August an excellent time to see Harlem in its most spirited mood. Check www.nycvisit.com for details.

New York International Fringe Festival (www.fringeny.com) The Lower East Side showcases its talent, with over 1,000 performances in comedy, dance, theatre and more taking place in the second half of August.

Wigstock Drag queens come out to play around Tompkins Square Park for this annual celebration of all things wiggy and womanly in late August.

September

US Open (www.usopen.org) Tennis lovers should hop on the subway and head to Flushing Meadow in Queens where the big names of international tennis take to the courts in September.

Broadway on Broadway On the Sunday after Labour Day, the cast from dozens of Broadway shows put on free performances in Times Square. Check www.nycvisit.com for details.

New York Film Festival (www.filmlinc.com/nyff/nyff.htm) Film premieres are screened at the Lincoln Center's Walter Reade Theater from late September until mid-October.

Festival of the Feast of San Gennaro (www.littleitalynyc.com) For 10 days in mid-September, the inhabitants of Little Italy honour the patron saint of Naples by toting his statue along Mulberry Street and eating like good Italians.

Medieval Festival For one day each September, Gothic revivalists come out in full gear to celebrate medieval culture at The Cloisters in Fort Tryon Park.

October

Columbus Day Parade The second Monday of October is a national holiday to celebrate the day Christopher Columbus discovered America. Again, the parade heads down Fifth Avenue.

DUMBO Art Under the Bridge Festival (www.dumboarts center.org) This eclectic group of artists converge Down Under Manhattan Bridge Overpass in mid October to showcase their art in over 250 galleries in Brooklyn. Check the website for details.

Greenwich Village Hallowe'en Parade
(www.halloween -nyc.com) The most fabulous street party of the year sees thousands of costumed locals living it up in ghoulish style. Get your kit on for this 31 October event.

November

New York City Marathon (**T** 1-212 860 4455) Approximately 35,000 entrants run through all five boroughs on the first weekend in November. Watch them finish in Central Park, if you don't feel like joining the race.

Macy's Thanksgiving Day Parade The country's biggest and most famous float extravaganza shimmies its way from Central Park down to Macy's department store. Millions of Americans watch it on television every year.

December

Rockefeller Center Christmas Tree Lighting The enormous tree is shipped in, decorated and lit at 1900 on the Tuesday after Thanksgiving. It's a festive affair, complete with live entertainment from well-known stars, singers and the Rockettes.

New Year's Eve in Times Square For those who love crowds and commotion, show up here to watch the ball drop along with mobs of other people.

Shopping

New York is material bliss so it's not surprising that many visitors come to the city just to max out their credit cards. New York's shops tempt even the most budget-conscious traveller with their huge choice. Uptown's designer shops and Midtown's department stores flash their expensive goods from swanky window displays, while Downtown has smaller boutiques, discount stores, bric-a-brac and offbeat speciality shops. Fifth Avenue, from 23rd Street down to 14th Street, features many of the retail chains typically found in shopping malls throughout the USA but there are unexpected delights, too, from the scrumptious food hall at Grand Central Terminal to Chelsea's fabulous, kitschy weekend flea market.

For fashionistas there's everything from punk to posh, couture to camp, thrift and second-hand to designer heaven. Vintage gear can be found in the East Village, the Lower East Side and Nolita, while high-end designers are flocking to open stores in the Meatpacking District.

Most shops are generally open seven days a week, from about 1000 until at least 1800 Monday to Saturday, with shorter hours on Sundays. However, boutiques in the East Village and Lower East Side may not open until noon on any day of the week, while other stores will keep on selling until the late evening. Before you go mad with your credit card, don't forget the whopping 8.25% sales tax that is tacked on to all purchases.

Antiques/flea markets

Chelsea Antiques Building, 110 W 25th St. *Subway F, V, 1, 2, 3 to 23rd St. Map 3, C4, p264* One hundred and fifty indoor stalls over several floors sell high-quality furniture, lamps, books and trinkets of all sorts.

Chelsea Flea Market (Annex Antiques & Flea Market), 6th Av at 25th St and 26th St. *Sat and Sun only. Subway B, D, F, Q to 23rd St. Map 3, C5, p264* Rummaging through two parking lots of bric-a-brac, hats, records, jewellery, antiques, clothing, shoes, art and handbags is like stumbling upon the outpourings of an old attic. Bargaining is expected and prices usually go down later in the afternoon. The 26th Street lot costs $1 to enter, 25th Street is free.

IS 44 Flea Market, Columbus Av between 76th St and 77th St. *Sat and Sun 1000-1800 only. Subway B, C to 72nd St. Map 5, H3, p268* The hundred or so stalls that fill this parking lot and school are hit or miss. Many creative gifts can be found, so can furniture, brooches, hot cider and some interesting bric-a-brac. Locals know this as the Columbus Avenue flea market.

Books and music

For used CDs and vinyl, head to Eighth Street, between First and Second Avenues, in the East Village, also known as St Mark's Place, which is dotted with interesting music stores. While there, you can pierce and tattoo every part of your body just like a rock star.

Alabaster Bookshop, 122 Fourth Av. *Subway 6 to Astor Pl. Map 3, F7, p265* This tiny, friendly, second-hand bookshop has a good selection at bargain prices.

Barnes & Noble, 33 E 17th St. *Subway L, N, Q, R, 4, 5, 6, W to 14th St-Union Sq. Map 3, E6, p264* This huge chain has books, magazines, music and movies. Apart from its huge selection, the best thing about this store is the café, which welcomes lingerers who pile up reading material and sit for hours.

Housing Works Used Book Café, 126 Crosby St, www.housingworks.org/usedbookcafe *Subway S, F, V, 6 to Broadway-Lafayette, N, R to Prince St. Map 2, A5, p262* The mahogany bookcases, spiral staircase and inviting café are just part of the reason New Yorkers linger here. All proceeds from the used, new and rare books go to a charity for homeless New Yorkers with HIV and AIDS. Free readings and live music events are hosted here.

Rizzoli, 31 W 57th St. *Subway N, R, B, Q to 57th St. Map 4, D6, p266* This beautiful old art, architecture and design bookstore is a cultural haven in the otherwise busy strip of Midtown.

The Strand, 828 Broadway. *Subway L, N, Q, R, 4, 5, 6, W to 14th St-Union Sq. Map 3, F7, p265* This long-running institution is every book-lovers dream, with over eight miles of books, many with sale prices. Be prepared to dig a little in the cramped, stuffed aisles.

Three Lives, 154 W 10th St. *Subway 1, 9 to Christopher St. Map 3, F4, p264* This charming little bookstore in the West Village is a welcoming place, where writers hang out and give readings. It's chock-full of biographies and independent books.

Norman's Sound & Vision, 67 Cooper Sq, nr St Mark's on 3rd Av. *Subway 6 to Astor Pl. Map 3, F7, p265* A vast selection of new and used CDs fill this music store, where Norman and his friendly staff will help you rifle through stacks of tunes.

Sam Ash Music, 163 W 48th St, between 6th Av and 7th Av. *Subway B, D, F, Q to Rockefeller Center. Map 4, F5, p266* One of many musical instrument shops along this stretch of 48th Street.

Tower Records, 692 Broadway. *Daily 0900-2400. Subway 6 to Bleecker St. Map 3, H7, p264* The main New York branch of the mega music chain has an array of music and is often visited by recording artists.

Virgin Megastore, 1540 Broadway. *Mon-Sat 0900-0100, Sun 1000-2300. Subway N, Q, R, S, W, 1, 2, 3, 7 to 42nd St-Times Sq. Map 4, F5, p266* This gigantic store stocks a vast selection of CDs, DVDs and vinyl, including some hard-to-find imports and world music.

Department stores

Barneys, 660 Madison Av. *Subway N, R to 5th Av. Map 4, C7, p267* Offering hip fashion at a price, Barney's is where urban folk with an unlimited budget come to shop. Watch out for bi-annual warehouse sales at Barney's Co-op store on 236 W 18th Street.

Bergdorf Goodman, 745 Fifth Av. *Subway N, R, E, F to 5th Av. Map 4, C7, p267* The beautiful, elegant building entices the old-school Uptown elite through its front doors. Admire the lavish store, especially the top floor home furnishings department but stay out of the way of women carrying their small dogs.

Bloomingdales, 1000 3rd Av.   *Subway N, R, 4, 5, 6 to 59th* St. *Map 4, C8, p267*   Big, brash and busy, this is probably the most-visited department store in town and sells everything from make-up to mattresses.

Henri Bendel, 712 Fifth Av at 56th St.   *Subway N, R, W to 5th Av-59th St.   Map 4, D6, p266*   This luxurious, trendy department store is like a jewellery box full of glittering treats .

Macy's, 151 W 34th St.   *Subway B, D, F, N, Q, R, V, W to 34th St-Herald Sq.   Map 3, A5, p264*   The world's largest department store is also the most difficult to get around. Skip Macy's and stick to the other, less chaotic stores.

Saks Fifth Avenue, 611 Fifth Av.   *Subway B, D, F, V to 47th-50th Sts-Rockefeller Center.   Map 4, E7, p267*   Classic department store selling clothes, shoes and accessories. Check out the lovely cosmetics section near the entrance.

Electronics

Electrical equipment is a good buy for European visitors, as it tends to be cheaper in the USA . However, before purchasing any electrical devices here, always check their compatibility with the system in your country.

The Apple Store, 103 Prince St at Greene St.   *Subway N, R to Prince St.   Map 2, A5, p262*   This glossy, tech-y dream store shows off Apple's latest goods in a former post office where interaction is encouraged. It also hosts seminars and has a genius bar upstairs where Mac users can get help.

B&H Photo-Video, 420 Ninth Av. *Subway A, C, E to 34th St-Penn Station. Map 3, A2, p264* All kinds of photography and video equipment are stocked in this conveyor-belt shop. The size may overcome you but the service will not. Closed on Jewish holidays.

J&R Music & Computer World, 15 Park Row. *Subway A, C, J, M, Z, 1, 2, 4, 5 to Fulton St-Broadway Nassau. Map 7, C3, p272* This is New Yorkers' first choice for anything to do with computers and electronics.

Fashion: designer and vintage

New York is fashion heaven. As well as flagship stores on Madison Avenue for the big names of international fashion, you'll also find boutiques selling pieces by designers straight out of the Fashion Institute of Technology. The choice of handmade, vintage and one-off clothing is particularly abundant around Nolita, the Lower East Side and the East Village (Ninth Street between Avenue A and Third Avenue). Unusual shoes can be found in SoHo and Nolita.

Betsey Johnson, 138 Wooster St. *Subway N, R to Prince St. Map 2, A4, p262* Fun, flirty, flowery attire for women. Ms Johnson is a New York institution.

Calvin Klein, 654 Madison Av. *Subway 4, 5, 6 to 59th St. Map 4, C7, p267* Clothes and home furnishings are sold in this classic, neutral-toned, minimalist American store.

DKNY, 655 Madison Av. *Subway 4, 5, 6 to 59th St. Map 4, C7, p267* Power suits and sneakers share space in Donna Karan's flagship store.

Edith and Daha, 104 Rivington St. *Subway F, J, M, Z to Delancey-Essex Sts. Map 2, A8, p263* This excellent second-hand shop has a vast collection of clothing, shoes, accessories and handbags, mostly dating from the 1960s to the 1980s.

Ina, 101 Thompson St. *Subway N, R to Prince St.* *Map 2, A4, p262*
High-end vintage clothes and accessories for women.

Jeffrey, 449 W 14th St. *Subway A, C, E to 14th St.* *Map 3, E2, p264*
Fancy footwear for men and women make Jeffrey the hottest shopping destination in the Meatpacking District.

Jimmy Choo, 645 Fifth Av. *Subway E, V to Fifth Av.* *Map 4, E7, p267* Heels, boots, slides and all kinds of strappy wonders at expectedly high prices.

Kirna Zabete, 96 Greene St. *Subway N, R to Prince St.* *Map 2, A5, p262* Funky, unusual store for women's clothing, shoes, accessories, candy and beauty products.

Marc Jacobs, 163 Mercer St. *Subway N, R to Prince St.* *Map 2, A5, p262* This is Jacobs' first boutique. It's housed in a former art gallery and is cool enough for trendy fashionistas not to miss its discreet storefront.

Mayhem, 441 E Ninth St. *Subway 6 to Astor Pl.* *Map 3, F9, p265*
Embrace your inner-rock chick.

Meg, 312 E Ninth St. *Subway 6 to Astor Pl.* *Map 3, F8, p265*
Funky dresses with a flair and atypical bridesmaids dresses.

Nicole Miller, 134 Prince St. *Subway N, R to Prince St.* *Map 2, A4, p262* Known for its cocktail dresses, this shop has something for any woman who wants to feel feminine.

Designer dummies
Funky fashion and footwear draws trendsetters to Jeffrey in the Meatpacking District.

Patricia Field, Hotel Venus, 382 W Broadway. *Subway, N, R to Prince St. Map 2, A4, p262* Crazy clubwear by the woman who designed clothes for *Sex and the City*.

Prada, 575 Broadway. *Subway N, R to Prince St. Map 2, A5, p262* Rem Koolhaas's funky store is distinguishable by the mannequins lined up in the window. Fun for a browse but highly expensive.

Ralph Lauren, 867 Madison Av. *Subway 6 to 68th St-Hunter College. Map 4, A7, p267* The old mansion that houses this store is the epitome of wealth and the home goods and clothing on sale will help you to part with some serious cash.

Vui Vui, 309 E Ninth St. *Subway 6 to Astor Pl. Map 3, F8, p265* Asian-inspired glamorous clothing and accessories.

Yellow Rat Bastard, 478-480 Broadway. *Subway N, R to Prince St. Map 2, B5, p262* Hip-hop and retro clothes and accessories for men and women. Whimsical T-shirts.

Fashion: discount

Bargain stores such as Loehmann's and Daffy's offer designer goods at incredible prices. Label-conscious shoppers should also visit ongoing sample sales, where designer names are hugely discounted; see www.dailycandy.com.

Century 21, 22 Cortland St. *Subway 1, 2 to Chambers St. Map 7, D3, p272* New Yorkers flock to this store, across the street from the World Trade Center site, to make the most of steep discounts on designer clothing, accessories and shoes.

Daffy's, 111 Fifth Av. *Subway L, N, Q, R, 4, 5, 6, W to 14th St-Union Sq. Map 3, D6, p264* "Where millionaires shop" is Daffy's motto, but it doesn't take a fortune to buy the designer goods at this local chain. Excellent deals on lingerie and clothes.

Loehmann's, 101 Seventh Av. *Subway 1, 2 to 18th St. Map 3, E4, p264* If you can face rummaging through the rails with crowds of other bargain hunters, some great shoes and clothes can be found here at a fraction of the normal price.

Food and wine

Chelsea Market, 75 Ninth Av, between 15th St and 16th St, www.chelseamarket.com *Subway A, C, E to 14th St. Map 3, E2, p264* A former Nabisco factory has been successfully converted in to a shopping arcade, selling a stunning choice of fresh fruit, vegetables, food, flowers, cheese, coffee and gifts. It's open till 2100 during the week and until 2000 at weekends.

Gourmet Garage, 453 Broome St. *Subway N, R to Prince St. Map 2, B5, p262* Gourmet foods at reasonable prices, including tasty sandwiches and an impressive cheese and olive selection.

Grand Central Market, Grand Central Terminal. *Mon-Fri only. Subway L, 4, 5, 6 to 42nd St-Grand Central. Map 4, G7, p267* This weekday food hall is stuffed with gourmet cheese, seafood, breads, desserts, fruits and flowers.

Greenmarket Farmers' Market, Union Sq, 14th St to 17th St between Broadway and Park Av South. *Mon, Wed, Fri and Sat. Subway L, N, R, Q, W, 4, 5, 6 to 14th St-Union Sq. Map 3, E6, p264* Upstate farmers sell all kinds of produce, including bread, fruit and organic cider.

Vintage New York, 482 Broome St. *Subway C, E to Spring St. Map 2, B5, p262* The only liquor store allowed to stay open on a Sunday, this tasting room and store sells food and wine from across the state of New York.

Zabar's, 2245 Broadway at 80th St. *Subway 1, 2 to 79th St. Map 5, G2, p268* A New York foodie institution on the Upper West Side. Visit just to see its vast selection and head for the second floor to buy any sort of kitchen-related device.

Gifts

Flight 001, 96 Greenwich Av. *Subway 1, 9 to 14th St. Map 3, F4, p264* Everything travel-related: bags, books, bottles and more.

Hiponica, 238 Mott St. *Subway 6 to Bleecker St. Map 2, A6, p262* Hip handbags that won't break the bank.

Pearldaddy, 202A Mott St. *Subway 6 to Bleecker St. Map 2, A6, p262* Delightful handmade freshwater pearl jewellery.

Random Accessories, 169 Thompson St. *Subway N, R to Prince St. Map 3, H6, p264* The best place for creative gifts from unusual baby items to key chains.

Tah Poozie, 50 Greenwich Av. *Subway 1, 9 to Christopher St. Map 3, F4, p264* If you need a plastic dashboard Jesus or other such kitsch items, this is where you'll find them.

Home and lifestyle

SoHo is the place to go for upscale home furnishings, from antique to modern. Check out **Moss** (146 Greene St) for industrial home accessories and **The Apartment** (101 Crosby Street) for stylish contemporary items. **Depression Modern** (150 Sullivan St) has 1930s furniture and **Dom** (382 W Broadway, Ste 1) has quirky inflatables at affordable prices. Head over to **The Bowery** if you're shopping for lighting or kitchen supplies.

ABC Carpet & Home, 888 Broadway. *Subway N, R to 23rd St. Map 3, D6, p264* Beautiful and expensive home furnishings span two buildings. Styles encompass shabby chic and Asian imports, ultra-modern and French country.

Crate & Barrel, 611 Broadway. *Subway 6 to Bleecker St. Map 3, H7, p265* The all-American take on classic furniture with a modern flair: dishes, rugs, paintings, sofas and other home accessories at reasonable prices.

Pottery Barn, 600 Broadway. *Subway N, R to Prince St. Map 3, H7, p265* The staple of yuppie life, this Cape Cod meets New York store sells furniture, bedding and home accessories.

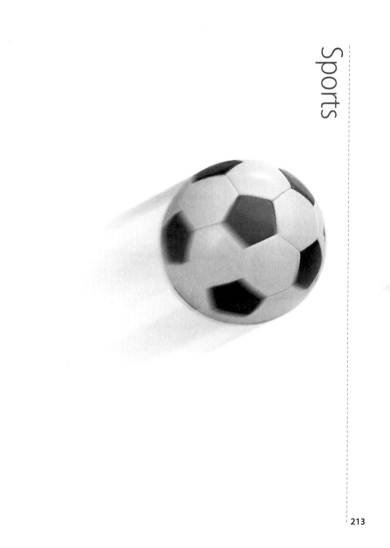

Walk by a sports bar on nearly any night of the week and you're sure to see either a baseball, football or basketball game on TV. You are also likely to notice New Yorkers sporting jerseys, hats and T-shirts that proclaim their allegiance to the Yankees or the Mets (baseball), the Knicks (basketball), or the Jets and Giants (football).

New Yorkers are known for being constantly on the go, so it's no surprise that they take great pride in keeping fit. In fact, the first question a New Yorker may ask a new acquaintance is "which gym do you belong to?" When they're not at the gym, the city's sporty types can be found jogging, cycling and roller-blading around Central Park or along the recently rejuvenated Hudson River Park on Manhattan's western border.

Baths

Tenth Street Baths, 268 E 10th St, **T** 1-212 473 8806, www.russianturkishbathscom *$22. Subway 6 to Astor Pl. Map 3, F9, p265* The Lower East Side and East Village were once home to dozens of Russian-Turkish steam baths. Now, just the 10th Street Baths remain. Popular since 1892 and recently refurbished, the baths attract all sorts to their renovated saunas, steam rooms and pool.

Bowling

Bowlmor Lanes, 110 University, **T** 1-212 255 8188. *$7.95 per round, $5 shoe rental. Subway 4,5, 6, L, N, Q, R, W to 14th St-Union Sq. Map 3, F6, p264* The DJ and bar at Bowlmor make it more like a club than a regular bowling alley and ensure a funky experience that's great for groups. On Monday nights between 1000 and 0300 there's unlimited bowling for $20, shoes included.

Gyms and sport centres

With nearly as many gyms as corner delis, it's easy to find a place to work out in New York. Many hotels will offer complimentary passes or discounts for local gyms, such as **New York Sports Club** (www.nysc.com), which is found in every neighbourhood. A standard day pass costs $25.

Chelsea Piers, 23rd St at the Hudson River, **T** 1-212 336 6666. *Subway C, E to 23rd St. Map 3, C1, p264* Four piers on the Hudson River have been converted into an enormous 30-acre recreational complex that's a dream for kids and adults, who come to ice-skate, swim, hit golf balls, rock climb, bowl, play basketball or hockey and use the spa. Day passes are sold for use of the fitness centre and spa; other activities are sold individually.

Sports

Equinox, www.equinoxfitness.com Posh gyms in locations all around town. Classes like Urban Conditioning and Will Power & Grace will leave you buffed. Day pass is $25. The Greenwich Village location has a swimming pool.

Ice-skating

Rockefeller Center, Fifth Av at 49th St and 50th St, **T** 1-212 332 7654. *Call for times and prices. Subway B, D, F, V to 47-50 Sts/Rockefeller Center. Map 4, F6, p266* Twirl around the famous rink, with hundreds of tourists watching you.

Wollman Rink at Central Park, 62nd St at Central Park, **T** 1-212 396 1010. *Call for times and prices. Subway F to 57 St. Map 4, C5, p266* Roller-skating or blading in the summer and ice-skating in the winter, against a million-dollar backdrop of Midtown.

Jogging

Central Park (see p91) is the most popular jogging space in town with 58 miles of pathways, but you could also try **Hudson River Park**, a wonderful strip overlooking the water from Battery Park up to 59th Street that's perfect for jogging, cycling and roller-blading, or **Riverside Park** (see p96), a lovely stretch of green space on the Upper West Side. **New York Road Runner's Club**, www.nyrrc.org, organizes group runs and is an excellent resource for information .

Kayaking

Kayaking at the Downtown Boathouse, Pier 26, between Canal St and Chambers St on the West Side Highway, **T** 1-646 613 0740, www.downtownboathouse.org *May-Oct Sat and Sun 0900-1800; call for times Mon-Fri. Subway 1, 9, 2, 3 to Chambers St,*

A, C, E to Canal St. Map 2, D2, p262 One of the most peaceful ways to see Manhattan is from the water. The Downtown Boathouse has a mission to provide free access to the Hudson River for everyone – as long as they can swim.

Roller-blading

Blades, **T** 1-212 787 3911, hires out roller-blades from various locations for $20 per 24 hours.

Yoga

Atmananda Yoga & Holistic Center, 552 Broadway, SoHo, www.atmamanda.com *Subway 6 to Astor Pl. Map 2, A4, p262* When the hurly-burly of the city gets too much, the beautiful denizens of SoHo recharge their spiritual batteries at one of the yoga centres in the area. This place offers classes for all abilities.

Jivamukti, 404 Lafayette St, 3rd Flr, **T** 1-212 353 0214, www.jivamuktiyoga.com *Subway 6 to Astor Pl. Map 3, G7, p265* This is the best-known yoga centre in the city. The likes of Madonna, Sting and Christy Turlington have all been seen in the lotus position here. Free introductory classes are given every month; check the website for details of prices and times.

Spectator sports

Basketball and ice hockey are the only major spectator sports that take place in Manhattan but baseball matches are an easy subway ride in either the Bronx (for the Yankees) or Queens (for the Mets). American football fans must head over to New Jersey to watch the Jets or the Giants. **Ticketmaster** (**T** 1-212 307 7171) sells tickets for all, though it's usually cheaper to try and buy tickets at the venue.

Sports

Giants Stadium, Meadowlands Sports Complex, exit 16W, Rutherford, New Jersey, **T** 1-201 935 3900. *Regular buses from Port Authority.* Both the New York Giants and the New York Jets play professional football here from September to the end of January.

Madison Square Garden, 7th Av between 31st and 34th Sts, **T** 1-212 465 6741. *Subway 1, 2, 3, 9, A, C, E to 34th St-Herald Sq. Map 3, A4, p264* The main sports arena in Manhattan is where you can sit courtside to watch the New York Knicks (basketball) dribbling and dunking in the summer or the New York Rangers (ice hockey) checking and deking from fall to spring.

Shea Stadium, 126th St at Roosevelt Av, Queens, **T** 1-718 507 8499, www.mets.com *Subway 7 to Willets Points. Map 1, F7, p260* This stadium is home to the New York Mets baseball team, regarded as the working-class, everyman's alternative to the Yankees and, usually, as the underdogs. A huge rivalry exists between Mets and Yankees fans, which becomes apparent whenever the two teams play. The Mets farm team, the minor-league Brooklyn Cyclones, play all summer at Coney Island.

Yankee Stadium, 161st St and River Av, The Bronx, **T** 1-718 293 6000. *Subway B, D, 4 to 161 St-Yankee Stadium. Map 1, D5, p260* Babe Ruth's former hangout is the most famous landmark in the Bronx. Since 1923, the New York Yankees, or Bronx Bombers as locals call them, have been cheered on by thousands of fans at this arena. Lou Gehrig, Joe DiMaggio and Mickey Mantle all played here, helping to amass 26 World Series' championships – you can see plaques commemorating them in Monument Park. If you're visiting New York during the baseball season from April to October, take the subway out for a taste of Americana. The music, overpriced beer and hot dogs will keep you entertained if the baseball game does not. The family atmosphere makes it a festive event for kids but beware, most games go on for at least a few hours.

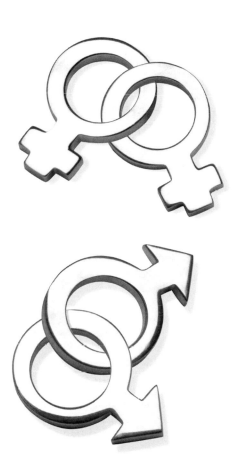

In the USA, New York is rivalled only by San Francisco in terms of its thriving gay and lesbian community. The defining moment came in 1969, when police raided a gay bar in Sheridan Square, where mourners were gathered after Judy Garland's death. The raid sparked a three-day uprising, known as the Stonewall Rebellion, which led directly to the establishment of the gay rights movement.

Chelsea, especially along Eighth Avenue, and the West Village are where most of the cruisy bars, clubs and restaurants are clustered and where many rainbow flags fly proudly. There are also a few gay clubs tucked into warehouses in the Meatpacking District, where a mixed crowd turns up to dance and party the night away. Kitschy, fun-spirited gay shops and bookstores are grouped around Christopher Street between Seventh Avenue and Hudson Street and the largest concentration of lesbian bars is on Hudson Street, north of Houston Street up to Bank Street. Check weekly listings in *HX* (Homo Xtra; www.hx.com, *HX for Her*, the *Village Voice* and *Time Out New York* for details of gay events in the city.

Sleeping

Most hotels in New York are gay-friendly, especially those in Chelsea and Greenwich Village, such as the **Abingdon Guest House** (see Sleeping, p120).

C Incentra Village House, 32 Eighth Av, **T** 1-212 206 0007. *Subway A, C, E to 14th St.   Map 3, F3, p264* This twelve-room guesthouse is charming and cosy. A fireplace, antiques and a piano fill the Victorian living room, making it a communal and welcoming place to rest or mingle.

Eating and drinking

Big Cup, 228 Eighth Av (between 21st and 22nd Sts), **T** 1-212 206 0059. *Subway C, E to 23rd St. Sun-Thu 0700-0100, Fri, Sat 0800-0200. Map 3, D3, p264* The campest café in town, with couches, cappuccinos, cupcakes and enough eye-candy to keep everyone happy.

Café Mona Lisa, 282 Bleecker St, **T** 1-212 929 1262. *Subway 1, 9 to Christopher St. Sun-Thu 1100-0200, Fri and Sat 1100-0300. Map 3, H5, p264* The big, comfy chairs, antique tables and lovely pastries, make this an ideal place to relax or have brunch.

Bars and clubs

Bar d'O, 34 Downing St at Bedford St, **T** 1-212 627 1580. *Mon-Fri 1800-0300, Sat and Sun 1900-0400. Subway 1, 9 to Houston St. Map 3, H4, p264* Dark and seductive, this hip lounge-bar attracts a mixed crowd of gays, straights and those in between. Famous for its weekend drag shows.

Gay and lesbian

Barracuda, 275 W 22nd St, **T** 1-212 645 8613. *Daily 1600-0400. Subway C, E to 23rd St. Map 3, D3, p264* Down-to-earth gays, retro decor and cocktails with a punch mean it's often standing-room only at Barracuda, especially when drag shows liven up the crowds.

The Cock, 188 Av A at 12th St, **T** 1-212 946 1871. *Daily 1900-0400. Subway L to 1st Av. Map 3, F10, p265* Dark, seedy and debaucherous, this long-standing East Village dive bar is where biker dudes gather.

Cubby Hole, 281 W 12th St, **T** 1-212 243 9041. *Mon-Thu 1600-0200, Fri 1600-0400, Sat 1400-0400, Sun 1400-0200. Subway A, C, E to 14th St, L to 8th Av. Map 3, F3, p264* Friendly lesbian neighbourhood bar with beer on tap, a jukebox and twinkly lights hanging above.

Hell, 59 Gansevoort St, **T** 1-212 727 1666. *Fri 1700-0400, Sat-Thu 1900-0400. Subway A, C, E to 14th St, L to 8th Av. Map 3, F2, p264* Velvety red decor, fabulous Martinis and a mixed crowd, ensure a sultry experience at this cavernous club-lounge.

Henrietta Hudson, 438 Hudson St at Morton St, **T** 1-212 924 3347. *Mon-Fri 1600-0400, Sat and Sun 1300-0400. Subway 1, 9 to Christopher St. Map 3, H4, p264* A good meeting spot with a pool table, jukebox and a friendly, casual atmosphere. It's bustling at night when the dancing kicks off.

Meow Mix, 269 E Houston St at Suffolk St, **T** 1-212 254 0688. *Daily 1900-0400. Subway F, V to Lower East Side-2nd Av. Map 3, H10, p265* Attractive lesbians and a few select men enjoy funk, hip-hop, reggae and house music from the DJs and events such as poetry readings. Thursday is glam girl night.

The Monster, 80 Grove St at Sheridan Sq, **T** 1-212 924 3558. *Mon-Fri 1600-0400, Sat and Sun 0200-0400. Subway 1, 9 to Christopher St-Sheridan Sq. Map 3, G4, p264* Two-floored club featuring a lively disco downstairs and a piano lounge upstairs. It attracts a wonderfully eclectic bunch of social animals and is considered one of the campest places to sing out Broadway tunes. Fun for those seeking the true spirit of the West Village.

Rubyfruit, 531 Hudson St at Charles St, **T** 1-212 929 3343. *Mon-Thu 1500-2300, Fri and Sat 1500-2400, Sun 1130-2400. Subway 1, 9 to Christopher St-Sheridan Sq. Map 3, H3, p264* Sofas, cheap drinks and low-key crowds make this a comfortable lesbian bar where all feel welcome.

Stonewall, 53 Christopher St, **T** 1-212 463 0950. *Daily 1430-0400. Subway 1, 9 to Christopher St-Sheridan Sq. Map 3, G4, p264* The site of the 1969 rebellion, this basic bar with a pool table is mostly special for its history.

Wonder Bar, 505 E 6th St between Av A and Av B, **T** 1-212 777 9105. *Daily 1800-0400. Subway F to 2nd Av, 6 to Astor Pl. Map 3, G10, p264* All sorts of attractive gays and lesbians mingle here with some straight folks. Candlelight and DJs with cool tunes make this feel less like a pick-up joint and more of a chilled, hip hangout.

xl, 357 W 16th St between 8th Av and 9th Av, **T** 1-212 995 1400. *Daily 1600-0400. Subway A, C, F to 14th St, L to 8th Av. Map 3, E3, p264* This three-floor bar is one of the most happening gay bars in Chelsea, thanks to topless bartenders, light shows, a 30-foot aquarium in the bathroom, attractive crowds and a lively pick-up scene. There are free performances by cabaret and Broadway stars on Monday nights.

Gay and lesbian

Festivals and events

Lesbian and Gay Pride Week and Parade (see also p197)
Manhattan buzzes with rainbow stripes, leather-clad men on
motorbikes and dressed-up transsexuals strutting their stuff.

New York Lesbian and Gay Film Festival, **T** 1-212 254 8504,
www.newfestival.org   Every June this festival screens a variety of
gay and lesbian films.

Shopping

Creative Visions/Gay Pleasures, 548 Hudson St, **T** 1-212 645
7573. *Subway 1, 9 to Christopher St-Sheridan Sq. Map 3, G3, p264*
Over 5000 gay and lesbian books, videos, CDs, gifts and cards.

Oscar Wilde Memorial Bookshop, 15 Christopher St, **T** 1-212
255 8097. *Subway 1, 9 to Christopher St-Sheridan Sq. Map 3, G4,
p264* Small bookstore that's chock-full of literature, magazines,
videos, accessories, flags and trinkets.

Directory

Gay & Lesbian Switchboard, **T** 1-212 989 0999, 1-888 843 4564,
www.glnh.org *Mon-Fri 1600-2000, Sat 1200-1800.*   Provides
counselling for those struggling to come out, details of gay and
lesbian organizations and information on bars, eateries and hotels.

NYC Gay & Lesbian Anti-Violence Project, 240 W 35th St
between 7th Av and 8th Av, **T** 1-212 714 1184, 24-hr hotline 1-212
714 1141, www.avp.org *Subway A, C, E, 1, 2, 3, 9 to 34th St-Penn
Station. Map 3, A4, p264* This project works with the police
department's bias unit. Volunteers give advice on getting help,
and counselling is available.

New York is a playground for kids who share its lickety-split attention span. From streetside performers and the tack of Chinatown to Christmas lights, gigantic toy stores, Central Park and the Bronx Zoo, the city is an explosion of images that will delight children of all ages. New York can also be surprisingly hospitable to young ones, who usually blend right into the chaos. Many museums offer reduced or free admission for children under the age of 12 and, although New York's formal restaurants can be unwelcoming to kids, more laidback venues tend to have an anything-goes attitude. Inflated balloons and colourful floats at the city's numerous festivals, especially the Macy's Thanksgiving Day Parade, will amuse smaller children, while teenagers can shop, ice-skate and hang out at the Rockefeller Center or peer into the MTV studios and do some celeb-spotting over at Times Square.

Kids

Sights and activities

American Museum of Natural History, (see p94).
The butterflies, dinosaurs and space centre will keep everyone
entertained for hours.

Astroland, Coney Island (see p111)   All sorts of bumper cars,
rollercoasters, cotton candy and stomach-churning rides line the
famous boardwalk in Brooklyn.

Bronx Zoo, Bronx River Parkway at Fordham Rd, **T** 1-718 367 1010,
www.bronxzoo.com   *Subway 2, 5 to Bronx Park East.   Apr-Oct
Mon-Sat 1000-1700, Sat and Sun 1000-1730; Nov-Mar daily 1000-1630.
Map 1, C6, p260*   The Congo Gorilla Forest, the newly opened Tiger
Mountain and 4000 other animals are exciting for zoo lovers. A kids'
section allows children to pet some of the calmer animals.

Bryant Park (see p74).   An old-fashioned carousel twirls in one
of New York's prettiest squares and children who ride will feel its
old-world charm.

Central Park (see p91)   Highlights for kids include the **Carousel**,
the **Children's Zoo** and the **Conservatory Gardens**, where a
whimsical statue portrays characters from the *Secret Garden*.
Children can sail little boats around **Conservatory Water** and
the bronze *Alice in Wonderland* statue is nearby for climbing.

Chelsea Piers, (see Sports p215).   Kids can have a ball in the
batting range, skate around the ice rink, flip out in the gymnast's
arena or play organized team games. Call ahead to see what's on
each day.

Kids

Children's Museum of the Arts, 182 Lafayette St, **T** 1-212 274 0986. *Subway 6 to Spring St, N, R to Prince St. Wed 1200-1900, Thu-Sun 1200-1700. $5. Map 2, B5, p262* This hands-on art house for kids will make parents want to participate too. Workshops and classes are given by art teachers in this five floor space, with collage-making, costumes, a performance space, sculptures and easels on hand to allow kids to express themselves freely. Artwork by kids covers the museum head to toe.

Children's Museum of Manhattan, 212 W 83rd St, **T** 1-212 721 1234. *Subway 1, 9 to 86th St. Tue-Sun 1000-1700, $5. Map 5, F2, p268* The engaging exhibits at this hands-on museum will hold the attention of even the smallest children. There's a room inspired by Dr Seuss where kids can make green eggs and ham, plus interactive cartoon characters, including Charlie Brown and Curious George. Fun with a capital 'F'.

Intrepid Sea-Air-Space Museum, *USS Intrepid*, Pier 86, 46th St at the Hudson River, **T** 1-212 245 0072. *Oct-Mar Tue-Sun 1000-1700; Apr-Sep Mon-Fri 1000-1700, Sat and Sun 1000-1800. $14, seniors and students $10, children 6-11 $7, children 2-6 $2, under-2s free. Subway A, C, E to 42nd St-Port Authority, then walk to the river. Map 4, G1, p266* A spy plane, submarine and other wartime devices surround this 900-foot aircraft carrier used in World War II. Many of the interactive exhibits will appeal to kids, or those adults interested in wartime history.

Museum of the City of New York (see p90). Old-fashioned board games, fire trucks and dollhouses sit next to historical exhibits of the city, making this an educational yet entertaining museum. The shop sells some great New York-themed toys.

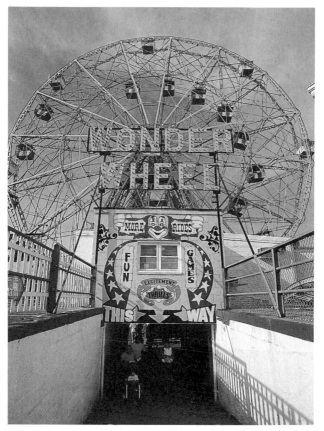

Wonder wheel
Children will be thrilled by the beachfront fairground rides at Coney Island's Astroland.

New York Aquarium, W 8th St and Surf Av, Coney Island, **T** 1-718 265 FISH. *Mon-Fri 1000-1700, Sat and Sun 1000-1730. $9.75. Subway D, F to W 8th St/NY Aquarium. Map 1, L4, p261* Dark halls connect the aquariums, which feature sea creatures in a fairly interesting display. Outside you can watch dolphin shows and feeding time for the sharks, walruses and sea otters.

Sony Wonder Technology Lab, Sony Building, 550 Madison Av at 56th St, **T** 1-212 833 8100, www.sonywondertechlab.com *Subway 4, 5, 6 to 59th St. Tue-Sun 1000-1800, Thu 1000-2000, Sun 1200-1800. Free. Map 4, D7, p267* Gizmos, gadgets and all sorts of high-tech television, games, music and film make for an excellent interactive space at this recently upgraded museum. Perfect for a rainy day in Midtown or for kids who want to make their own video game. Free movies geared towards children are shown daily in the museum's cinema at 1800.

Child-minding services

Babysitters' Guild, 60 E 42nd St, **T** 1-212 682 0227. Babysitting services from $12 an hour plus travel costs, with a four-hour minimum.

Pinch Sitters, 799 Broadway, Ste 204, **T** 1-212 260 6005. Specializes in providing emergency babysitters, within an hour of calling. Four-hour minimum, rates vary.

Airline offices
See Travel Essentials, p24.

Banks and ATMs
In Manhattan, banks are found on every other block. Most are open until 1600 Monday to Friday and until 1200 on Saturdays. The most common banks are **Chase Manhattan Bank** and **Citigroup**. ATM machines are abundant; you'll even find them in corner shops and convenience stores. As long as your bank is linked to the Cirrus or Plus ATM networks, you should be able to withdraw money anywhere for a small fee, usually $3 and up.

Bicycle hire
See Travel Essentials, p31.

Car hire
Driving around Manhattan is not recommended but if you require a car for an out-of-town excursion, note that car hire companies in the USA require drivers to be at least 25 years old and to hold a valid US or international driving licence. The following have outlets around the city: **Avis**, **T** 1-800 230 4898, www.avis.com **Budget**, **T** 1800 527 0700, www.budget.com **Dollar Rent A Car**, **T** 1-800 800 3665, www.dollar.com **Hertz**, **T** 1-800 654 3131, www.hertz.com.

Consulates General
Australia, 150 E 42nd St, **T** 1-212 351 6500. **Belgium**, 1330 Sixth Av, **T** 1-212 586 5110. **Canada**, 1251 Sixth Av at 50th St, **T** 1-212 596 1628. **Denmark**, 1 Dag Hammarskjöld Plaza, **T** 1-212 223 4545. **France**, 934 Fifth Av, **T** 1-212 606 3600. **Germany**, 871 UN Plaza, **T** 1-212 610 9700. **Ireland**, 345 Park Av at 51st St, **T** 1-212 319 2555. **Italy**, 690 Park Av, **T** 1-212 737 9100. **Japan**, 299 Park Av, **T** 1-212 371 8222. **Netherlands**, 1 Rockefeller Plaza at 49th St between 5th and 6th Av, **T** 1-212 246 1429. **New Zealand**, 780

Third Av, **T** 1-212 832 4038. **Spain**, 150 E 58th St, **T** 1-212 355 4080. **Sweden**, 1 Dag Hammarskjöld Plaza, **T** 1-212 583 2550. **UK**, 845 Third Av between 51st and 52nd St, **T** 1-212 745 0200.

Credit card hotlines
If your credit card is lost or stolen cards, call the following numbers: **American Express**, **T** 1-800 528 4800; **Diners Club**, **T** 1-800 234 6377; **Mastercard**, **T** 1-800 826 2181; **Visa**, **T** 1-800 336 8472.

Cultural institutions
Alliance Francaise, 22 E 60th St, **T** 1-212 355 6100.
Asia Society, 725 Park Av at 70th St, **T** 1-212 288 6400.
Center for Jewish History, 15 W 16th St, **T** 1-212 294 8301.
Goethe Institute, 1014 Fifth Av at 82nd St, **T** 1-212 439 8700.

Dentists and doctors
For a list of dentists and doctors in your part of town, refer to the *Yellow Pages*. **DOCS** runs a respected walk-in doctor service at the Beth Israel Medical Center (55 E 34th St, **T** 1-212 252 6000) for a flat fee of $80-300. Check the *Yellow Pages* for other locations.

If you require cheap dental work, consider the **NYU College of Dentistry** (345 E 24th St, **T** 1-212 998 9872), where supervised final-year students use you to practise their techniques. They also provide emergency care after hours (**T** 1-212 998 9828) for a fee.

Disabled
Since 1987, all newly constructed buildings in New York City must provide facilities for the disabled, including specially adapted restrooms and entrances. Many older buildings have also had to comply with this law. For details of facilities at cultural institutions in the city, a helpful resource is the **Hospital Audience's** guide **T** 1-212 575 7660, www.hospaud.org   All Broadway theatres are equipped with devices for the hearing impaired. Call **Telecharge**,

T 1-212 239 6200, to reserve tickets for wheelchair seating in Broadway and Off-Broadway venues. In addition, the non-profit organization **Big Apple Greeter**, **T** 1-212 669 8159, has volunteers who help any person with disabilities see New York City; reserve a volunteer three weeks ahead of your visit.

Electricity

The US uses 110-120V, 60-cycle AC current, rather than the 220-240V, 50-cycle AC used in Europe and elsewhere. To use any electrical device from abroad in the US (except for plug-in shavers), you will require an adaptor, which can be purchased at airport shops and many stores. Most hotels provide hair dryers.

Embassies

See Consulates General, p232.

Emergency numbers

For **ambulance**, **police** and **fire** services, call **T** 911, for free from any telephone.

Hospitals

To find the nearest hospital, consult the *Yellow Pages*. Having traveller's health insurance for your trip is crucial as the cost of care in the US is exorbitant. The East side of Manhattan is lined with well-run, large hospitals including the **New York University Medical Center** (462 First Av, **T** 1-212 263 5550). On the West Side try **St Vincent's Hospital** (153 W 11th St at 7th Av, Greenwich Village, **T** 1-212 604 7998).

Internet/email

The many branches of the **New York Public Library** offer free internet access in half-hour slots. Internet cafés provide access for anywhere from $1 to $15 an hour. **easyEverything** is the cheapest, with rates as low as $1 per hour depending on the time of day. **easyEverything**, 234 W 42nd St, **T** 1-212 398 0724. *Daily 24 hrs. Subway A, C, E, 1, 9, N, R to 42nd St-Times Sq.* **News Café**, 107 University Pl, **T** 1-212 353 1246. *Mon-Fri 0730-2000, Sat and Sun 0830-2100. Subway L, N, R, W, 4, 5, 6 to Union Sq.*

Branches of **Kinko's** are scattered every few blocks around the city and have computers, photocopiers and just about any kind of print service you'd need. They are open 24 hours daily.

Left luggage
The strict security constraints now in operation in the USA mean that there are no public places to leave luggage. Bags can normally be left for a while at your hotel, but take all valuables with you.

Libraries
The **New York Public Library** has numerous branches all around town. The main Humanities and Social Sciences library is at 42nd Street and Fifth Avenue (**T** 1-212 930 0830). Anyone is welcome in to the libraries to browse but to obtain a library card you will have to show proof of residence in New York.

Lost property
Call the police is you lose something on the street or in another public place. If you leave something behind on the subway or bus, contact the MTA-New York City Transit (**T** 1-212 712 4500).

Newspapers
The main broadsheet is *The New York Times*, the nation's most prestigious paper daily with the best and most in-depth national and international news. The recently established *New York Sun* is conservative in tone and far less global in its news coverage. Two daily tabloids, the right-wing *New York Post* (owned by Rupert Murdoch) and the centrist *Daily News*, have been around forever and are what you'll see many locals reading on the subway in the morning. Since the 1920s *The New Yorker*'s long and intelligent

articles have been considered among the best examples of high-quality weekly journalism. The *New York Observer* is a salmon-coloured weekly featuring articles on New York's most powerful and elite circles. For weekly listings and information about what's on in the city, the best sources are the left-leaning *Village Voice* (free), the *New York Press* (also free) or *Time Out New York*. Just about any newspaper from around the globe can be found in New York at newsagents.

Pharmacies (late night)

CVS, Duane Reade and Rite Aid are the main pharmacies around the city and have several 24-hour locations: **CVS**, 342 E 23rd St, **T** 1-212 505 1555; **Duane Reade**, 224 W 57th St at Broadway, **T** 1-212 541 9708; **Rite Aid**, 542 Second Av at 31st St, **T** 1-212 213 9887; call **T** 1-800 RITE AID for other locations.

Police

To find the nearest police precinct, or for general information about police services, call **T** 1-646 610 5000. In an emergency, dial 911.

Post offices

Most post offices are open Monday to Friday and Saturday mornings and are closed on Sundays and holidays. However, the **Main Post Office**, 8th Av between 31st and 33rd St, **T** 1-212 967 8585 is open 24 hours daily.

Public holidays

Most government offices, banks and post offices are closed on public holidays, but many stores, restaurants and museums remain open.

    New Year's Day (1 Jan). **Martin Luther King Jr Day** (3rd Mon in Jan). **Presidents' Day** (3rd Mon in Feb). **Memorial Day** (last Mon in May). **Independence Day** (4 Jul). **Labor Day** (1st

Mon in Sep). **Columbus Day** (2nd Mon in Oct). **Veterans' Day** (11 Nov). **Thanksgiving Day** (4th Thu in Nov). **Christmas Day** (25 Dec).

Religious services

Anglican/Episcopal, Cathedral of St John the Divine, 1047 Amsterdam Av. **Buddhist**, Eastern States Buddhist Temple of America, 64 Mott St. **Jewish**, Temple Emanu-El, 1 E 65th St at 5th Av. **Muslim**, Islamic Cultural Center & Mosque of New York City, 1711 Third Av. **Roman Catholic**, St Patrick's Cathedral, 50th St and Fifth Av.

Student organizations

Although New York isn't quite on par with some European destinations when it comes to student discounts, the International Student Identity Card (**ISIC**) will provide cheaper access to many sights, theatres, buses to the airport and other attractions in the city. A card can be obtained from STA Travel (see p238) on proof of student status. British students who want to work in New York should contact the British Universities North American Club (**BUNAC**; www.bunac.org/uk), a program that arranges for recent students to work in the USA.

Taxis

You don't need to worry about hiring a yellow taxi in advance, just look for the light atop the cab to see whether it's vacant. If you want a private car that will come to your door at a designated time, **Tel Aviv**, **T** 1-212 777 7777 or **Carmel**, **T** 1-212 666 6666, both run reliable services.

Telephone

Public phones can be found on street corners. Most take quarters ($0.25) for local calls of up to three minutes and accept credit cards for other numbers.

Time
New York is on Eastern Standard Time, which is five hours behind Greenwich Mean Time, one hour ahead of Central Time, two hours ahead of Mountain Time and three hours ahead of Pacific Time.

Tipping
See Travel Essentials, p28.

Toilets
New York has never quite grasped the concept of public conveniences. Toilets can be scarce so be sure to take advantage of those in museums, cafés and restaurants.

Transport enquiries
MTA New York City Transit travel information hotline, **T** 1-718 330 1234, is available 24 hours a day. For airport and airline enquiries, see Travel Essentials, p24 and p25.

Travel agents
American Express Travel Service, 295 Park Av South, **T** 1-212 691 9797; call for details of other branches. **STA Travel**, 10 Downing St, West Village, **T** 1-212 627 3111; call for details of other branches. See also Travel Essentials, p24.

Background

A sprint through history

1524	Giovanni da Verrazano is the first European to sail into Manhattan.
1609	Henry Hudson sails into New York harbour and claims the land for the Dutch.
1624	The colony of New Amsterdam is established and the first Dutch settlers arrive.
1626	Peter Minuit, the governor of the colony, buys Manhattan from the Indians for $24 in trade goods.
1643	Peter Stuyvesant becomes governor of the Dutch colony of New Amsterdam.
1664	The British gain control of New Amsterdam, renaming it New York.
1689	War breaks out between England and France and New York becomes a battleground in four French and Indian Wars.
1735	John Peter Zenger establishes the right to free speech in the *New York Weekly Journal*.
1763	The Treaty of Paris is signed, ending the French and Indian Wars.
1776	The Declaration of Independence is signed. The Revolutionary War takes place and the British occupy New York.
1783	The British leave New York after being defeated.
1789-1790	Manhattan serves as the capital of the United States of America. George Washington is inaugurated as president in New York.

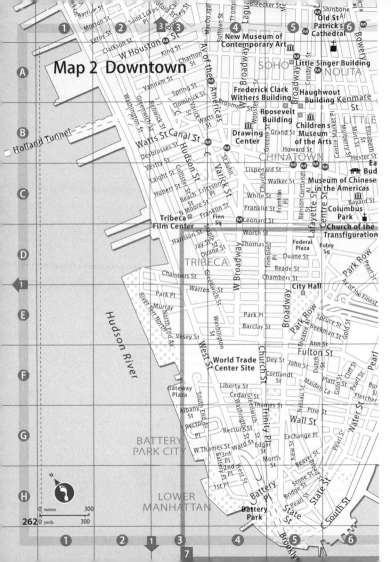

Map 2 Downtown

A
B
C
D
E
F
G
H

Barrow St
Morton St
Leroy St
Clarkson St
W Houston St
King St
Charlton St
Vandam St
Spring St
Dominick St
Broome St
Watts St Canal St
Desbrosses St
Vestry St
Laight St
Hubert St
Beach St
N Moore St
Franklin St
Harrison St
Jay St
Duane St
Chambers St
Warren St
Park Pl
Murray
North End Av
River Terr
Vesey St
Gateway
Plaza
Albany
St
Rector St
W Thames St
1st Pl

Saint Luke's
Pl
Leroy St
Downing St

Morton St
Bedford
Cal

Sullivan St
Bleecker St
Thompson St
Laguardia Pl
Sullivan St
Broadway

**New Museum of
Contemporary Art**

SOHO

NOLITA

Shinbone
Old St
Patrick's
Cathedral

Bowery

Little Singer Building

**Frederick Clark
Withers Building**

**Haughwout
Building** Kenmare
St

**Roosevelt
Building**

**Children's
Museum
of the Arts**

LITTLE

**Drawing
Center**

Grand St
Howard St

CHINATOWN

Ea
Bud

Hester St

Mott St
Elizabeth St
Mulberry St
Centre Market Pl

Lispenard St

**Museum of Chinese
in the Americas**

Walker St
White St
Franklin St
Leonard St

**Tribeca
Film Center**

Finn
Sq

Bayard St

**Columbus
Park**

**Church of the
Transfiguration**

Worth St
Thomas St
Duane St
Reade St
Chambers St

Federal
Plaza

Foley
Sq

TRIBECA

City Hall

Park Row

Park Pl
Barclay St

Av of the Finest

Spruce St
Beekman St
Ann St

Fulton St

Dey St
John St
Cortlandt St
Liberty St
Cedar St
Thames St

**World Trade
Center Site**

Dutch
Gold St
Platt St
Maiden La
Nassau St
Pine St

Wall St

Exchange Pl

Beaver St
New St

Morris St
Edgar
Battery
Pl

W Thames St Ward St

2nd
Pl

Stone St
Bridge St
Pearl St
State
St

**Battery
Park**

**BATTERY
PARK CITY**

**LOWER
MANHATTAN**

Hudson River

Holland Tunnel

**Haughwout
Building**

Washington St
Greenwich St
Renwick St
Hudson St
Varick St
Wooster St
Greene St
Mercer St
West Broadway

Av of the Americas

Watts St
St John's Ln
Collister St
Crosby St
Franklin Pl
Cortlandt Al
Benson
Lafayette St
Centre St
Mulberry St
Mott St

Broadway
Church St
Trinity Pl
Greenwich St
West St
Washington St
South End Av

Park Row
Theatre Al
Broadway

Water St
Pearl St
Front St
Gold St
Fletcher St
Burling Slip
South St

0 metres 300
0 yards 300

262

1
2
3
4
5
6

7

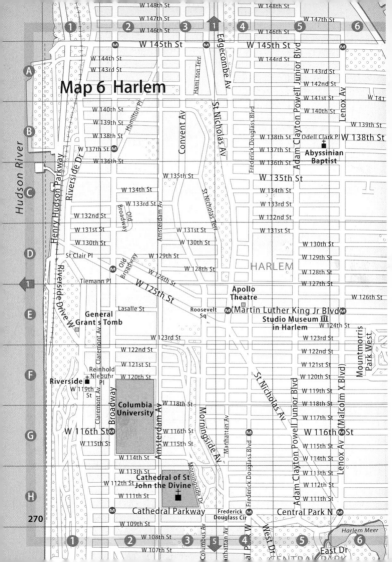

Map 6 Harlem

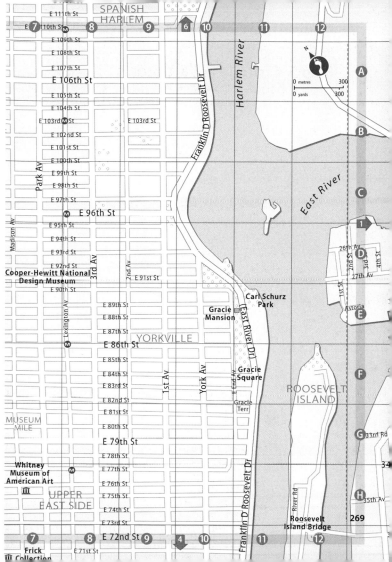

E 111th St

E 7 110th St   8   9   6   10   11   12

E 109th St

E 108th St

E 107th St

E 106th St

E 105th St

E 104th St

E 103rd M St   E 103rd St

E 102nd St

E 101st St

E 100th St

Park Av

E 99th St

E 98th St

E 97th St

E 96th St

Madison Av

E 95th St

E 94th St

E 93rd St

E 92nd St

Cooper-Hewitt National
Design Museum

E 90th St

E 91st St

Lexington Av

3rd Av

2nd Av

E 89th St

E 88th St

E 87th St

YORKVILLE

E 86th St

E 85th St

E 84th St

1st Av

York Av

E 83rd St

E 82nd St

E 81st St

E End Av

E 80th St

MUSEUM
MILE

E 79th St

E 78th St

Whitney
Museum of
American Art

E 77th St

E 76th St

UPPER
EAST SIDE

E 75th St

E 74th St

E 73rd St

7   8   E 72nd St 9   4   10   11   12

Frick
Collection

E 71st St

Harlem River

East River

Franklin D Roosevelt Dr

N

A

0 metres   300
0 yards   300

B

C

1

26th Av

2nd Av

3rd

4th St

D

27th Av

1st St

Astoria

E

East River Dr

Carl Schurz
Park

Gracie
Mansion

Gracie
Square

Gracie
Terr

ROOSEVELT
ISLAND

F

G

33rd Rd

34

Franklin D Roosevelt Dr

River Rd

H

35th Av

Roosevelt
Island Bridge

269

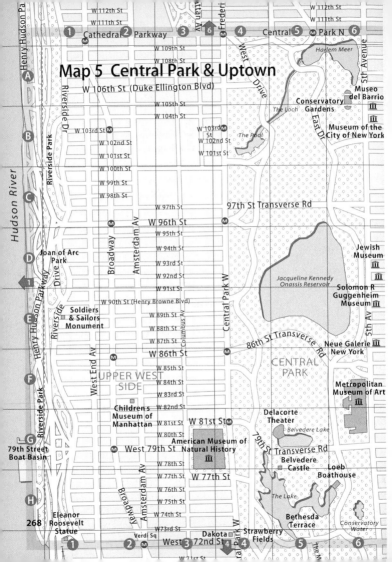

Map 5 Central Park & Uptown

268

Henry Hudson Pa

W 112th St
W 111th St

① Cathedral ② Parkway ③ ⓜ ④ Central ⑤ Park N ⑥

itan Av

Frederi

ⓜ

W 109th St
W 108th St

Harlem Meer

Ⓐ

West Drive

5th Avenue

W 106th St (Duke Ellington Blvd)

W 105th St
W 104th St

The Loch

Conservatory
Gardens

Museo
del Barrio

Museum of the
City of New York

East Dr

W 103rd St ⓜ

Ⓑ

Riverside Park

W 102nd St
W 101st St
W 100th St
W 99th St
W 98th St

W 103rd
St

ⓜ

The Pool

W 102nd St
W 101st St

Riverside Dr

Hudson River

Ⓒ

W 97th St

97th St Transverse Rd

Riverside Park

W 96th St

ⓜ

Broadway

Amsterdam Av

W 95th St
W 94th St
W 93rd St
W 92nd St
W 91st St

ⓜ

Jewish
Museum

Ⓓ

Joan of Arc
Park

Jacqueline Kennedy
Onassis Reservoir

Solomon R
Guggenheim
Museum 🏛

Central Park W

5th Av

Henry Hudson Parkway

❶

Riverside

W 90th St (Henry Browne Blvd)

Ⓔ

Soldiers
& Sailors
Monument

Riverside

Columbus Av

W 89th St
W 88th St
W 87th St
W 86th St

ⓜ

86th St Transverse Rd

Neue Galerie 🏛
New York

West End Av

ⓜ

Ⓕ

UPPER WEST
SIDE

W 85th St
W 84th St
W 83rd St
W 82nd St

CENTRAL
PARK

Metropolitan
Museum of Art
🏛

Riverside Park

Children's
Museum of
Manhattan

W 81st St ⓜ

Delacorte
Theater

Belvedere Lake

Ⓖ

79th Street
Boat Basin

ⓜ

W 80th St

West 79th St ⓜ

American Museum of
Natural History
🏛

79th St Transverse Rd

Belvedere
Castle

Loeb
Boathouse

W 78th St
W 77th St

Ⓗ

W 76th St
W 75th St
W 74th St

The Lake

Broadway

Amsterdam Av

Eleanor
Roosevelt
Statue

Bethesda
Terrace

Conservatory
Water

❶ ❷ Verdi Sq ❸ West ❹ ⓜ ❺ ❻

Dakota

Strawberry
Fields

tral Park

W 72nd St

W 71st St

The Ma

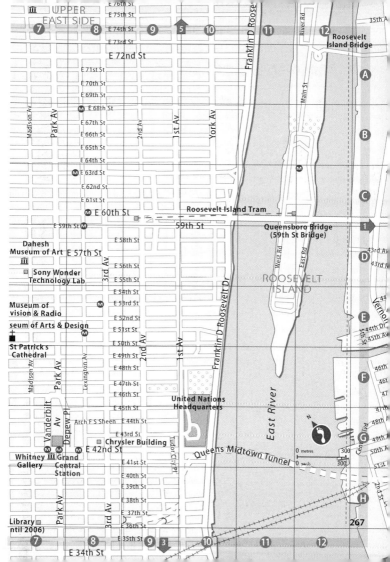

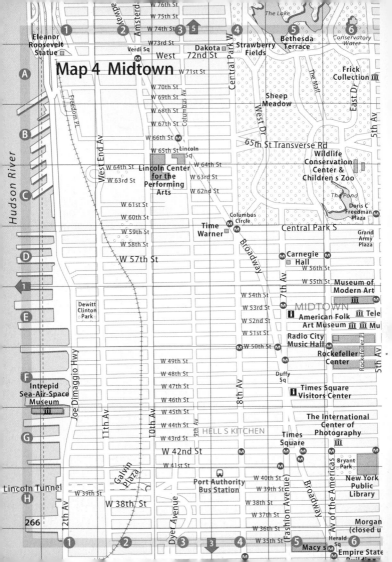

Map 4 Midtown

Eleanor Roosevelt Statue

Verdi Sq

West 72nd St

Dakota

Strawberry Fields

Bethesda Terrace

Conservatory Water

Frick Collection

The Lake

The Mall

Sheep Meadow

West Dr

65th St Transverse Rd

Wildlife Conservation Center & Children's Zoo

Lincoln Center for the Performing Arts

Columbus Circle

The Pond

Doris C Freedman Plaza

Time Warner

Central Park S

Grand Army Plaza

Carnegie Hall

Museum of Modern Art

MIDTOWN

American Folk Art Museum

Tele

Mu

Dewitt Clinton Park

Radio City Music Hall

Rockefeller Center

Rockefeller Pl

Duffy Sq

Intrepid Sea-Air-Space Museum

Times Square Visitors Center

The International Center of Photography

HELL'S KITCHEN

Times Square

New York Public Library

Bryant Park

Lincoln Tunnel

Galvin Plaza

Port Authority Bus Station

Herald Sq

Macy's

Morgan (closed u

Empire State

266

Hudson River

Freedom Pl

West End Av

Columbus Av

Amsterdam

Central Park W

5th Av

East Dr

Broadway

7th Av

8th Av

9th Av

10th Av

11th Av

12th Av

Joe Dimaggio Hwy

Dyer Avenue

Fashion Avenue

Av of the Americas

Broadway

W 76th St
W 75th St
W 74th St
W73rd St
W 71st St
W 70th St
W 69th St
W 68th St
W 67th St
W 66th St
W 65th St
W 64th St
W 63rd St
W 62nd St
W 61st St
W 60th St
W 59th St
W 58th St
W 57th St
W 56th St
W 55th St
W 54th St
W 53rd St
W 52nd St
W 51st St
W 50th St
W 49th St
W 48th St
W 47th St
W 46th St
W 45th St
W 44th St
W 43rd St
W 42nd St
W 41st St
W 40th St
W 39th St
W 38th St
W 37th St
W 36th St
W 35th St

Lincoln

A
B
C
D
E
F
G
H

1
2
3
4
5
6

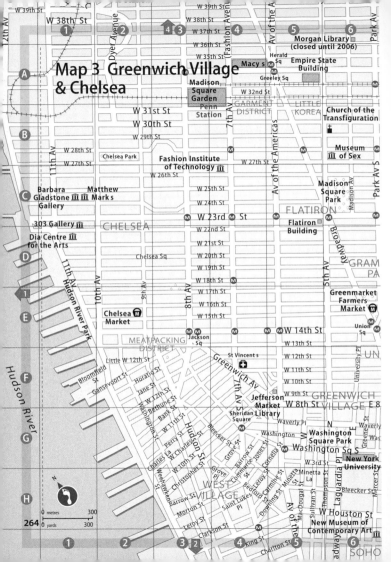

Map 3 Greenwich Village & Chelsea

W 39th St
W 38th St
W 37th St
W 36th St
W 35th St
Macy's
Herald Sq
Greeley Sq
Empire State Building
Morgan Library (closed until 2006)

Madison Square Garden
Penn Station
W 32nd St
W 31st St
W 30th St
W 29th St
W 28th St
W 27th St
W 26th St
GARMENT DISTRICT
LITTLE KOREA
Church of the Transfiguration
Museum of Sex

Chelsea Park
Fashion Institute of Technology

Barbara Gladstone Gallery
Matthew Mark's
303 Gallery
Dia Centre for the Arts
CHELSEA
W 25th St
W 24th St
W 23rd St
W 22nd St
W 21st St
W 20th St
W 19th St
W 18th St
W 17th St
W 16th St
W 15th St
FLATIRON
Flatiron Building
Madison Square Park
GRAM PA

Chelsea Sq
Chelsea Market
MEATPACKING DISTRICT
Jackson Sq
Greenmarket Farmers Market
Union Sq

W 14th St
W 13th St
Little W 12th St
Bloomfield St
Gansevoort St
Horatio St
Jane St
W 12th St
Bethune St
Bank St
St Vincent's
Greenwich Av
W 12th St
W 11th St
W 10th St
W 9th St
Jefferson Market Library
W 8th St
GREENWICH VILLAGE E 8

Hudson River
Hudson River Park
11th Av
10th Av
9th Av
8th Av
7th Av
Av of the Americas
5th Av
Broadway
Madison Av
Park Av
Fashion Avenue

Washington St
Charles St
Perry St
W 11th St
W 10th St
Christopher St
Weehawken
Barrow St
Morton St
Leroy St
Clarkson St
Sheridan Square
Grove St
Bleecker St
Commerce St
Jones St
Barrow St
Redford St
Leroy St
Carmine St
Downing St
Minetta St
Saint Luke's Pl
Waverly Pl
Washington
Washington Square Park
Washington Square S
W 3rd St
Bleecker St
MacDougal
Sullivan St
Thompson St
Laguardia Pl
Minetta La
New York University
Waverly
Washington Sq

WEST VILLAGE
W Houston St
New Museum of Contemporary Art
King St
Charlton St
SOHO
Mercer St

264

N
0 metres 300
0 yards 300

A B C D E F G H
1 2 3 4 5 6

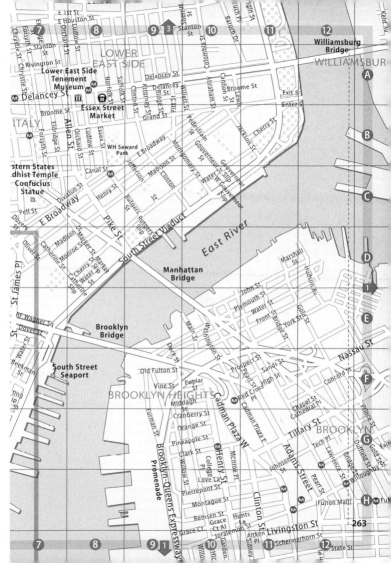

LOWER EAST SIDE

E 1st St
E Houston St
Stanton St
Rivington St
Chrystie St
Forsyth St
Orchard St
Ludlow St

Lower East Side
Tenement
Museum
Delancey St

Essex Street
Market

Delancey St
Delancey St

Broome St
Norfolk St
Suffolk St
Clinton St
Attorney St
Ridge St
Pitt St
Willett St

Williamsburg
Bridge

WILLIAMSBUR

Exit St
Enter St

Broome St
Eldridge St
Allen St
Orchard St
Ludlow St
Essex St

WH Seward
Park

E Broadway
Jefferson St
Madison St
Clinton St

Federal Plaza

Broome St
Cannon St
Lewis St
Columbia St
Baruch Dr

Abraham St
Jackson St
Cherry St

Gouverneur St
Water St
Gouverneur St Slip
W Gouverneur
Slip

East River

ITALY

Forsyth St
Eldridge St

Canal St

stern States
dhist Temple
Confucius
Statue

Division St
E Broadway

Pell St
Dover St

Henry St
Rutgers St
Rutgers Slip

Pike St

South Street Viaduct

Marshall
St
Hudson Av

Oliver St

St James Pl

RF Wagner Sq

Dover St

Madison St
Market St
Monroe St
Cherry St
Water St
Catherine St
Catherine Slip

**Manhattan
Bridge**

John St
Plymouth St
Water St
Front St
Bridge St
York St
Gold St

1

Nassau St

Beekman
St

**Brooklyn
Bridge**

Washington St
Main St
Dock St

Prospect St
Pearl St
Sands St
High St

Marshall St

Concord St

ting
ip

**South Street
Seaport**

Old Fulton St

Vine St
Poplar
St

Furman St

BROOKLYN HEIGHTS

Middagh
St
Cranberry St
Orange St
Pineapple St
Clark St
Willow St
Henry St
College
Pl
Monroe Pl
Love La
Pierrepont St
Montague St
Remsen St
Grace
Ct Al
Joralemon St
Grace Ct
Aitken
Pl

Red Cross
Pl

Cadman Plaza W
Cadman Plaza E

Chapel St
Cathedral Pl

Tillary St

Adams Street

Clinton St
Johnson St
Pearl St
Willow St
Hunts
La
Sidney
Pl

Tech Pl
Lawrence St
Bridge St
Duffield St
Gold St
Fair

BROOKLYN

Willoughby

(Fulton Mall)

Fu

Brooklyn-Queens Expressway

Livingston St
Schermerhorn St
State St

1811	The Commissioners' Plan to develop New York in a grid layout between 14th Street and Washington Heights is approved by the state legislature.
1812-1814	The British fight the Americans in the War of 1812 and are defeated.
1837	Financial ruin wipes out all but three of New York City's banks.
1839	The anti-rent movement begins. Tenant farmers refuse to pay rent to their wealthy landowners, thus establishing renters' rights.
1843	Immigrants begin pouring into the city.
1860	Abraham Lincoln is elected President.
1861-1865	The American Civil War. New York sends more men and money to the Union (North) army than any state.
1863	Draft Riots break out in New York in response to conscription laws, which allow the rich to buy their way out of military service. Over 1,000 people are killed in the riots.
1865	The Union army wins the Civil War, slavery is abolished. New York grows as an important manufacturing centre.
1883	Brooklyn Bridge is completed.
1886	The Statue of Liberty is unveiled as a gift from France to the USA.
1892	Ellis Island opens as an immigration stop.

1895	The New York Public Library is founded.
1898	The five boroughs of New York are incorporated to create the second-largest city in the world.
1900	The city introduces elevated trains (els).
1907	Taxis with meters are introduced to the city streets.
1909	As unions become active, 20,000 women strike for better working rights and conditions in factories and sweat shops.
1911	146 women die in a fabric factory belonging to the Triangle Shirtwaist Company. This leads to the creation of the International Ladies' Garment Workers' Union.
1917	The USA enters World War I. Soldiers set sail for Europe from the ports of New York.
1920	Women win voting rights. Prohibition makes alcohol illegal.
1925	Jimmy Walker is elected mayor. The Jazz Age sees the rise of speakeasies and bootleg liquor.
1929	The Wall Street stock market crashes on 29 October, instigating a period of financial meltdown across the country, known as the Great Depression.
1930s	President Roosevelt introduces the New Deal, which aims to provide new jobs for the unemployed through public works projects. New York's mayor Fiorello La Guardia fights corruption and develops the city's social services.
1939	The World's Fair takes place in Corona Park, Queens.

1941	The USA enters World War II.
1945	The war ends. New York develops as a media and cultural centre and thrives as one of the busiest ports in the world.
1946	New York is chosen as home for the United Nations.
1950s	The Great White Flight. Middle class New Yorkers begin moving to the suburbs leaving behind a slowly deteriorating city. Manufacturing plants close, restaurants, stores and landmark buildings are left empty.
1970s	The economy sours and businesses continue to close. Unemployment grows and many people leave the city.
1975	New York hits a low point financially and nearly declares bankruptcy. Crime is rampant.
1977	A serial killer known as the 'Son of Sam' stalks the city streets. A massive power blackout occurs, enabling rioters to loot millions of dollars of merchandise from businesses around the city.
1978	Mayor Ed Koch vows to improve the city's finances.
1980s	AIDS hits New York. So does the crack cocaine epidemic, causing crime to rise dramatically and welfare and law enforcement services to be stretched thin. Mayor Koch tries to establish order and revitalize the city. Meanwhile millions are being made on Wall Street by the new 'yuppies'.
1987	Wall Street crashes again.

1990	David Dinkins becomes the city's first black mayor.
1993	Terrorists try to blow up the World Trade Center. Rudolph Giuliani is elected mayor, the first Republican in the post for 28 years. He promises to tackle the city's crime problems by introducing a 'zero tolerance' campaign.
1997	Technology boom and the internet revolution form the basis for a period of economic prosperity. Crime rates continue to drop.
2000	Hilary Rodham Clinton is elected as Senator of New York. The city begins to enter an economic downturn.
2001	The World Trade Center is destroyed in a terrorist attack on September 11th. President George W Bush declares a War on Terror. Republican Mike Bloomberg is elected New York mayor.
2002	New York finds itself in a recession as the War on Terror continues. Unemployment rises and the city teeters financially with huge budget deficits.
2003	Mayor Bloomberg raises property taxes and cuts back on many services in an effort to avoid city bankruptcy. The war in Iraq breaks out, in the face of large-scale protests in New York. A slow recovery in jobs and tourism brings the city back to its feet. A blackout on 14 August leaves the city without power for more than a day. Crime rates continue to fall to all-time lows.

Art and architecture

1624-1664	The Dutch construct wood-frame buildings in the colonial style with gables and tile roofs.
1664-1783	Under British control the city gains some stately Georgian structures, although few remain today.
19th century	US architects adapt British designs to create their own Federal style. Cast iron becomes fashionable and popular as a cheap but decorative building material.
1857	Frederick Law Olmstead and Calvert Vaux map out plans for Central Park.
1868	A competition is held for the design of the Equitable Life Building, the first office building to use the passenger elevator.
1870	The Metropolitan Museum of Art is established.
1873	Economic depression causes a halt in the construction of tall buildings.
1888	The Lincoln Building on Union Square is built, one of the last skyscrapers to be constructed without a steel skeleton frame.
1890-1920s	The beaux arts period, or the Gilded Age, sees the construction of many of the city's landmark buildings including the New York Public Library, Grand Central Terminal, the Municipal Building and the original Pennsylvania Station (torn down in 1965). The construction of Grand Central causes business to shift to Midtown. The architecture firm of McKim, Mead & White are responsible for the design of a significant proportion of buildings up

until World War I. Blue-blood families such as the Rockefellers and Vanderbilts flock to New York to build palatial homes.

1903 The Flatiron Building (then the Fuller Building) is completed. At only 20 storeys, it nevertheless becomes an icon of the skyscraper era to follow.

1909 The Metropolitan Life Building on Madison Square Park is completed and is, briefly, the world's tallest building.

1913 The Woolworth Building is completed. It remains the world's tallest building until 1929.

1916 The 1916 Zoning Law is passed to regulate the shape of skyscrapers in order to maintain proper air and light on city sidewalks.

1929 The Chrysler Building is completed and takes over from the Woolworth as the world's tallest skyscraper. The Museum of Modern Art opens.

1930-1949 Many consider this to be the golden age of New York's skyline. The Chrysler Building, the Empire State Building, the McGraw-Hill Building and Rockefeller Center are all constructed during the Great Depression. Art deco deluxe buildings with ornamented façades become fashionable. At the same time, civic planner Robert Moses starts ripping through neighbourhoods with 416 miles of highways, changing the cityscape forever.

1950s Following the success of the modernist glass Lever House at 390 Park Avenue, the German architect

Ludwig Mies van der Rohe teams up with Philip Johnson to build the Seagram's Building (375 Park Av) as New York's testament to modernism. The United Nations headquarters is also built.

1959 Frank Lloyd Wright's Guggenheim Museum opens, casting its unique spiral down Fifth Avenue.

1970s Construction of the World Trade Center begins.

1980s Transition from modern to post-modern designs. The Sony Building (550 Madison Av) by Philip Johnson is a testament to the new style.

1990s High-rise buildings continue to go up, including Trump Tower, the world's tallest residential structure.

2001 The World Trade Center is destroyed by terrorists on 11 September, 2001.

Future plans Although, enormous skyscrapers fell out of favour for a short time immediately following 9-11 and some companies moved their headquarters out of the city, high-rises, both residential and commercial, continue to go up all around the city. The 'Twin Towers' are to be replaced by the equally tall Freedom Tower designed by Daniel Libeskind. A twin-towered Time Warner building will open in 2004 on Columbus Circle but plans to turn the beaux arts post office building into a train station are on hold for budgetary reasons.

Books

Fiction

Asbury, H, *The Gangs of New York*, (1928), Thunder's Mouth Press. Tour through the violence, poverty, crime and corruption of New York's underbelly in the late 1800. Mixture of fact and fiction.

Auster, P, *New York Trilogy*, (1994), Penguin. Three dark, thrilling detective novellas combining film noir atmospherics and suspense. Contemporary New York classics.

Capote, T, *Breakfast at Tiffany's*, (1958), Penguin/Random House. A compelling depiction of Uptown life in 1940s New York.

Ellis, Bret Easton, *American Psycho*, (1991), Simon& Schuster. A serial killer prowls the streets and clubs of 1980s Manhattan.

Ellison, Ralph, *Invisible Man*, (1897), Penguin/Random House. Harlem in the 1950s is the setting for an exploration of black cultural identity.

Fitzgerald, S, *The Beautiful and the Damned*, (1922), Scribner. A destructive marriage, involving alcoholism and greed, portrays New York nightlife and reckless attempts to achieve material wealth.

James, H, *Washington Square*, (1881), Penguin. Upper-class New York life is eloquently portrayed in this novel, set just before the Civil War on the northern edge of Washington Square Park.

Jamowitz, T, *Slaves of New York*, (1986), Pan Books Ltd. Excellent portrayal of the grungy, bohemian life of a struggling artist in New York in the 1980s.

Lethem, J, *Motherless Brooklyn*, (1999), Vintage. Brooklyn provides the backdrop to this detective story about a loss of innocence and betrayal. Orphan misfits and Tourette's syndrome are part of the compelling mix.

Morrison, Toni, *Jazz*, (1992), Alfred A Knopf. Relives the music and excitement of the Harlem Renaissance.

Parker, Dorothy, *Complete Stories*, (1995), Penguin. Witty and moving tales of New York, many focusing on women.

Salinger, JD, *The Catcher in the Rye*, (1951), Bantam. Holden Caulfield's adolescent wanderings around New York.

Selby Jr, Hubert, *Last Exit to Brooklyn*, (1966), Paladin/Grove Weidenfeld. Disturbingly vivid account of the drugs, sex and violence of 1960s Brooklyn.

Wharton, E, *The Age of Innocence* (1920), Modern Library. This tragic story of impossible love in upper-class New York is a Pulitzer Prize-winning classic.

Wolfe, T, *Bonfire of the Vanities* (1987), Bantam. Excellent insight into city life in the 1980s and its racial problems. Wealthy Wall Street bond trader runs down a black man in the Bronx, sparking a trail of mayhem.

Non-fiction

Burrows, E and **Wallace**, M, *Gotham*, (1998), Oxford University Press. Two volumes cover every inch of New York history from prehistoric days to the end of the 1990s. Written in a lively manner.

Irving, W, *A History of New York*, (1809). Satirical look at colonial New York, written under the pseudonym of Dietrich Knickerbocker.

Jackson, K, *The Encyclopedia of New York City*, (1995), Yale University Press. Columbia University historian has amassed this enormous collection of history and titbits presented in dictionary format with photos.

Riis, Jacob, *How the Other Half Lives*, (1890), Scribner. Shocking account of the poverty in the Lower East Side in the late 1800s. The book, along with Riis' friendship with Roosevelt, caused the city to rethink the way immigrants were living at the time.

White, N, *AIA Guide to New York City*, (2000), Harcourt Brace Jovanovich. The most comprehensive architectural book on New York guides readers through every interesting street and alley of all five boroughs.

Films

Film directors are giddy about New York, with many of them using the city as the focus of social and political films. Woody Allen, Spike Lee, Sidney Lumet and Martin Scorsese are only a few of the directors that call the city home.

Annie Hall, Woody Allen, (1977). This New York classic is an Oscar-winning tribute to the city, from childhood in Coney Island to adulthood in Manhattan. Equally notable is *Manhattan* (1979), shot beautifully in black and white with a Gershwin soundtrack.

Breakfast at Tiffany's, Blake Edwards, (1961). Follow Audrey Hepburn as Holly Golightly as she dawdles over jewels, climbs fire escapes and throws parties on the Upper East Side.

French Connection, William Friedkin, (1971). Epic cop thriller with Gene Hackman and plenty of atmospheric shots of Brooklyn.

The Godfather II, Francis Ford Coppola, (1974). The classic prequel follows Vito Corleone's immigrant experience in Little Italy.

King Kong, John Guillermin, (1976). Not the first King Kong but this version, starring Jessica Lange, is a highly entertaining romp through New York.

Midnight Cowboy, John Schlesinger, (1969). One man's journey to make it in the big city is overcome by another man's struggle in this touching drama.

On the Waterfront, Elia Kazan, (1954). Marlon Brando stars in this epic film of corruption on the docks. Great views of Manhattan.

On the Town, Stanley Donen, Gene Kelly, (1949). Frank Sinatra and Gene Kelly sing 'New York, New York' at the Rockefeller Center in this celluloid musical-comedy.

Out of Towners, Arthur Hiller, (1970). Jack Lemmon's hilarious attempts to relocate to tough New York.

She's Gotta Have It, Spike Lee, (1986). A comedy romance that traces a Brooklyn woman experiences dating three men. Possibly Lee's best film to date.

Smoke, Wayne Wang (1995). Interwoven stories of Brooklyn, scripted by Paul Auster and starring Harvey Keitel as the owner of a cigar store.

Sweet Smell of Success, Alexander Mackendrick, (1957). New York's most powerful newspaper columnist sets out to ruin a jazz musician. Black and white classic with Burt Lancaster and Tony Curtis. Excellent shots of Times Square.

The Taking of Pelham One, Two, Three, Joseph Sargent, (1974). Walther Matthau keeps this suspenseful thriller edgy and funny. Perfectly set in New York's subway.

Taxi Driver, Martin Scorsese, (1976). Robert De Niro plays the psychotic East Village cab driver on a self-destructive tour of the city. Wonderful and eerie.

Wall Street, Oliver Stone, (1987). Charlie Sheen and Michael Douglas show New York's 1980s greed at its peak.

The Warriors, Walter Hill, (1979). Considered the best film portrayal of a gang story spanning the Bronx to Coney Island.

Index

Credits

Footprint credits

Text editor: Sophie Blacksell
Map editor: Sarah Sorensen

Publisher: Patrick Dawson
Series created by Rachel Fielding
Cartography: Claire Benison, Kevin
Feeney, Robert Lunn
Design: Mytton Williams
Maps: Footprint Handbooks Ltd

Photography credits

Front cover: Alamy
Inside: Susannah Sayler (p1 Empire
State Building, p5 Statue of Liberty,
p33 Flatiron Building, p103 Brooklyn
Botanic Garden)
Generic images: John Matchett
Back cover: Susannah Sayler
(Brooklyn Bridge)

Print

Manufactured in Italy by LegoPrint.
Pulp from sustainable forests.

Footprint feedback

We try as hard as we can to make
each Footprint guide as up to date as
possible but, of course, things always
change. If you want to let us know
about your experiences – good, bad
or ugly – then don't delay, go to
www.footprintbooks.com and send
in your comments.

® Footprint Handbooks and the Footprint
mark are a registered trademark of
Footprint Handbooks Ltd

Publishing information

Footprint New York
1st edition
Text and maps © Footprint Handbooks
Ltd March 2004

ISBN 1 903471 93 1
CIP DATA: a catalogue record for this
book is available from the British Library

Published by Footprint
6 Riverside Court
Lower Bristol Road
Bath, BA2 3DZ, UK
T +44 (0)1225 469141
F +44 (0)1225 469461
discover@footprintbooks.com
www.footprintbooks.com

Distributed in the USA by
Publishers Group West

Complete title list

For a different view…
choose a Footprint

Over 100 Footprint travel guides
Covering more than 150 of the world's most exciting
countries and cities in Latin America, the Caribbean, Africa, Indian
sub-continent, Australasia, North America, Southeast Asia, the
Middle East and Europe.

Discover so much more…
The finest writers. In-depth knowledge. Entertaining and accessible.
Critical restaurant and hotels reviews. Lively descriptions of all the
attractions. Get away from the crowds.

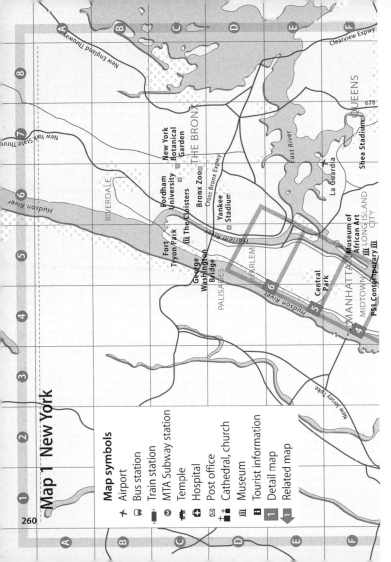

Map 1 New York

260

Map symbols

✈ Airport
🚌 Bus station
🚆 Train station
Ⓜ MTA Subway station
✡ Temple
✚ Hospital
✉ Post office
✝ Cathedral, church
🏛 Museum
ℹ Tourist information
1 Detail map
1 Related map

New England Thruway
Clearview Expwy
New York State Thruway
New York Botanical Garden
THE BRONX
QUEENS
678
Hudson River
East River
RIVERDALE
Fordham University
Bronx Zoo
Cross Bronx Expwy
Yankee Stadium
La Guardia
Shea Stadium
Fort Tryon Park
The Cloisters
George Washington Bridge
Harlem River
HARLEM
LONG ISLAND CITY
Museum of African Art
PALISADES
MANHATTAN
Central Park
MIDTOWN
PS1 Contemporary
Hudson River
New Jersey Tpke

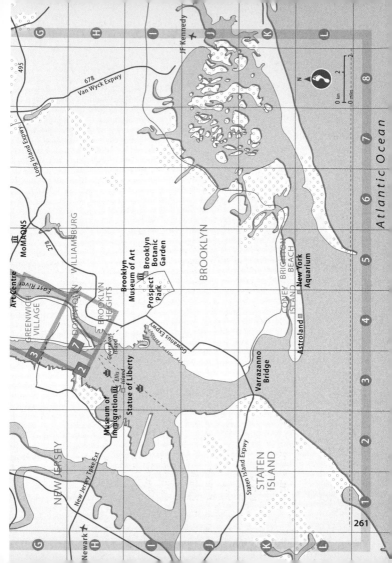